FLYING HIGHER

a true story by

MORTEN S. BEYER

Order this book online at www.trafford.com
or email orders@trafford.com

Most Trafford titles are also available at major online book retailers.

© Copyright 2009 Morten S. Beyer.
All rights reserved. No part of this publication may be reproduced, stored in a retrieval
system, or transmitted, in any form or by any means, electronic, mechanical, photocopying,
recording, or otherwise, without the written prior permission of the author.

Note for Librarians: A cataloguing record for this book is available from Library
and Archives Canada at www.collectionscanada.ca/amicus/index-e.html

Printed in Victoria, BC, Canada.

ISBN: 978-1-4251-6652-6 (Soft)
ISBN: 978-1-4251-6653-3 (e-book)

Library of Congress Control Number: 2009939676

*We at Trafford believe that it is the responsibility of us all, as both individuals
and corporations, to make choices that are environmentally and socially sound.
You, in turn, are supporting this responsible conduct each time you purchase a
Trafford book, or make use of our publishing services. To find out how you are
helping, please visit www.trafford.com/responsiblepublishing.html*

*Our mission is to efficiently provide the world's finest, most comprehensive
book publishing service, enabling every author to experience success.
To find out how to publish your book, your way, and have it available
worldwide, visit us online at www.trafford.com*

Trafford rev. 10/23/2009

Trafford PUBLISHING®   www.trafford.com

North America & international
toll-free: 1 888 232 4444 (USA & Canada)
phone: 250 383 6864 ♦ fax: 812 355 4082 ♦ email: info@trafford.com

Acknowledgements

This book would never have come into being without the enormous support group's encouragement. Linda Ware typed it, transcribing the text from the Olivetti Portable to the digital age. Bill Whiteside researched the pictures, and a lot of the facts, Wayne Hill spent hours scanning pictures and offering expert advice along with a liberal flow of wine and dinners. Cathy Randall did fine editing work, and helped with the organization of the text. Louise Randolph, Eileen McDonough, Keith Skriver, and Carl C. Mueller carefully read and corrected the text, checking commas, capitals and facts.

Marielle Fares and Adil Reghioui translated a bit of Arabic conversation.

Our lucky day chance encounter with Lisa Pampillonia brought in our accomplished graphic artist.

Bob Agnew, Patti Williams at the Smithsonian Air and Space Museum, and Jeff Kochan all abetted in various ways, and to all I offer the most heartfelt thanks. The collective efforts of these talented people have produced this anecdotal history of the air transport world.

The pictures of the Ford Tri-Motors are printed courtesy of M. Kelly Cusack – www.EverythingPanAm.com

Some of the pictures in this book were obtained from open sources such as Wikipedia. Unfortunately, we could not locate all the photographers, despite our best efforts. We apologize for any problems that may be caused by the use of these images.

Morten Beyer

✈
CONTENTS
Flying Higher

CHAPTER I

In the Beginning

Father and Mother

O tto and Clara were meant to make a difference — and did. Mother was the youngest of six daughters of Morten Mortensen, a Danish immigrant, and had three younger brothers as well. All grew up on a homestead chicken farm in Petaluma, California in the first decade of the 20th Century. Clara put herself through the University of California at Berkeley before heading east to teach at Bryn Mawr in Pennsylvania. During World War I, she was in Washington, involved in the war effort and the fledgling women's suffrage movement. It was during these war years that she met Otto Beyer, then a young Army major helping manage aircraft production at the Government arsenals.

Otto was born in 1886, the first son of German emigrant parents in Hoboken, New Jersey. His father was an inventor credited with developing the huge stamping machines used to manufacture the steel bodies of the first mass produced automobiles. Reportedly, he made a lot of money and lost it all. Father never talked about him and none of us ever met him.

After graduating from Lehigh University as a civil engineer Otto worked in the railroad industry until World War I, when he was commissioned and placed in charge of a production division of the war effort. His first wife died in the flu epidemic of 1918, after which he met Clara. They were married in 1920.

Following the end of the war, Otto became convinced that the logical principles of engineering could be applied to industrial relations. He used these principles to settle the often long and brutal strikes affecting industry, particularly the railroads.

Otto and Eleanor Roosevelt

At this time, the Baltimore & Ohio Railroad was engulfed in a bitter dispute in the locomotive shops, and the union leaders asked Otto to intervene and seek a settlement. He went to Dan Willard, enlightened president of the B&O, and asked for an opportunity to "mediate" the strike. Willard agreed.

The idea of "mediation" was a new one at the time. Previously, strikes were the result of frustrated workers led by politically inspired left-leaning activists confronting intransigent management who used force, police, the Army and National Guard, and private armies of "goons", to break the strike. Otto was convinced that by mediating between the legitimate demands of labor and management, peaceful solutions could be found. It was a revolutionary idea applied in a non-confrontational manner.

In order to avoid any suspicion of conflict of interest, Otto always insisted on working for the unions and was paid by them, relying on his reputation for fairness and even-handedness to win the concurrence of management.

The first problem was always to win the respect and confidence of the workers, to make sure that he was not thought of as just another union-buster in different clothing. By carefully listening to the union grievances, generally involving management's lack of concern over safety issues and the union's suggestions for improvements, Otto was able to build a list of constructive suggestions to management which, when accepted, became the basis of agreements and strike settlements and later prevention.

In 1926 Otto crafted a proposed Railway Labor Act which created a National Mediation Board to help resolve transportation labor disputes at the national level. The mediator's role was that of an honest broker between the parties, as opposed to an arbitrator or judge who handed down binding decisions. Congress passed the act, and a few years later Otto was appointed Chairman of the NMB, a post he held until World War II.

In the 1930s, as the infant airline industry was just beginning to spread its wings, jurisdiction over airline labor unions was also assigned to the NMB, a factor of future importance to me.

The NMB continues to this day, with jurisdiction over airlines, bus lines (such as they are) and the atrophied railroad industry. More and more, the NMB is seen as a politicized "tool of labor," an instrument to extract even greater concessions (read higher wages, more work rules, fewer hours) from management which has grown more artificial with the passage of time. As Father used to tell me: "The Railway Labor Act requires negotiaion in good faith. It does not require that you give the unions anything" – advice that airline management ignored too often.

During World War II, Otto was a member of the War Labor Board, with responsibility for transportation labor, and at the end of the war once again became a member of the NMB. He died in 1948 at the age of 62 as a result of a botched kidney operation and was buried in a full military dress funeral at Arlington. Frances Perkins, former Secretary of Labor, gave the eulogy.

Mother returned to Government service in 1930 as Deputy Director of the newly founded Children's Bureau, an agency devoted to stopping child labor and generally improving child welfare, before anybody had heard of "child welfare". With the increasingly deepening depression hard upon the nation, there was much to do.

With Roosevelt's election and the appointment of Frances Perkins as Secretary of Labor, Clara was transferred to the Labor Department as Deputy Director of the Division of Labor Standards, an administration generally devoted to enforcement of the wage and hour laws nationwide. Clara held this position until her first retirement in 1957, serving as the functioning head of the division under a string of figurehead male directors. The current practice of employing women in top level posts had not yet been implemented.

Upon "retiring" from the Department of Labor, Clara assumed a second 20-year career with the Department of State with the International Cooperation Administration. Her mission was administering the U.S. Government programs designed to aid in the development of women's institutions abroad. She traveled constantly, even visiting me while I was in Saudi Arabia during the 1960s. Following her second retirement in 1987, Clara continued to

Clara Mortensen Beyer

maintain an active interest in women and labor affairs worldwide, entertaining her wide circle of friends until her death in 1990 at the age of 98.

Clara and Otto made a difference and imbued us children with a sense of duty and responsibility.

In the Beginning

I was born in New York City on November 13, 1921, first son of Otto Sternoff Beyer and Clara Mortensen Beyer. We moved to Washington, D.C. in 1923, living above Rock Creek Park. My first memories as a child were of the lions in the zoo across the creek roaring fearsomely in the night.

In June of 1925 my parents bought Spring Hill Farm, Virginia, a Revolutionary War-era plantation house on 40 acres near Spring Hill, 12 miles west of Washington. The house was large, with seven bedrooms, two living rooms and a large dining room, all with fireplaces. Large and livable as it was, it lacked full indoor plumbing, central heat, and electricity until the coming of the Rural Electrification Administration a decade later. A huge leaky water tower stood at the south end of the house, fed by a hand-started one-cylinder gas engine pumping water from the dug well. Work was immediately begun under the direction of my then young Uncle Fred to modernize the house.

He installed a wood/coal-fired furnace, a hot water radiator heating system, indoor toilets (fortunately, before winter made the trek to the outhouse unacceptably uncomfortable), and a pressure water system which still relied on the water tower as the source. Now at least, we had the minimum comforts of country living.

Cooking was done on a huge cast iron wood stove, with some six separate "lids" providing interior access to the firebox and cooking space. This stove also provided hot water for a decade until electricity came and a conventional water heater could be installed. The coal furnace also provided hot water in a separate system from the hot water radiators.

Illumination was provided by candlelight or by kerosene wick lamps – a perpetual source of danger that once or twice almost resulted in serious fires when the lamps exploded. The six-party telephone line – though not private – worked well. If the phone rang with one long, then two short rings, we knew the call was for us.

The dirt roads to the farm were primitive: dusty in summer, muddy in foul weather, and all but impassable in winter. A ford through Carper's Creek was negotiable except after a thunderstorm, when a three-foot torrent of muddy water made the creek impossible to cross. The Great Falls branch of the Washington and Old Dominion Railroad provided frequent, reasonably

Haying at Spring Hill Farm

reliable, and cheap access to Washington via the terminal in Rosslyn where it connected with the DC streetcar system. The U.S. mail was delivered by motorcycle in summer. However, when winter made the roads impassable, the mailman delivered the mail on horseback.

In the fall, thirty tons of coal were delivered under our great oak tree to feed the furnace. As kids we trundled endless wheelbarrow loads up to the house and dumped them down the chute to the coal bin in the basement. The fireplaces and kitchen stove had prodigious appetites for wood, devouring 25 to 30 cords a season. In the beginning our woods had scores of dead chestnuts, killed in the blight of 1918. Having clean, bright and warm wood, these trees swiftly fell to the axes and shad-belly saws of the black men we hired each fall to lay in the winter supply.

Spring Hill had been the "Massa House" in the days of slavery – only 65 years prior to this time. The Spring Hill community consisted mostly of Blacks descended from the old farm slaves and several of the elderly persons, who had been born in the Massa House basement. Many of the old ties still existed, and initially we drew most of our household and farm help from Spring Hill; Bertha, the cook, crippled by arthritis until she walked perpetually bent ninety degrees at the waist; Jim and George, twins of great dignity who still wore their Army uniforms of 1918; Julia, the washer woman, two hundred fifty pounds and gaining. These people and many more day laborers worked for us on the early farm.

Animals were quickly added: three cows for fresh milk, cream, butter and buttermilk; two horses for plowing and hauling, and 300 chickens to sustain my mother's "eggs by mail" business. In these days before

Mort and Clara

supermarkets, "eggs by mail" was a practical solution for those who wanted fresh eggs on a reliable basis. Mother's clients included three Supreme Court Justices.

Transportation was provided by a single Model T which negotiated the dirt road to Great Falls Pike, a paved, single lane toll road to Washington via Chain Bridge. Both the bridge and the Pike had a 5¢ toll, collected by gatekeepers manning a long pole (balanced by a box of stones) blocking the road. In 1928 my parents bought the toll road for $400 and deeded it to the County, hoping it would be improved in the future.

Public schools were segregated and the nearest white school was located in McLean, then a small crossroads on the Old Dominion Railroad three miles down the track from our house. Our parents refused to send us there, instead hiring live-in tutors and using the Calvert correspondence course curriculum for many years.

In later years we three boys attended Sidwell Friends School in Washington, going in each morning with our parents when they drove to work, and returning with them at night. After we had completed the 8th grade we were each shipped out to the George School, a Quaker boarding school in Newtown, Pennsylvania.

In the early farm years, before Mother returned to work in the Children's Bureau and the Labor Department, our Spring Hill home, complete with cows, horses, pigs and hundreds of chickens, was a subsistence farm. The orchard yielded apples, cider and applesauce by the gallon. Mason jars of peas, beans, and squash filled the basement, while jellies and jams crowded the shelves above the potato bins.

A huge lawn surrounded the house. We had to mow the lawn by hand with a reel mower until at last we acquired a gas-driven Toro. An enormous black oak, reputed to be the largest in America, covered more than an acre of ground and was twelve feet in diameter. Today, fifty years after we left the farm, it is still standing.

And so we three boys, Donald, Richard and I grew up in a relatively sheltered and bucolic atmosphere on the farm.

Cutting Fire Wood

Each fall we cut, sawed and split wood to make the thousands of logs and pieces of stove wood we would need for the winter. Felled chestnut and oaks were sawed into logs with our 8 foot, two-man "shad belly" saws, so called because their deep bellies were much wider than the ends. Razor sharp, these long handsaws could cut wood almost as fast as today's ubiquitous chain saws. But a man had to know how to swing one, not too fast, not too slow, not too much pressure, not too little. The rhythm was the thing.

Once cut into logs, wedges and "gluts" (heavy wooden wedges) quickly opened up even the biggest trunks, reducing them to manageable sections that were dragged from the woods by horses. Down by the barn the buzz saw had been erected, powered by a huge old single stroke gasoline engine driving a five foot fly wheel, which in turn ran the belt to the saw. A tilting table carried the log sections into the saw blade, cutting through a foot of wood in a few seconds. "Catchers" stood at the side of the saw, grabbing each piece as it was cut and carrying it to the woodshed for stacking.

These ponderous heavy, slow engines had a characteristic sound: chuff ...chuff ...boom! ...chuff ...chuff ...boom! Compression, ignition, power, exhaust, intake, compression, ignition. Reliable and simple, they did immense work on America's farms in the early years of the century. A few still exist today.

Figgin Andy, Moon, and Jug Haid were the names of some of the younger Blacks who worked with us. They usually showed up on wood cutting day to pick up a dollar or two helping out. Dancing and cavorting, they sometimes appeared heedless of the perils of the big buzz saw. Wood cutting day also brought out all the stray dogs, hoping for a hand out, a spare bone or a piece of leftover lunch. Thus, a good bit of chaos and confusion reigned as more steadfast souls proceeded with the job at hand.

The operation was in full swing one bright fall day and the black boys were getting a bit boisterous. Threats to shut down the saw went unheeded as the more playful catchers bounced around. In an instant there was a cry,

Mort and his brothers

Chief Justice William H. Taft administering the oath of office to Herbert Hoover on the East Portico of the United States Capitol on March 4, 1929.

and then stunned silence. Jim hollered to George to shut down the engine. Figgin Andy lay under the saw blade, his arm severed, too shocked to cry.

We quickly moved him away and George frantically sought a rag to use as a tourniquet. Figgin Andy moaned as the seriousness of his accident sank in. George rose from getting the tourniquet in place, at the same time saying, "Thinks that will do it." I went to the house to call the Volunteer Fire Department at McLean, who responded within a few minutes, the long low wail of their siren rising swiftly. As the truck rolled up, the medical aide jumped off and surveyed the scene. "Where is the arm?" he said. We looked at each other and then under the saw ... no arm. A frantic search all around the area failed to turn up the arm. There was a long silence and then someone asked tentatively, "Where are the dogs?"

Inauguration, 1929

March 4, 1929 was Inauguration Day. The United States was at the peak of the Twenties boom, with a chicken in every pot, and two cars in every garage. I was eight years old and taking a keen interest in the world around me. My mother was an official of the Children's Department, a new U.S. Government social agency. Over the years she and my father had cultivated many friends among the movers and shakers of government, politics, industry and labor. Among my mother's best friends were Justice Louis Brandeis and his wife Elizabeth, a relationship that went back even before his appointment to the Supreme Court.

Justice Brandeis was entitled to two tickets to sit on the portico of the Capitol during the 1929 Inauguration ceremony. Unfortunately, he was ill and unable to attend. He gave the tickets to my mother who took me to the ceremony with her.

I vividly remember the occasion, solemn yet optimistic, as Herbert Hoover was sworn in as our Nation's 30th President. Hoover had beaten Democrat Al Smith 21.3 to 15.1 million votes, or 444 to 87 in the Electoral College, and rode into office on a wave of good will. We were seated just to the left at the rear of the podium with the Supreme Court Justices. The invocation droned on and finally Hoover strode in, elegant in a top hat and cut-a-way, followed by the dour departing President Calvin Coolidge.

The ceremony was relatively brief and dignified, ending with the band playing the National Anthem. President Hoover's inaugural address was simple and forgettable, promising the continuation of the good times, which few indeed doubted.

Canadian National

My father was a railroad man. He was trained as a civil engineer with a degree from Lehigh University. In World War I he organized the U.S. Army's munitions manufacturing depots, producing the shells for the Western Front. After the War he put his engineering skills to work settling labor disputes on the railroads, always working for the unions. He devised the technique of "mediation" in which the legitimate concerns of both parties were considered as an alternative to the strikes and pitched battles which so often occurred between the workers and the company goons and armed Pinkerton detectives during the '20s.

In 1925 Sir Henry Thornton, president of the Canadian National Railway, hired my father to solve the violent and intractable labor strife that shut down the railroad's shops in Winnipeg and other locations. After long months and years of patient mediation, Otto finally brought peace to the Canadian National. As a reward, Sir Henry gave the family his personal rail car for a trip from Toronto to Prince Rupert, British Columbia. The trip included two weeks at the CNR's Jasper National Park Lodge and a cruise to Alaska on their cruise line.

Mother, Father and the three boys, ages 8, 6 and 4, drove from Washington to Toronto in our new Model A Ford Phaeton convertible sedan. It was the summer of 1929. The Ford went into the baggage car and we boarded Sir Henry's private car, which was attached to the end of the train. For days we rolled across the vastness of Canada, sitting on the observation platform as we passed through the forests of Ontario, the plains of Saskatchewan and Alberta. We stayed two days at the Calgary Stampede before hooking up again for the trip through the Rockies to Jasper National Park, where we were ensconced in the Royal Suite at the lodge. On the train we had our own chef and porter who prepared meals and made us comfortable. I will always remember the huge plates of fresh calves' liver, bacon and onions, which were devoured with youthful enthusiasm.

Once ensconced in the magnificent lodge at Jasper, we went exploring on the lakes in high-powered speedboats and climbed bear trails up the mountains. We rode in 16-cylinder Rolls Royce touring cars up the road to the foot of the glaciers on Mt. Edith Cavelle for more exploring in the ice caves.

On reaching the Pacific Ocean, we boarded the HMS Prince Rupert and sailed for Alaska, stopping at Sitka, Juneau, and finally Skagway – the jumping off point for the Gold Rush miners crossing White Pass to the Klondike. This had occurred a scant twenty five years before, and while hiking up the pass one could still see the bones of dead horses and discarded tools and packs, and other relics of the great Gold Rush stampede. On the sheer rock cliff behind the town was painted the likeness of Soapy Smith, the local bad man who had terrorized Skagway during the Gold Rush, until he was gunned down in a local barroom brawl.

Our cruise ended in Vancouver, where we reclaimed our car from the CNR terminal. The family then drove leisurely down the Pacific coast, passing the great volcanoes of the Cascade Range, and even climbing the newly opened road into Crater Lake, breaking out onto the awesome view. Just some 7,000 years ago, an eruption had blown the entire top off of Mt. Mazama, leaving a crater about ten miles across and several thousand feet deep. The crater subsequently filled with water from melted snow, creating a magnificent blue lake. As eager youngsters we were impressed, and I have been twice again on subsequent trips.

Our trip ended, for the time, north of San Francisco where we visited my grandmother, then in her 70s, and several of our aunts and uncles. We stayed a few weeks in the mountain cabin of my Uncle Ez (for Ezra), a gigantic 6'8" recluse, who lived by himself far up in the Mendocino Mountains. Ez was not there at the time, having retreated even further into the mountains for the summer, so I never had a chance to meet him. After a month in California we started our trek back to the East Coast in our Ford Phaeton.

Trans Continental in a Model A – 1929

The family trip back across the U.S.A. on U.S Highway 40 was far different from the trip out in Sir Henry Thornton's private rail car. The paved road ceased to exist at Modesto, where we turned east to climb into Yosemite

National Park - a then unspoiled and magnificent wilderness of enormous cliffs and tall trees. We passed the legendary Giant Sequoia tree that was so big the road was built right through its base. East of Yosemite over Tioga Pass, the road degenerated to a single lane, loose gravel track cut out of the sheer walls of the mountains. Below us and around every unmarked curve was an abyss several thousand feet deep. One skid or miscalculation and you were gone! My father did not drive at this time so mother was at the wheel, always aggressive, hour after hour. From the 10,000 foot high Tioga Pass we descended to Mono Lake, surrounded by volcanic peaks and desert sands, and then on to Reno, a sinful city, then noted for its easy divorces.

We stayed in tourist homes, which today are called "bed and breakfasts." There was usually only one hotel in town, down by the railroad depot. Motels were unheard of, but a few "cabins" were appearing on main routes - 10 x 12 foot shacks with no facilities (water, toilets, heat, etc.), only a couple of iron beds. We drove down the side streets looking for the "tourist home" signs, knocked on the door, sized up the hosts while they looked us over, and then moved in. Rooms with breakfast were $2.00 a person. Gasoline came in tall hand-cranked pumps with sight gauges on the sides, for ten cents a gallon.

There were no paved roads between Modesto and St. Louis except in the cities. U.S. 50 and U.S. 40 were gravel, dirt, and mud depending on the weather. Huge plumes of dust followed every car on the open road, and we arrived each night covered with grit and grime. Our route took us from Mono Lake to Reno and then east across the desert of northern Nevada and through the Great Salt Lake desert on U.S. 40 to Salt Lake City, an oasis in the journey. It was early October and the weather was turning bad as we headed for Denver, choosing the northern route via Cheyenne, Wyoming in order to avoid the 11,000 foot passes over the Rockies on Route 40. Snow was already a problem and if you got stuck, you were likely to stay stuck for quite some time. Even so, we faced several days of snowy weather and slow progress as we crossed the high passes between Rock Springs and Rawlins. Sometimes we were uncertain if we would reach the next town by dark.

East of Denver we encountered our worst condition.

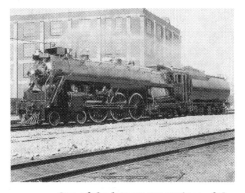

One of the last steam engines of the Canadian National

U.S. 40 turned into a muddy, rutted battle. Over many miles all of us, including the three kids, had to get out of the Phaeton and push while mother charged at full power into the gumbo ahead. There was no way around, no way back. So pushing, digging, backing and charging again, we went ahead. On one day we made only 30 miles through the mud. Where we now take interstates for granted, then there were only rutted roads, hardly better than the wagon trails of the pioneers. For hours on end we would not see another car, let alone a truck. At the end of these days we arrived at our tourist home destinations covered with mud from head to foot and needing both a bath and clean clothes. It took three weeks to make the 2,000 mile journey from California to St. Louis, where at last paved roads appeared and we could average 200 or 300 miles each day.

Tires were also a problem in the late '20s. We carried four spares, but it was not uncommon to have two or three flats or blowouts in one day. Inner tube patching kits, jacks, tire irons, and hand tire pumps were all required equipment for the touring motorist. AAA produced nice little strip maps, but tow trucks and tire repairs were still a generation away. So we all played our parts: jacking, pulling lug nuts, scraping the tubes, breaking the tires loose, patching, pumping-pumping-pumping, and finally getting it all back on.

Inauguration Day, 1933

Franklin D. Roosevelt was elected President in November, 1932 by an overwhelming 22.8 million votes compared to 15.8 for Hoover. The electoral vote was even more lopsided: 472 to 59. Norman Thomas, the Socialist, got 884,000 votes. The country was in deepening depression, and few today can contemplate the depths of misery and disillusion which prevailed. Twelve million unemployed despaired with hardly any social support net. Bands of hobos roamed the country, demanding food and clothing from hapless citizens. The Bonus Army, some 12,000 World War I vets, came to Washington to demand a bonus payment for its war service, only to be driven from the flats of Anacostia where it had set up a squatters' city. General Douglas MacArthur, then Chief of Staff of the U.S. Army, mobilized a division of troops to burn the Bonus Marchers' tent city and drive them out of Washington. The Nation's financial system tottered on the brink as Hoover strove valiantly, but ineffectively, to turn the tide. Roosevelt bided his time, refusing to take any action from his election in November until his swearing in March, 1933.

With my parents in government in Washington, I was all eyes and ears as these events unfolded. I remember the truckloads of hobos driving up to our house, and three dozen of them massing on the porch, selling old magazines and demanding a handout. "Ma'am, I have a button here … would you sew a shirt on it for me?"

Inauguration Day, March 4th, dawned cold and rainy. This time I did not have a seat on the portico, but stood alone, far out in the great crowd below the East Portico, cold, miserable and dripping wet from the rain. The hours dragged on. It was SRO and only the early birds got within hearing distance. Megaphones and speakers were set up, but sound quality was poor and Roosevelt's voice, when it finally came, was weak and tinny.

Roosevelt's was a message of hope. "We have nothing to fear but fear itself," was the unforgettable line. The crowd was moved, and it seemed as if a great sullen weight had been lifted from everyone's shoulders. I well remember the "100 Days" – the Bank Holiday, the National Recovery Administration (NRA), Works Progress Administration (WPA), Public Works Administration (PWA), Civil Aeronautic Administration (CAA) and all the rest. The nation began to move and stir again. It was not to reach the economic levels of 1929 until we began to gear up for WWII.

By the time of the 1936 Landon campaign, Roosevelt's second term, I was attending my first year of prep school at George School. At the school we took an active interest in politics, with more Republicans than Democrats present. The Landon campaign took over an old country store in Newtown, and ran their local "return to basics" campaign from there. Only Maine and Vermont supported Landon, and the unfortunate candidate went down 523 to 8 electoral votes – the most lopsided vote in U.S. history.

The charismatic Roosevelt was once again the President of a trusting America, and the Beyers were enthusiastic supporters once again. I attended the inauguration, standing with the massed thousands in front of the Capitol and then later, along the parade route. I have no memory of the speech, only the grinning politician in his top hat in his limousine as it rolled back to the White House.

The Death of Huey Long

In the summer of 1935 Huey Long, the flamboyant populist Senator from Louisiana, loomed large on the political horizon of the United States. Promising to reorganize government for the benefit of the "common man," the "Kingfish" was posing an ever-greater threat to President Roosevelt and his liberal policies. Many saw Huey Long as a potential Mussolini, and it was an almost certainty that he would challenge Roosevelt for the Democratic nomination for President the next year. My parents loathed Huey Long, and dinner conversations were often laced with denunciations of his latest outrageous pronouncement.

We spent summer vacations those days on the Atlantic shore, at Rehoboth Beach, Delaware, a then sleepy little town. We would rent a house for a month or so, and we kids would play in the sea, go crabbing, or search the sand dunes behind the Cape Henlopen Light for traces of Black Beard's treasure which legend said was buried there.

One August afternoon my father went to the local store to get a few groceries and the newspaper. When home, he burst through the door in high agitation, waving the paper.

"Jesus Christ, Clara, Huey Long has been shot!" he yelled.

"Is he dead?" mother called from upstairs.

"No," my father replied.

"Aw, Hell!" was her response.

Huey died a few days later.

Geneva Student

Shuffleboard on board the SS George Washington

In the summer of 1938 I was 17, Mother was appointed to head the U.S. Delegation to the International Labor Organization (ILO) in Geneva. The ILO was a part of the League of Nations, of which the U.S. was not a member. But we did send delegates to affiliated organizations such as the ILO. Mother was selected due to her long association with the U.S. Department of Labor and the labor movement. Chief U.S. Labor delegate was Denny Lewis, brother of John L. Lewis.

Mother had a First Class cabin on the SS George Washington. I was confined to the tourist section, somewhere between the engine room and the water line. Locked doors separated First, Cabin and Tourist classes, one of the reasons so many lower class passengers were lost on the Titanic, Lusitania and others. I managed to solve this by using the steel ladders welded to the outside structure of the ship. Look right and left, all clear, swing out over the rail onto the ladder and climb like a monkey two decks to First, then back over the side to go see what Mother was up to.

Once in Geneva I enrolled in an International Relations course at the University of Geneva. The institution provided a small cell of a room that at one time must have belonged to a monk of the lowest order in the castle that served as a dorm. My five-foot-six inch bed was a foot short of my requirement, since I was already close to six-foot-six. There I learned to sleep curled up, so bed length was never again a problem.

My fellow students came from virtually all over the Continent, and some beyond – England, France, Italy, Germany, Scandinavia and more. I was the sole American, and arrived with strong opinions about events like the on-going Spanish Revolution, Fascism, Democracy, and Communism. I found to my amazement that the other students had strong opinions too. None could understand our violent society, including strikes, lynchings, and the killing of the Indians. They could not understand our morality about foreign countries. Other students were strong believers in their cultures. The British were superior, sometimes arrogant, effete, and often leaned towards Communism. The French were a race unto themselves. The Germans, proud of what Hitler was doing for their economy, their country and their pride, were totally oblivious to the evils of Nazism. The dour Scandinavians were filled with dread for the future. The Swiss considered themselves safe and superior in their little fortress. We would argue vociferously far into the night. Few, if any, minds were changed. But I did learn a good bit of conversational French and German. I also learned that people have differing cultures, different views, and that these must be understood and respected, even if not accepted.

When Father joined us in August I withdrew from the University and we set out by train for Germany, Denmark, and Estonia whence our ancestors had come, stopping in Norway, Sweden and Finland along the way.

Hitler's Reich

During my two months at the University in Geneva I gained a new appreciation for the intensity with which European students supported their national policies. This was particularly true of the young Germans at the University, who were empathetic in their support of Hitler and the revival he had brought to Germany's economy and national pride.

My Father joined us in August, and we proceeded by train to Germany where some of his family lived in Kassel and Essen. These industrial cities seemed prosperous, but not opulent. Small parades were frequent, with bands of black- or brown-shirted para-military Nazi troops striding by, usually with flags and sometimes a small band. I remember laughing at one of these pompous demonstrations only to feel someone tugging at my elbow and shaking his head vigorously. "Nein, nein, nicht lachen mein herr ..." and then he was gone. I was more careful after that.

The German family members were distant relatives but we did not have much in common. Essen and Kassel were virtually totally destroyed by Allied bombs in the war a few years later, and we never heard from any of these good people again.

From the Rhine River valley we took the train to Berlin, then the largest and most opulent city in Europe. We were impressed by the prosperity, hustle and bustle on the streets, and by the grandeur of the monuments, museums and palaces. We spent almost a week touring them.

Late one Sunday morning there came a great roaring outside our hotel facing the Unter den Linden Strasse, a vast eight-lane avenue bisecting the city and running through the Brandenburg Gate. Going to the balcony we looked out on the most impressive military parade I had ever seen. Down the avenue swept rank on rank of tanks and armored troop carriers, all moving at 35 miles an hour and in perfect formation. In the tens and hundreds they swept by, filled with grim-faced soldiers staring straight ahead. Flags flew from the radio masts and banners fluttered from the buildings above the streets — red, white and black Swastikas everywhere.

And then came the Luftwaffe, in tight echelons of a dozen planes each, right down on the treetops. Their roar was fearful indeed, and the absolute precision with which they held formation made them doubly impressive as they swept down the avenue at 300 feet. In thirty minutes the show was over, and people again trooped into the streets. But the impression this demonstration of military power and precision made on me was lasting.

Journey to Estonia

From Berlin, Mother, Father and I journeyed on to Denmark, where we found my Mother's old family homestead in Northern Jutland. Her father had emigrated to the United States in the 1870s as a young man, first to Hawaii (then an independent Kingdom) and then to California where he married and raised nine children on a farm near Petaluma. The heirs of his family still owned and farmed their little homestead in Denmark much as they had three quarters of a century before. I was impressed by the intensity with which Danish farmers (and northern Europeans in general) farmed their few acres, extracting more produce from one acre that we could in the U.S. from ten.

From Denmark we took the night boat to Oslo, Norway, then the train to Stockholm, and finally another night boat to Finland's capital of Helsinki. Everywhere we went in Scandinavia there was a pervasive dread of the war to come. A pharmacy in Oslo had a window display of gas masks, their huge black eyes and cold breathing tubes staring out ominously. 1938 saw the Nazi takeover of Austria, and the Sudentenland and the Munich Pact, along with the fear of war and all the things it would bring. Bombing, gas, and invasion were the primary topics of conversation. Finland had lived as a Russian province from the early 1800s until it won its freedom after World War I. But St. Petersburg was only a few miles away, and few Finns doubted that Communist Russia craved to restore its rule at the first opportunity. While most of Europe had eyes fixed on Berlin, the Finns' were rightly glued on Moscow. Everywhere we looked preparations were being made for the inevitable defense of Helsinki and the freedom of Finland.

My father's paternal ancestors, the Sternoff family, had been members of the German Hanseatic League, who had effectively dominated the commerce and society of the Baltic States for several hundred years under both Swedish and later Russian dominion. His people had come from central Estonia, some 100 miles south of Tallin, the capital. Father had only the foggiest notions of family names and places since the family had been forced to flee to Germany following the attempt by young revolutionaries to assassinate Czar Alexander I in April, 1866. His grandfather was implicated in the attempt and sent to Siberia to mine salt. Nobody ever heard from him again, and his wife fled to Germany with the children, including my grandfather.

I made my first airplane flight from Helsinki to Tallin across the Gulf of Finland. Early in the morning we took a taxi to the airport, where we boarded a Lufthansa Junkers J-52 Trimotor. The aircraft carried 15 passengers in single seats on both sides of the aisle. It looked as if it had been made of corrugated sheet iron (which it was), and both Ford and Fokker copied the design for their Trimotors. The J-52, unlike the Fords and Fokkers, was a low wing aircraft and the passengers in the front had to clamber over the wing spar across the floor in mid-cabin. Cold and noisy, rattling like a tin lizzie, the Junkers taxied out, revved up its engines and off we went. The flight took about 30 minutes, landing on a grass strip at Tallin after an uneventful crossing. The sight from the air of old Tallin with its castle, walled city, cathedrals, moat and fortified harbor was a striking conclusion to my first flight.

Years later I repeated this story at an international conference, only to be challenged by a Finnair executive who said I was dead wrong. "Lufthansa never flew the route to Tallin. That was a Finnair plane you took!" he stated. I assured him that it was a Lufthansa indeed and a few weeks later I received a letter of apology with a pictorial history of Finnair, showing that indeed in 1938, the Tallin route was flown by Lufthansa's J-52s.

We found lodging at Tallin's best hotel and my father headed for the catacombs of the Cathedral where all of the family records of the Hanseatic Germans were reportedly kept. After several days of research assisted by the librarian he found what he was looking for, the location of the Sternoff family estate in Central Estonia.

Meanwhile, I went exploring all the back alleys and side street shops of Tallin, a fascinating treasure trove of history. I bought several million old Czarist Rubles (some of which I still have), old swords, helmets and so forth.

Estonia became a free nation for the first time following the Bolshevik revolution, but was ruled by a highly socialist government. The big estates that had survived the recent war were partitioned and given to the peasants. In many cases the peasants burned the great manor houses when their owners were evicted. Slowly, however, the former owners were putting their estates back together again as the new peasant owners proved incapable of managing their land, fell into debt, and had to sell. And, as in the case of the Finns, the Estonians lived in dread of the day when the Russians would come again. Many Estonians had been caught up in the war and revolution and were only now coming back from Russia after two decades in captivity.

We hired an Estonian taxi, a small, non-descript vehicle of ancient and unknown manufacture in deplorable mechanical condition. Our driver, however, was a determined individual who, once he understood where we wanted to go, set off at a good rate of speed, down what may best be described as "unimproved roads", toward our destination. Several hours later we arrived. The old manor house was nothing but a ruined foundation overgrown by weeds and second growth trees. Local citizens spoke only Estonian and Russian and my father's efforts to communicate in German were a failure. We wandered around among the ruins of the former "Great House," the barns, sheds and other relics of the past. It was growing late and we had no place to stay.

At this point an old white-haired lady appeared, impeccably dressed in the finery of a former age. She introduced herself in perfect German as a neighbor and father explained our pilgrimage. The lady was the wife of General von Rennenkampf, leader of the Russian Imperial Army at the Battle of Tannenberg, where he was defeated in the early days of World War I by the Germans, led by General Ludendorf and Von Moltke. Her husband was long dead, as were his German adversaries, and now she was living alone in the remnants of her estate in Central Estonia. She, too, had lost her land and the peasants had burned her great house. She lived in the former coach house, surrounded by her relics and attended by a few remaining relatives who had survived the revolution.

Madame von Rennenkampf invited us to her coach house home where we were seated among the mementos of her past, gorgeous tapestries, deep rugs, a huge vase (a present from the Tsar depicting the victory at Tannenberg), old furniture, desks, tables, chairs and cabinets. It was an amazing display of the glories of the past and of the survival of this old lady and her memorabilia. She told us of her family history and that of our family during the tempestuous times of the late 1800s, of the years leading up to World War I, the Bolshevik Revolution and finally of Estonia's independence. Her supply of good vodka was adequate and I was introduced to the pleasure of that wonderful liquor. Father had a good bit more and grew increasingly expansive as the night wore on.

We spent the night on small mattresses on the floor of the living room crowded around the fireplace. In the morning we were roused with coffee and the aroma of ham and eggs, Russian style. After the hearty breakfast and extensive farewell, we entered our taxi (whose driver had slept in the barn) and headed back to Tallin. From there, the ferry took us to Helsinki for the voyage to Stockholm and on to Hamburg for the trip on the US Lines SS George Washington back to the United States.

Most of our fellow passengers were Jews fleeing the growing Nazi terror in their homeland. ✈

CHAPTER II

College Days

Mother Bloor

I arrived at Swarthmore College on a cool crisp September morning in 1939 and was billeted in the old "Prep School" buildings down in the village, along with 50-odd other students. Most considered the main dormitory more prestigious, as it was closer to the main campus and the fraternity houses, as well as closer to the old "Main" building where the girls were. The Prep School was a ten-minute walk under the railroad tracks and up Crum Walk to the campus proper, but it suited me fine.

The next few days were spent in course selection, switching from engineering to economics as a major, getting books and supplies, and going through orientation. The lovely stately old campus, magnificent trees, and fine buildings all made a favorable impression on me after the somewhat cramped and seedy facilities at George School.

The United States Postal Service (USPS) maintained an official station on the campus. We had our own Swarthmore College postmark, and full facilities. I received my box and key but was somewhat surprised to find the box stuffed with propaganda from the American Student Union, a then Communist-leaning organization with cells on many campuses. This material was not franked and, on inquiry, I found that the Post Office was staffed entirely by students (except for the Postmistress), and that most, if not all, of these students were members of the Campus Young Communist League. Thus, with great regularity our student boxes were stuffed with reading material not officially sanctioned by the USPS.

World War II had just begun. Hitler and Stalin had signed their Pact and their troops were sweeping across Poland. Feelings among the students were running high between Isolationists, pro-British Interventionists, Quaker Pacifists, Communists and even a few leaning toward the Axis.

The College administration was caught on the horns of the usual dilemmas. Some faculty members identified with one side or the other. The Quaker traditions bespoke peace and tolerance. Freedom of speech was encouraged – up to a point. I was fresh from a summer in Europe in 1938. I had visited eight countries and seen the moral and military bankruptcy of Britain and France first hand. In Switzerland I had talked with dozens of students from every country and seen the awesome might of the Nazi forces on display. I had visited my father's ancestral home in Estonia and heard their fears for the future.

At this moment the Young Communists had invited Mother Bloor to speak at Swarthmore. Mother Bloor was a tough, articulate survivor of America's early communist movement – the International Workers of the World, Bill Hayward and the rest. She was an outspoken advocate of the Party line. The crew in the Post Office packed every box with announcements of her coming, which was approved by the College.

I felt that this was too much. I picked up a copy of the flyer, announcing Mother Bloor's speech and wrote a brief letter, requesting anonymity, to the *Philadelphia Inquirer* explaining that I and other students were concerned over the use of the campus as a platform for the communists. Unfortunately, the Bloor speech was allowed to take place on a fine Saturday afternoon, filling one of the largest halls on campus.

The *Inquirer* covered the event and the Sunday edition of the paper carried a front page story and a cartoon. The headline screamed "Red Addresses Swarthmore." The rival *Philadelphia Bulletin* followed up with a story of its own. Upset by the publicity, the outraged Alumni on whom the College depended so heavily for endowments, began calling in increasing numbers, forcing the Administration to issue a statement explaining their position.

An immediate investigation was launched. The reporter responsible for the article was quickly discovered and he immediately read my letter to the dean of the college, ignoring my request for anonymity.

The next day I was called into Dean Hunt's office and seated before a cold and angry man.

"Morten, does thee realize what thee has done?" he inquired.

Figuring he had me dead to rights, I said "yes." We had several minutes of discussion about the effects of the press stories on the college, my position that I had just been passing on information which had been illegally stuffed in all of our mailboxes, and my feeling that I had done nothing wrong, however embarrassing it turned out to be.

After a moment to gather his thoughts the dean said: "Morten, I am sorry, but we are going to have to withdraw thee from the college."

I turned to him and replied, "Dean Hunt, have you thought about what tomorrow's headlines are going to look like?"

Again several moments of silence, and then Dean Hunt rose, shook my hand and responded, "Morten, thee are right. But please, try not to embarrass us again."

I was to prove worthy of his trust four years later when I graduated with Honors, as you will see.

The Graduate

Tug 'O War

My tenure at Swarthmore secure, I switched from my entry major of engineering to economics, with minors in political science and history, subjects which I found increasingly fascinating as the world spun into World War II. My courses in these subjects and English went well, but foreign languages proved stubbornly incomprehensible. The teachers were doctrinaire Europeans whose major concerns were grammar and conjugation – not speaking, understanding or reading. Nevertheless, I managed to scrape by.

Campus social life largely revolved around the fraternities (frats) and sororities that vied for desirable freshmen. I was "rushed" by all six, but became increasingly disdainful of the fraternity attitude, instead joining the large group of "non frats" and becoming their leader of sorts. Non frats were non-believers such as I, and the rejects and culls spurned by the upper classmen who made the annual fraternity selections. Not too many years later the frats were barred from the campus.

Part of the annual "initiation" of the freshmen was the Crum Creek Tug-of-War. Crum Creek was a 50-foot wide muddy creek that meandered through the western edge of the campus. The freshmen were assembled on the far side of the woods and the upper classmen on the meadow below Clothier, the campus cathedral. Only boys participated, the girls came to watch, cheer and jeer.

The big day dawned, a fresh Saturday. We "froshes" trailed across the Crum Creek bridge. We were well represented – a little "get out the troops" activity having paid off. However, a seeming vast horde of upper classmen assembled across the creek from us, promising us a quick and ignominious dunking in the cold muddy waters.

Seeing that we were greatly outnumbered and taking advantage of the crowd, I looped our end of the rope low around the trunk of a small tree and tied it firmly. The tug began and slowly we were dragged, yelling and howling, toward the edge of the water... until the rope tightened on the tree and the upper classmen's progress came to a halt. They strained in vain, and the frosh kept yelling and pulling with might and main, effectively disguising the fact that the rope was tied to a stump.

As the minutes passed, more and more upper classmen let go and went to chat up the girls who had gathered on their side. We saw our chance and quietly passed the word up and down the line. "Frosh, one, two, three, PULL!" With a great heave we all dug in together and the line began to move. Faster and faster, harder and harder we pulled as we dragged the depleted remnants of the upper classmen team through the muddy creek in defeat. In the melee that followed, a quick-witted freshman untied the rope so that no evidence of our trickery remained.

What Helps Business

In December of 1939 the American Student Union (ASU), a communist-led nationwide student activist group called for a march on Washington to protest the United States' increasing tilt toward England in the growing World War II in Europe. The Hitler-Stalin Pact and Russia's subsequent invasion of Finland placed this so-called student group firmly in the Communist camp, opposed to U.S. participation against the U.S.S.R. The ASU had once been considered a harmless socialist group, but was now more militant and strident.

The Young Communist League chapter at Swarthmore organized a small group to join the march. I and several of my like-minded friends thought it might be interesting to go along.

The ASU's previous credentials insured it a good reception in Washington. Meetings were held in the giant gilt and purple, 1,000-seat auditorium of the U.S. Department of Labor. President Roosevelt invited the students to the White House, where he would address them on the South Lawn. Mrs. Roosevelt and John L. Lewis, president of the Council for Industrial Organization (CIO) and the most powerful labor leader in the U.S., were to address the group at the Labor Department auditorium. A major parade was organized down Pennsylvania Avenue following the White House visit. It was a demonstration of the influence that the communists and their fellow travelers had in Washington in those days.

It was quickly apparent how far to the left the group's leadership had gone. Moderates were expelled from the leadership in organizational meetings. Resolutions were passed opposing any aid to the Allies, particularly Finland, fighting for its life against the Russian invasion. Slogans like "millions for jobs, but not one cent for defense" abounded. My group from Swarthmore sat quietly and bided its time.

The 1,000-odd delegates trooped up to the White House on the morning of the second day and assembled on the South Lawn. President Roosevelt was wheeled out on the South Porch in his wheelchair. He then stood and addressed the group about political responsibility, the Finnish War, and other subjects the students did not want to hear about. They booed him loudly, roundly and repeatedly - on his own lawn, yet! To us it seemed strangely uncouth and a display of bad manners.

Later that afternoon John L. Lewis addressed the delegates. He was due at 3:00 P.M. but was not there. At 3:30 an aide said he was on the way, a statement repeated over and over for the next hour and a half. The crowd grew more and more restive and more hyped up waiting for the great "John L." It was a technique perfected by Adolph Hitler, who learned that by delaying his appearance he could key up his supporters to a frenzy of anticipation. At last the rear doors of the auditorium burst open and in came John L. Lewis, striding down the aisle to the podium. With a great roar, the audience rose as one to welcome their hero. Lewis mounted the rostrum and poured on a stem winder speech about the rights of labor and the working man. The students loved it. Lewis, his leonine mane shaking in the spotlight, loved it and then he was gone.

The next day Eleanor Roosevelt addressed the group and gave them a first class verbal spanking for their conduct, lack of manners and lack of tolerance for the opinions of others. Hers was a masterful performance. I enjoyed it immensely, but I doubt if many members of the ASU leadership appreciated frank talk from a person who understood them far better than they understood themselves.

Strike!

Father and Mother both held influential positions in the Roosevelt administration and were generally partisans of the labor movement. I had vivid memories of the labor leaders who joined our Sunday dinners at the farm. John L. Lewis, Sam Gompers, and Walter Reuther were all shining idols.

Chester, Pennsylvania was a boomtown dominated by the massive Baldwin Locomotive Works and the Sun Oil refineries and ship building company. The town was served by the *Chester Times* newspaper, a rugged repository of Republican (if not Neanderthal) virtue. Its workers were badly treated and poorly paid. One day they went out on strike. The company hired scabs to replace the strikers. The union brought up strong-arm squads from Sun Shipbuilding to hold the picket lines.

The union leadership asked the Swarthmore students to support the strike. We heeded the call and one cold winter morning four of us took the early bus to Chester and the Times Building. In front of the building stood a solid phalanx of the Chester Police, some 90 strong, clad in their great coats and hats. Each wore his Colt .45 and swung a three-foot long mahogany club. Twenty feet in front of them stood the union men, a ragged collection of newspaper staff looking weak, puny and undernourished. Side by side with these men were the strong arm union goons from the shipbuilding crews: big, brawny and ugly and armed with steel rods. One or two ladies in shawls furtively flitted up and down the line bringing coffee and perhaps a donut. An occasional ill-tuned song rose from the union ranks:

"Solidarity forever. Solidarity forever,
For the union makes us strong ..."

Or a plaintive:

"Oh, I dreamed last night that I saw Joe Hill, a-standing by my bed ..."

The singing faded away as a growing sense of futility prevailed. In contrast to the strong blue line which was letting the strikebreakers in and out and seeing that they came to no harm, the union pickets seemed weak and disorganized. A cold fog drifted in from the river, casting an even grimmer hue over the scene.

Heeding the words of the Reinhold Niebuhr who said, "Give me the strength to change what I can, and to accept that which I cannot," we slunk back to the campus, much wiser for our lesson in Civics 101.

Construction Days – Building the Pentagon

Summer 1941 was a time to earn some money. As soon as Swarthmore let out for the summer I returned to Virginia, looking for a job that suited an unskilled but motivated young man of nineteen. Since Mother was then a senior executive of the United States Department of Labor, she called a friend in the department who put us in touch with the President of Local 1054 of the Hod Carriers and Common Laborers Union of America (now the Laborers' District Council of Washington, D.C.). They invited me to visit the Union Hall on 4th and C Streets, NW.

The hod carriers supplied all of the unionized day laborers required by contractors on major governmental and private projects in the area. Wages were a munificent $0.90 per hour – a fortune in those days – with time-and-a-half for overtime and Saturdays and double-time on Sundays and holidays. Contractors called or visited the Union hiring hall to select the workers they wanted and other hopefuls hung around the projects as the day began, hoping to be picked up.

After a brief and friendly chat with the union president, I was ushered to the cashier's window to sign up as a union member. Membership was $5.00 and the dues were $5.00 per month. I joined.

Each morning I lined up with the other hopeful workers in the basement of the Union Hall which served as the hiring hall, waiting room and poker alcove. Contractors came and went, selecting the qualified men they knew. I was not among those chosen and so spent the day in idle conversation with my fellow rejects. Virtually the entire union membership was black, and being a common laborer and hod carrier was about as far up the union scale as a black man could aspire. Carpentry, plumbing, masonry and other trades were effectively closed to Blacks. Thus I, as a lone white youth, was somewhat of an oddity among the hod carriers. There was no hostility and we bantered and talked of the projects under way and our hopes to land a job on one. Occasionally I would join the perpetual game of poker. Black Jack or Five Card Stud were games of choice. They were better players than I and participation in the games proved unprofitable for me.

After a few days the Union president came down to visit us. A huge, well-dressed and imposing black man, his authority commanded respect.

"How ya doin?" he asked me with a nod of recognition.

"No job yet," was my reply.

"Well, let's do sumpin about dat, come along with me," he answered.

I followed him out to the parking lot, where a not-so-new but well kept and impressive black Cadillac sedan stood under the only shade around.

"Git in," he said, and I did. He drove slowly to the first major project close by, the building of the Statler Hilton Hotel at 16th and K Streets. The Cadillac swung in through the fence surrounding the excavation and carefully descended the truck ramp to the bottom. We stopped and the Union president leaned out, waving a worker over.

"Git me da boss," he said, and the man obediently trotted off looking for the project manager, who soon appeared.

"Yes sir," he said respectfully to the Union leader. "What can I do for you?"

"Well, dis young man, see, he need a job. Now do you have sumpin fo' him here?" The white foreman, looking uncomfortable, shuffled his feet a bit and started to say "No."

The Union boss cut him off saying "Sho, you got plenty fo' him to do here. Sign him up."

"Yes, Sir," said the unwilling foreman. I got out, was led to the office (a trailer perched precariously over the pit), signed up and given a badge. Since mine was obviously a "made work" situation, I was put to picking up trash in the excavation: broken boards, chunks of steel, tangles of wire, paper and bottles thrown over the fence. By quitting time the "hole" was all picked up and I proudly turned in my badge for the night, going home happy after my first day at a "real job."

Promptly at 7:30 the next morning I showed up at the Statler Hilton project and went to the office trailer to pick up my badge. The clerk inside the check-in window asked my name, checked his roster, and said indifferently, "Sorry, Bud, you been laid off. No more work for you here … Here's your pay," pushing a small brown envelope toward me which contained $5.40 for the six hours I had worked the previous day. "Sign here," he said. I signed the receipt, pocketed the pay envelope, and disconsolately headed to my car to drive to the Hiring Hall. That was the way it was. Union workers got good wages, but were hired and fired at the whim of the foreman, an experience I would repeat several times that summer.

However, the next job was not long in coming. Tompkins, a major contractor, was building additional "war temporaries" as the two-story, wood and asbestos shingled office buildings were called that soon stretched in multiple rows from the Washington Monument to the Lincoln Memorial. New space was urgently needed to house the rapidly growing staff of the navy as the U.S. geared up for the impending war. Only a few years earlier there had been plans to tear down the World War I Temporaries that still scarred the Mall, but now we were building more.

By bus and car we streamed out of the Hiring Hall and headed for the Tompkins office at 17th and Constitution. Application blanks required name, address, and Social Security and Union membership numbers. The mostly black members of the Hod Carriers and Common Laborers did just that. We toted lumber, mortar, bundles of shingles and tons of nails from ground level to the higher floors where white (mostly red-neck) carpenters sawed, hammered, trowelled, braced and nailed the rising structure in place. Chief architectural instruments were their squares, levels and tape measures. A hod carrier was not even permitted to touch one of the tools of these highly skilled and even better paid artisans.

Obviously, I was somewhat of an oddity in this crowd. A white college student working with the negroes. But I was always treated with respect and consideration. When the day dragged on in heat, humidity and sweat, there was always someone willing to lend a hand with an extra big board, or give a few words of encouragement or banter: "Hey there, Slim, you gonna make it okay?" "Sure, thanks."

Much of the work of my crew consisted of carrying 16-foot 2" x 8" timbers of fresh sawed yellow pine for framing and ceilings up to the second and third floors. The normal load was two boards and we shuffled in single file up the ramps with our loads, then going back down empty handed to get the next. As I became more accustomed to the work, I tended to increase my load to three boards at the same time increasing my walking speed, often passing other crew members marching to a slower drum. Surprisingly, this produced no hostility in my black crew members, but rather a degree of amusement.

"Slim whutcha carrying three boards for?"

"Sam, I guess I am comfortable carrying three boards."

"Slim, whutcha walking so fast fo'?"

"Heck, Sam, I'm just walking my normal pace"

"Slim, I done many a hour just walking."

Pressure to speed up the work continued. Occasionally the foreman would stop to urge greater efforts.

"Why don't you move it ...We ain't got all day!"

Such entreaties did not seem to produce any visible effect. Work days increased to 10 hours and six-day work weeks were common, which gave us 40 hours of straight time and 20 hours of overtime or 70 hours' pay each week. I would go home at night exhausted, take a shower, eat a quick dinner saved for me by Julia, the cook, and head for bed.

One evening, as I was hoisting the last load on my shoulder for the long climb to the roof, I looked down the face of the building. There, a hundred yards away, stood a crane idle and unused. It had been there for several days. I completed my load and sought out the foreman.

"Mr. Foreman, can I make a suggestion?" I asked.

"Why don't you mind your own goddam business, what is it?"

"Well, sir, if you fired up that crane down there you could lift all of these boards up on the roof much faster and with less labor."

"We don't want your fuckin' no good ideas," he replied and strode off.

Arriving at the office the next morning, I noticed that most of my fellow workers were standing around disconsolately talking to themselves. I went briskly to the window to punch in and get my badge only to be told "Sorry, Slim, no more work for you here. Go get your pay." As I left the project I stopped to look down the face of the building. Where we had been working the day before the crane was picking up one bundle of lumber after another and slowly lifting them to the roof.

I soon got another job, at the Pentagon, rising on the Hoover Flats just across the Potomac. There were other jobs as well, such as clearing forests for the expansion of Ft. Belvoir and building piers at the Naval Station at the foot of South Capitol Street. Sometimes we spent days waiting in the hiring hall, playing poker. The summer passed soon enough and, in early September, I returned to Swarthmore for my sophomore year.

The Origin of Two-Tone Paint Schemes

In the beginning, all cars were painted a single color. Henry Ford's Model T was black. Period. That was the only color you could get. Later, with the Model A, the Chevy, and big cars such as the Buick, Auburn, and LaSalle, you could get a variety of colors – usually conservative blue, brown, or maroon. But occasionally you could get red or cream.

In the summer of 1941, using my extraordinary wages from working for the union, I bought a 1936 rumble seat Ford V8 convertible for $275 cash. A few more dollars bought a spotlight (a necessity in those days) and a new, solid yellow paint job.

A few weeks later I and another car coming from the opposite direction attempted to negotiate a curve on a narrow country road. Both of us were going too fast. I lost my two left fenders in a tangle of tin. New fenders from Ford were expensive and the local junkyards had no used ones on hand. So, for $4.50 each, I purchased two Ford fenders from Sears. Unfortunately for me, when they were delivered I discovered they were painted black, the only color available.

With the help of several local boys in the neighborhood I installed the new fenders in no time, and then went looking for the auto painter who had painted my car yellow. But, looking at the little yellow convertible with the black fenders, I decided it looked sharp. In fact, it looked better that way than all yellow. So I painted the other two fenders black also. And that was the way she stayed, as far as I know the first two-tone paint scheme on a car.

Inauguration Day – 1941

January 20, 1941 was a beautiful day. President Roosevelt was being sworn in for his third term. I came down from Swarthmore for the weekend to hear him and watch the parade. His speech from the East Portico of the Capitol was unimpressive. He was promising peace while preparing to involve the U.S. in the war. Hitler's armies were in firm control of Europe, with the U-boats taking a greater and greater toll on Allied shipping. The British were hanging on grimly, managing to stall the German conquests short of victory and hoping for Roosevelt's planned intervention sooner rather than later.

Roosevelt used the Inauguration Day parade as an opportunity to display America's awesome military might to the world. Divisions of tanks and armored cars made up the bulk of the parade, interspersed with the usual high school marching bands, Legion posts from World War I, and others. An aerial display of U.S. fighter and bomber aircraft was planned as well. Remembering vividly the tremendous military show that the German forces had put on in Berlin three years previously, I expected an impressive display.

Roosevelt rolled by in his open car, waving and beaming his famous smile to the cheering crowds who jammed the sidewalks from the Capitol to the White House. But then things began to slow down. Gaps opened up in the parade ranks as some of the tanks' engines overheated and ground to a halt, smoking and clattering. Mechanics rushed to fix them or tow them out of the way. Soldiers in the armored cars grew tired of the delay and became thirsty as well. They piled out of their stalled vehicles to visit the local liquor stores for a six-pack or two, then spent the rest of their time during the parade swilling from the bottles and tossing the empties to the crowd.

At last the Army Air Corps and Navy planes appeared above us. In the German display a few years before, the aircraft had screamed down the parade route at housetop level, providing a thunderous climax to the show. But not here in Washington. The aircraft were ordered to remain above 5,000 feet in altitude for safety reasons, and so we craned our necks to watch a few dozen tiny silver specks crawling across the sky in ragged "V" formations.

It was hardly an impressive demonstration and made one wonder how high a price the United States would have to pay once war came to match the fighting efficiency of our foes.

War!

On December 7th, 1941 the Japanese struck Pearl Harbor. Swarthmore students huddled in small groups to analyze and discuss the news. Roosevelt declared the deed a "*day of infamy*", but to some of us it appeared that the United States had forced Japan's hand with our strangling blockade – cutting Japan off from the oil, food and raw materials it needed to survive. Nonetheless, a wave of patriotic fervor swept the campus, and a few days later all but a few conscientious objectors boarded a train at the Swarthmore rail station for the trip to Philadelphia to volunteer.

First I chose the Navy, where we were subjected to intensive intellectual and physical screening. We spent the day dressed only in our skivvies, going from desk to desk to give our life histories and undergoing physical examinations. I was rejected for being too tall – 6 feet 6 ½ inches in my bare feet. Obviously I would not fit in a submarine or destroyer. I had also suffered from an asthmatic condition since childhood and this did not enhance my prospects.

Rejected by the Navy, I tried both the Army and the Marines, but suffered a similar fate in both. After a few weeks I accepted my "4 F" draft classification and returned to college to study and sit out the war in a civilian capacity.

As the end of the War neared and manpower requirements increased, my Draft Board decided that I was "fit," and demanded I report for duty. However, by this time I had been employed by Pan Am for two years and had an "Essential" classification. Thus, I was spared doing garrison duty in Europe or Japan.

Tires, Tires and More Tires

During most of my Swarthmore College days I held various part time jobs. In 1940 I made an agreement with Mr. Hintlian the Rug Merchant, an Armenian rug dealer in the Village, to use his rug truck to meet the Pennsylvania Railroad mail trains passing through Swarthmore delivering the U.S. mail, then to be transferred to the Post Office.

In those days the *Pennsy* ran some twenty trains a day between Media and Philadelphia via Swarthmore. Eight of those trains carried U.S. mail. My job was to meet these trains and deliver the mail to and from the Post Office. The first train arrived at 5 P.M. and the last at 6 P.M. Each carried mail cars with postal personnel who bagged and prepared the mail.

So at 4:45 A.M. I rolled out of bed to the jangle of the alarm clock, slipped on whatever clothing the weather dictated, and took off with Hintlian's red Dodge truck for the station, hoping to beat the train by enough time to get the high wheel baggage cart ready to receive the mail. The train rolled in huffing and puffing and the U.S. mail clerks threw out the night's accumulation of mail sacks, slammed the door and rolled west to Media. I transferred the sacks to the truck, drove to the Post Office, unloaded the mail on the back platform, and returned to my dorm in time to dress for breakfast and class.

The return train arrived at 7 A.M. to pick up the outbound mail, and again I was there with the night's accumulation from our Post Office going into Philly. So it went throughout the day. I would watch the clock and, as the train approached and I heard the whistle, I would depart from class or seminar and head for the station to meet the train. I earned $200 a month doing this, a magnificent salary in those days.

I also used Hintlian's truck to deliver rugs for him between trains and to deliver steamer trunks and other large packages arriving by Railway Express at the station. But then one day the U.S. Post Office decided that this vital function should be performed by their own employees because they were not deterred by sleet, storm or night, etc. So I was replaced with a special new mail truck and three full-time postal drivers.

Next I went to work as the auxiliary driver at Railway Express which was the equivalent of UPS and FedEx. We had our office on Main Street opposite the Railroad Station and I continued to deliver trunks, parcels and other shipments arriving at off hours.

With the advent of World War II, America lost its sources of natural rubber as the Japanese overran the rubber plantations of Malaysia and Sumatra. An emergency program was instituted to get patriotic Americans to turn in all of their old tires to the U.S. Government. Railway Express was the handling agency. People with tires to turn in brought them to the RR Express offices where they were to be inventoried. The donor was given a receipt about 18 inches long and promised $2.00 per tire. I was honored with the task of heading this operation at Swarthmore starting right after New Year's Day 1942.

We opened our doors on the first day and people poured in carrying their used, discarded, old tires. Each was given his receipt and the tires were labeled and carried to the back warehouse. All day the tires poured in and the paperwork got more and more behind. I finally closed the doors at midnight and spent the rest of the night sorting out paperwork and stacking tires. At 8 A.M. I opened up again to a new horde of patriotic tire donors. This went on for three days and nights. I spent the entire 72 hours in the RR Express office receiving, labeling, processing and piling up tires, taking in thousands of them until the entire warehouse was filled to the ceiling. I finally gave out, went back to the dorm and collapsed for twelve hours of sleep.

In subsequent days we shipped the tires out to the government warehouses for processing and after a month they were all gone. I made an enormous amount of double time for my seventy-two hour stint, keeping the office open and processing tires in my first contribution to the war effort.

Eventually the U.S. developed a synthetic rubber and no longer depended on recycling old tires. But for a few months, our efforts to collect and reprocess old tires made us feel as if we were really contributing to the war effort.

Homer Lea

At Swarthmore I was an avid student of history. I spent many hours in the library stacks reading *Harpers Weekly* of the Civil War period. *Harpers* was considered the *Time* and *Life* magazine of that era. Their reporters covered all the great battles and their artists made magnificent steel engravings of the battle scenes. I also was enthralled with the doctrine of "Geopolitics" founded by Pareto, an Italian philosopher of the last century who believed in the survival of the fittest and the genetic superiority of peoples of the temperate climates over those of the tropics. Another author was Halford J. McKinder, an Englishman who shared similar thoughts.

One day in mid-1941, far back in the library stacks where few students ever ventured, I found two little volumes. Both were almost unread in the 30-odd years they had rested there. One bore the flamboyant title *The Valor of Ignorance*, and the other *The Day of the Saxon*. They were written by Homer Lea who further research showed to be the son of a Confederate Colonel who had emigrated to California following the fall of the South. In the late 1880's Lea grew up as a deformed hunchback with dreams of military glory. When America engaged the Spanish in the War of 1898 Lea volunteered, only to be laughed out of the recruiting office.

Frustrated and humiliated, Lea sought solace among the San Francisco Chinese who were actively supporting the Freedom Movement in China. Ruled by the corrupt and ruthless Dowager Empress, China was in a state of constant rebellion and chaos.

The Western Powers, Russia and Japan fought constantly with each other and with the Chinese over rights to Manchuria, Korea and China itself. A revolutionary movement under Sun Yat Sen slowly gathered momentum. In 1900 the Dowager Empress declared war on the foreigners and Christians in Peking and the Chinese in San Francisco sent Homer Lea to China to help organize a local army to raise the siege and free the Westerners. Homer Lea placed himself in command of a rag-tag native Chinese army and marched on Peking, raising the siege and freeing the European ambassadors and their staffs along with thousands of Chinese Christians.

Homer Lea was introduced to Sun Yat Sen and discussed with him his strategy for winning China for a democratic government. After days of discussion, an impressed Sun Yat Sen said to Lea: "Young man, when I become president of China, I will make you my chief of staff." Lea's reply was "Make me your chief of staff now and I will make you president of China." Sun Yat Sen accepted, and twelve years later, on February 12, 1912, the Boy Emperor resigned and Sun Yat Sen became the first president of China.

In the intervening years Homer Lea led a seemingly unending struggle across the vastness of China leading fighting between Sun Yat Sen's troops, the Emperor's forces, local warlords, the Western Powers, Russians, Japanese, and others. The Japanese destroyed the Russian fleet at Vladivostok and seized Korea and Manchuria. Wars waxed and waned across China.

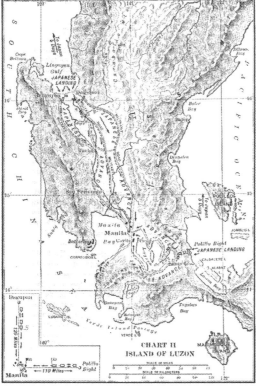

Map of Luzon

All during this period Homer Lea was writing his two books. The *Valor of Ignorance* foretold the convergence of U.S. and Japanese interests in the Pacific. It was published in 1907. *Valor* set forth the reasons why Japan and the United States were inevitably on a collision course for power in the Pacific and made the most extraordinary series of predictions, outlining the Japanese strategy. Each phase of the predicted war to come was outlined, including the very beaches on which the Japanese would land in the Philippines and how many days it would take them to reach Manila. Homer Lea was off by one day. The strategy of a land attack on Singapore down the Malay Peninsula and across the Straits of Jahore was spelled out with maps as well, pointing out that all the British guns faced the sea. And finally, the attack on Pearl Harbor was also outlined, though lacking aircraft, for all to read.

Lea felt that the political and economic convergence of the interests of Japan and the United States made war in the Pacific inevitable. No one in the U.S. ever paid any attention.

Homer Lea's books were required reading in the German and Japanese staff schools and military war colleges. The Russians also read them. After Pearl Harbor someone went looking for the two volumes of Lea's work in the West Point library. They were there, but had never been read.

The second book by Lea was published in 1912, called *The Day of the Saxon*, it predicted the coming of World War I in Europe and the conflict between the Central Powers and the Allies – England, France and Russia. The book outlined the inevitable political and economic convergence between these two groups of nations and contrasted the economic and political drive of the Germans with the decadence and decline of the Allies on the one hand, and the glacial expansion of Russia on the other. Again, it set forth the tactical and strategic objectives of the Central Powers and forecast that they eventually would be defeated but would rise again to renew their attack. And finally, *The Day of the Saxon* forecast the disintegration of the British Empire – then seemingly at the height of its power.

These two books by the deformed hunchback Homer Lea were by all odds the most penetrating analysis of world political-economic-military relationships that I have ever read. They had then, and have today, a profound influence on my thinking about what has happened in the last seventy-five years and what will happen in the future. Homer Lea had absolutely no equal as a geo-political strategist of the 20th century. Would that we had heeded him then – and today.

Homer Lea had planned to write a third book, *The Swarming of the Slav*, dealing with the expansionist proclivities of the Russians.

He dealt at some length with the subject in *The Day of the Saxon,* pointing out from his vantage point in 1910, when the Czarist Empire was crumbling from within and without, that Russia would continue its relentless expansion regardless of the form of government it was under. This proved true under Lenin, Stalin and their successors and, despite the temporary setback following the collapse of the U.S.S.R., it is most likely to continue again.

Homer Lea died in China in 1912 of tuberculosis at the age of thirty-nine. He had achieved some of the glory to which he had aspired. He became a general of the armies of China. He made Sun Yat Sen president of China. He laid out a strategic map of the future that was followed almost to the letter by America's enemies and ignored by our allies and ourselves. He was a long way from San Francisco and the days when he was laughed out of the U.S. Cavalry recruiting office.

Beat Haverford!

Swarthmore was a school where athletics was second only to academic excellence. We had good football teams and were always in the top form of the Ivy League. But, we did not play Haverford College, another Quaker College located some ten miles away. Swarthmore was coeducational and represented the liberal wing of the Quaker faith. Haverford was men only, and cleaved to the more conservative wing of the faith. For years the two colleges had not played each other in football due to some long-forgotten misunderstanding.

The college administrations thought it would be a good idea to bring the two teams together again. In "Morning Meeting" students were informed of the momentous decision and urged not to perform ungentlemanly acts against students of the other college, which would embarrass our schools.

Saturday was to be game day. As the day approached, college spirit ran high on the two campuses. Rallies were held on the theme "Beat Haverford!" More behavioral warnings were issued. On Thursday night a delegation of enthusiastic Haverford students visited Swarthmore and desecrated the campus with signs saying "Beat Swarthmore" up and down McGill Walk. In the wee hours dormitories were entered and graffiti (mild by today's standards) adorned the walls – "Swarthmore stinks!"

Student anger swept the campus. Outraged at the insult to our honor, it was obvious that we "had to do something." The Deans appealed for calm: "Thee has to understand and turn thy other cheek."

I kept a somewhat illegal car off campus, my 1936 Ford convertible. A group of us decided that retribution was in order and justice must be done, a feeling reinforced by several beers at "The Plushies," a small local tavern out on Lansdowne Pike. At 2 A.M. two carloads of us set out for Haverford.

It was a bright moonlit night, with patches of clouds bringing minutes of total darkness. We drove slowly up College Avenue and onto the Haverford campus, where all were sleeping soundly (we hoped). The Haverford football stadium, such as it was, lay to our right and we drove out, hiding the cars under the bleachers. A sharp carpenter's saw soon attacked the feet of the wooden goal posts, and within two minutes the posts at the north end of the field were eased to the ground and the cross bar wrenched off.

The three 20-foot long posts and cross bar were placed on top of my convertible (the roof was down) and tied firmly to the front and back bumpers. So far, so good. We eased out of the driveway and down College Avenue toward Swarthmore. A black cloud obscured the moon as we rounded a corner, only to encounter a Haverford Police car coming the other way on the narrow road. We were well past the police car when the officer realized what he had seen in his headlights, the Haverford goal posts en route to Swarthmore. Lights! Siren! I floored the accelerator and shot ahead with my precious cargo of five students and three goal posts. The police car struggled to turn around on the narrow road as we crested a small hill, shut off our lights, and drove through an open fence into a large welcoming pasture. We came to rest behind a hedge out of the moonlight.

The police car screamed past our hiding place, hotly pursuing the other car with the rest of our party. We slipped back onto the road and headed for another, less used road back to Swarthmore, arriving 30 minutes later without further incident. An occasional distant siren reminded us that someone might be looking for us. Our partners were apprehended a mile or so away, taken to the Haverford Police station, booked for speeding and released.

Back at college, we drove straight to the front of the main building where McGill Walk reached the massive portico. The posts were quickly untied and the cross bar reinstalled. A shovel appeared and in half an hour two holes awaited the posts. A roll of oil cloth and a paint brush produced a beautiful 18-foot "BEAT HAVERFORD" sign which was affixed between the posts as we raised them proudly and headed for our dorms.

Early risers saw our handiwork, and we believed it gave the campus a real morale boost. After a desultory investigation, the Deans decided to do nothing and say nothing. I suspect they had a pretty good idea who was responsible but, after all, Haverford had struck the first blow with its graffiti. On that day, and many more to come, Swarthmore beat Haverford in football.

I was graduated from Swarthmore in February 1943, receiving a Degree with Honors in Economics – with minors in Political Science and History. The College featured a unique Honors program under which the brightest students were invited to participate in a self-study program. You studied all week in the library or your room, then produced a weekly essay on the subject you were emphasizing, such as *Vauban's Fortresses, The 19th Century Maginot Line*, or the *Economics of Fascism*. Final examinations were given orally by professors from other colleges. They quizzed you in general on your fields of study. A broad general knowledge of your subjects and a quick wit were necessary ingredients for obtaining a good grade. It also paid to take a quick read on the examiner's political and social leanings, and give him the answers he wanted to hear.

Dogs, Dogs, Dogs

I was graduated from Swarthmore in February 1943 under an accelerated wartime program, receiving a degree with Honors in Economics, with minors in Political Science and History. Having been turned down for military service by all three services and classified 4-F by my Draft Board, I sought employment in my favorite business, the airlines.

In early February of 1943, I applied to TWA, American Airlines and Pan Am for a job. While these applications were pending I stayed at Swarthmore Village and worked full time for Railway Express. My job as the junior driver was to meet the morning inbound train, unload all shipments, and bring them to the distribution dock where the senior union drivers loaded them in their trucks for the daily suburban runs.

Once the old timers were away from the dock, we sorted the remaining odd packages and got the list of pickups. I met the noon trains at Darby and picked up some miscellaneous shipments that I was to deliver. One of the major daily inbound shipments was live dogs destined for the Lederle Laboratories where they manufactured serum for wartime diseases. Unfortunately, many of the dogs were dead on arrival, due to delays in shipment and lack of food and water. Nonetheless, as Railway Express drivers we were obligated to deliver the dogs - dead or alive. They were invariably shipped C.O.D. and Lederle objected mightily to paying for dead dogs they could not use. I could only sympathize and offer the complaint forms to fill out for a refund. As we made our way through the back streets of the Lansdowne area where Lederle was located, we were invariably pursued by packs of stray dogs. This gave rise to an idea! I picked up a bunch of meat bones from one of our grocery drops and placed them at the front entrance to my truck. Immediately dozens of hungry dogs appeared and went for the bones. The door was slammed, and truck and dogs headed to Lederle along with our usual shipment of dead animals. This time when the shipping supervisor started to give me a bad time about the shipment of dead dogs, I interrupted him:

"Sir, I may have an answer for you ..."

"Yeah, what is it?"

"I have some replacement dogs I will gladly sell to you."

"Let's see 'em."

I took him out to the truck full of strays and he surveyed the cargo. The lab needed the dogs for their serum and experiments and here they were - no questions asked.

"How much?"

"Ten bucks each."

After a few outraged sputters and grumbles he agreed, paid me $90.00 cash for the substitute dogs, signed for the dead dogs, and I left.

A few weeks later I received word that I had been accepted by Pan American Airways in Miami and left Railway Express, thus ending a profitable enterprise. ✈

CHAPTER III

Pan Am

Joining Up

The U.S. airlines had lost about half of their fleets and more of their airmen to the war. The aircraft were conscripted as transports for military personnel and cargo as part of MATS, the U.S. Army's mighty Military Air Transport Services, and many of the airlines operated contract services, using their own pilots and planes for MATS during the war. The remaining civil transports flew increased hours to make up for the loss of aircraft. All travel was controlled by "military priorities," and seats were scarce. Civilian passengers were likely to get bumped at any time, reduced to waiting or to jamming themselves into over-crowded trains instead.

Father was the Director of the Transportation Manpower Division of the War Labor Board and knew all of the airline presidents on a first name basis: C.R. Smith (American), Ralph Damon (TWA) and others. A believer in the school of "It's who you know that gets you someplace…and what you know that keeps you there," he unhesitatingly contacted these executives to advise them that his #1 son was available and interested in a job with their airlines.

A letter came from the office of the president of American Airlines, C.R. Smith, inviting me to report to the Personnel Office at LaGuardia Airport in New York. An American Airlines ticket from Philadelphia to New York was enclosed with the letter. I showed up for the early morning flight, boarded the shiny red-white-and-blue over silver DC-3, and flew to New York. Several hours of interviews with Personnel and a physical exam produced an offer to join American as a Ramp Agent in New York at $100 per month. A few weeks later a similar procedure produced an offer to work with TWA as a ticket counter agent at a similarly generous wage. I was not enthusiastic.

Mrs. Anne Archibald was Vice President in Washington for Pan Am. A short dumpy woman of fifty something, vain but unprepossessing-looking, Mrs. Archibald had gotten her job when her husband, Col. Bill Archibald, Ret. who had held the job, suddenly died. Anne showed up at the office the next day, plunked herself down in his chair, announced "I am in charge," and for the next ten years she was. Anne Archibald may not have looked like much but looks were deceiving. She demanded a fresh bouquet of roses on her desk every morning along with all the incoming mail, opened and neatly stacked. Anne had the coldest pair of ice blue eyes of anybody I ever knew and she ran her office with ruthless efficiency. She went through the mail, assigning each letter to a specific employee with instructions that the answer was to be on her desk by 4 P.M. Then began her daily round of calls, requests, favors to be done for Pan Am. "George, who is our man on the House Foreign Affairs Committee?" In every government bureau and legislative office Anne Archibald had "our man" who for one reason or another acted as an unofficial agent of Pan Am's foreign policy. In many smaller countries and possessions in the Caribbean, Central and South America, Pan Am's station manager had more influence than the American Ambassador, and so it was a two-way street. When the government wanted something done abroad, they often came to Pan Am's Anne Archibald.

At 4 P.M. the answered mail piled up on Anne's desk for signature, each task completed as requested, and no excuses thank you. She was one of the most effective persons I ever knew.

So one day in April, I was ushered into her office, thanks to an appointment made by my father. We chatted briefly and she turned and called, "George, get me Henry Snyder in Miami." Snyder was division manager of the Eastern Division of Pan Am. "Henry, Anne here...Fine, thank you...Henry, I am

Dinner Key with the Pan Am Terminal

sending you a young man named Morten Beyer and I want you to find him a job...Yes, that's right...Thank you..." I thanked her and left.

A job in Miami with Pan Am sounded much more attractive than loading DC-3s on the ramp at LaGuardia. Pan Am was still flying the Clippers to South America and operated the Africa Orient Division, supplying the U.S. forces in China and North Africa. Definitely preferable.

On May 10, 1943 I started out for Miami in my little yellow and black Ford convertible, carrying everything that I might need for my new life. I drove straight through, some thirty-two hours. Speeds were limited to 35 mph by wartime regulations, and headlights had to be hooded to prevent the Germans from spotting highway traffic. This was actually a problem in coastal

The Sikorsky S-42

areas where Nazi submarines were sinking tankers in great numbers, finding them outlined against the lume of the lights from the coastal roads and towns despite the blackout. During the long night I kept awake by picking up hitchhikers to talk to and drinking several thermoses of coffee.

Arriving in Miami, I found a two-dollar room in a motel and fell into bed for twelve hours of sleep. The next morning, as directed, I headed for the Aviation Building in Coconut Grove, a graceless three-story yellow stucco building on Biscayne Boulevard, which served as headquarters for the Operations Department of the Eastern Division of Pan American Airways.

Operations were conducted with flying boats from the Marine Terminal a few blocks away, and with land planes operating from the 36th Street airport ten miles to the north at the edge of the Everglades.

My new boss was Captain James (Jim) McLeod, Operations Engineer. Our staff consisted of a draftsman, a secretary and another assistant. Our office was responsible for relations with the CAA (now FAA), manuals, aircraft performance, weight and balance, and instrument approach procedures for Pan Am's far-flung airports and seadromes. Incidentally, we were also given responsibility for screening the dozens of new pilots who were joining the company. Jim had been a line pilot until a series of accidents (he was co-pilot) dampened his enthusiasm for flying. Jim joined Pan Am in the mid-30s and had been one of the pilots on the first trans-Atlantic flights of the giant Boeing 314 Clippers in 1939.

I was put to work designing aircraft instrument approach charts into Caribbean and South American airports. In 1943 all of our aircraft to ground communication was still by Morse code, so each plane carried a radio operator. Radio navigation capabilities were in their infancy and airport instrument approaches were time consuming. Radio directional beams were non-existent, or did not work well due to terrain and other factors, and could not be relied upon. Pan Am, therefore, developed a technique called "boxing" the station and gradually letting down for final approach. With many airports deep in mountain valleys or close to giant peaks, approaches had to be carefully laid out.

The procedure was as follows: the aircraft approached the airport using its high frequency directional "loop" antenna to guide it over the airport on a specific heading. Overhead the radio station sent a "null" sound, and the aircraft radio loop indicated the aircraft was moving away from the station. At this point the aircraft assumed a specified magnetic heading for two minutes at a set speed – 150 mph. At the end of two minutes the aircraft would make a "procedure turn" (30° bank) to the left to a new heading 90° or at a right angle to the original course. This track was held for two more minutes when another procedure turn was made to the left for 90°, making the aircraft's course 180° but five miles to the right of the station. The aircraft now proceeded for four minutes, again made a left procedure turn and flew four more minutes. Continuing in this manner, the aircraft "boxed" the station to verify its location. It then continued to box the station and descend until it reached a defined approach altitude. At this point it turned directly in toward the station on a defined heading following the Direction Finding Loop's indications and descending to the specified minimum approach altitude. If it broke out of the clouds the approach was continued visually to landing, and if not it was aborted and the aircraft climbed out on an approved heading designed to avoid any surrounding mountains and proceeded to the alternate airport.

My job was to design and draw these instrument approach "boxes," specifying headings and minimum approach altitudes. Over the next year we developed dozens of airport charts, incorporating them in our manuals. I had never seen a single one of these airports at the time, although I subsequently did, and wondered a little at the temerity with which I had designed the instrument approaches. Fortunately, we never experienced an accident due to use or misuse of our instrument approaches.

My office also calculated fuel minimums and scheduled flight times for all route segments, striving to increase payload without compromising safety. In the days of the piston aircraft, added fuel meant less passengers: 100 extra gallons of gasoline weighed 650 pounds, translate into three or four lost passengers.

A passenger offloaded in Miami on a Rio flight cost Pan Am thousands of dollars. Every passenger and his bags were weighed. Fat passengers (over 220 lbs) were charged extra fare – a 400-pound man paid a double fare and got two seats. Weight was money and we reviewed every item of the ship's

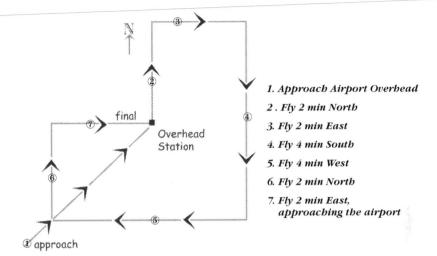

1. *Approach Airport Overhead*

2. *Fly 2 min North*

3. *Fly 2 min East*

4. *Fly 4 min South*

5. *Fly 4 min West*

6. *Fly 2 min North*

7. *Fly 2 min East,*
   approaching the airport

equipment to reduce weight.

In my position I was exposed to the other departments, marketing and scheduling, finance, maintenance, dispatching and flight control. At night and over weekends I spent hours on the hangar floor and in the shops, working on aircraft and engines. In operations I helped calculate weight and balance documents, ran the teletypes and screened flight plans. On the ramp and on the beaching crew, I helped dock flying boats and loaded passenger and cargo flights. Ferry flights and training flights gave me opportunities to ride the jump seat, and sometimes pilot the aircraft. Regulations and restrictions were much looser, union rules did not impede someone such as myself from helping out, and I gained a wealth of practical information. In two years I knew more about the actual operations of the airline than probably anyone else, because I had done all the jobs myself.

I moved rapidly up the ladder, as it were, becoming Assistant Superintendent of Stations, responsible for all of Pan Am's 50 down-line airports in Central and South America; Assistant Superintendent of Seaplane Services; and finally Superintendent of Scheduling, responsible for schedule planning and the day-to-day operational control of the airline, crew and aircraft scheduling.

Certifying the Cubana Ford Tri-Motors

In 1943 the war was reaching its climax. In the Pacific, McArthur and the Navy were island hopping toward Japan, and in Europe the Allies prepared for D-Day while Hitler's armies began to crumble in North Africa and Russia.

Airlift was scarce in the U.S. and every resource was pressed into service.

Pan Am's Cuban affiliate Cubana was operating its small domestic services with a half-dozen ex-Pan Am Ford Tri-Motors which had once been used in main line service. Built in 1929, these aircraft were still capable of carrying 3,000 pounds of cargo, and we needed the lift between Miami and Havana. Our traffic people made a deal with Cubana to fly a daily cargo flight for us with the old Tri-Motors. The only problem was that the U.S. Civil Aeronautics Administration demanded that we prove the operation was safe. These aircraft had been in service 15 years without any significant problems, but the CAA inspectors insisted. So, in my capacity as Assistant Operations Engineer with less than a year's experience with airplanes in any form, I was sent to Havana to obtain the necessary data to certify the operation. We needed aircraft weights, takeoff and landing field performance, one-engine out flying characteristics, fuel consumption, maintenance records and so forth. I had to write an operations manual satisfactory to the CAA – and do it in a week so that we could start the service.

Cubana's operations did not require all this paperwork and procedure, so much of it had to be done from scratch. Aircraft takeoff and landing performance was measured at Rancho Boyeros Airport at Havana using a surveyor's tape. Fuel consumption was measured by dip-sticking the tanks after demo flights. Maintenance and service manuals were adapted from DC-3 manuals and tailored to the simpler requirements of the old Fords. In a week we had our manuals ready to submit. Since nobody at the Miami Springs CAA Office had ever seen a Ford Tri-Motor, they all knew less about it than I did, and were not in a good position to second-guess us. We dropped a few well-timed hints about the military importance of the flights we were going to conduct, and our service proposal and manuals were approved promptly.

The next morning we all trooped out to 36th Street to see our first Ford land and, sure enough, in it came – on time. It was quickly loaded with war priority cargo, taxied out to the near end of the runway, and in 600 feet it was airborne and on its way to Havana, two hours away.

Commenting on my relative inexperience, my friend Johnny Donahue, the Pan Am Station Manager in Miami, said, "Mort, a good man is a guy who can figure out a new job faster than anybody else can figure out he don't know it."

Tommy Hand's Bar

Pan Am's flight crews hung out at Tommy Hand's Bar. Located on SW 8th Street (now Calle Ocho in Little Havana) and 38th Avenue, the bar was convenient to Coral Gables, Coconut Grove and Miami Springs where so many

Pan Am pilots lived. The bar was circular in shape and Tommy held forth in the center, dispensing booze, news, gossip, commentary and advice. Tommy Hand was an institution among the flight crews and his establishment was always full. Tommy was known for his frank talk and sharp wit. Tommy Hand stories abounded. One night a junior captain brought

Tri-Motor

Jimmy Walker, Pan Am's new Operations Manager (equivalent to today's Senior Vice President – Operations) in and introduced him to Tommy. Tommy stared at the new executive a few moments and a dead silence fell over the crowd.

"Get the son of a bitch out of here," said Tommy in a voice all could hear.

"Bu-bu-bu but why?"

"Look, dummy, he's bad for my business... You bring your goddamn new chief pilot in here and all the copilots leave... Now you bring this bastard in and all the captains leave!! You are ruining my business. Get him outta here!"

Jimmy Walker and his escort left.

Not many ladies visited Tommy Hand's, but one who did was Mrs. Eddie Musick, widow of the pioneer Pan Am captain who was killed when his S-42 Clipper exploded at Samoa while pioneering the Pacific routes. Now middle aged, she was left without any pension or support by the company when Eddie was killed. She was reduced to cadging drinks in Tommy Hand's, and occasionally arranging a date for a hungry pilot from among a group of young ladies she managed. Some of us thought she got a raw deal from Pan Am.

Loading the China Clipper

In late 1943, New York headquarters transferred the last of the three Martin M-130 "China Clippers" to Miami. The second M-130 had just been lost when it flew into a mountain in northern California in bad weather. The first one had disappeared without a trace in the western Pacific just before the war. The M-130 was a high wing, four-engine seaplane that carried about 50

The China Clipper (Martin M-130)

passengers in six compartments in the hull. Cargo was carried in a forward compartment over the sea wing, which was a distinctive feature of the Martin M-130. The aircraft had been used to inaugurate Pan Am's first trans-Pacific air service from San Francisco to Manila. Planned service to China was interrupted by the Japanese conquest of most of the country in 1938.

We did not know quite what to do with our new long-range plane. The ultimate plan was to open a new route to Leopoldville in the Belgian Congo via the Caribbean, South America and West Africa, but this was delayed by German submarine activity threatening our bases. We finally elected to put the M-130 on a six-day a week run from Miami to Cristóbal on the northern coast of Panama, an eight hour nonstop flight each way. The plane was scheduled to depart Miami at midnight, arrive in Cristóbal at dawn, make a quick turnaround for unloading, reloading and fueling, and then return to Miami by late afternoon. But getting the aircraft loaded and out of Miami proved to be a daunting task and every flight ran six to eight hours late because the ground crews could not get the plane loaded. Numerous flights were canceled due to these delays and backlogs of priority passengers and cargo built up (it was wartime and everything traveled priority). Operations Manager Jimmy Walker assigned me to fix the problem.

That night I went to the Dinner Key Marine Terminal (now the Dade County, Florida executive building) to size up the situation. The China Clipper was moored at the far end of one of the piers at which we docked our seaplanes because it was too big to fit at the close-in docks. A long narrow walkway led from the terminal area to the aircraft. Entrance to the aircraft was through a single hatch on the top of the aft fuselage through which the passengers entered and left, the crew boarded, and the cargo and passenger supplies were loaded and unloaded. The aircraft had an exit over the sea wings amidships, but this could not be used given the docking arrangements in Miami. A great deal of the aircraft's load was high priority cargo – as many as fifty to a hundred pieces a night, plus baggage and mail sacks.

The rear entry hatch was the bottleneck. We had a crew of 30-odd loaders who carried boxes, cartons, mail sacks, pieces of baggage, catering boxes and everything else from the terminal out along the dock to the aircraft. They clambered up onto the top of the fuselage and made their way down the stairs into the rear cabin. There they shuffled their way forward, through five bulkhead doors, until they at last reached the cargo compartment, deposited their loads, and then made their way back against the oncoming loaders until they at last reached the dock and terminal. The result was, of course, chaos and delay. It took six hours to load the aircraft in this fashion.

In Cristóbal, Panama, there was no such problem. The aircraft moored next to a large floating barge. The passengers entered and exited through the rear exit and the cargo was handed out through the sea wing exit and piled directly onto the barge. Passengers and cargo were transferred to shore by lighters, and the entire loading and boarding process took about an hour. But wartime security regulations and the FAA (then CAA) made such practical solutions impossible in Miami. Another solution had to be found.

After an hour of watching the chaos and confusion as the loaders struggled to carry their cargo to the hold and return for more, I positioned myself at the top of the cabin entry stairs. Six loaders were assigned below to pass the cargo, human chain fashion, from one compartment forward to the next when I handed it down. The rest of the loaders were positioned as a human chain along the dock, passing the boxes, bags and sacks from one to the other rather than carrying them individually. Things began to move. I yelled at the topside loaders to move it along faster, and sped up the below-decks loaders by passing the cargo down to them even faster and faster.

Within 30 minutes we had the China Clipper loaded and the cargo tied down. We were already delayed from the previous night's operation and from the time lost before we set up our human chain. But we got within two hours of the scheduled takeoff time, and the return flight was also about two hours late.

The next night I was there again as the China Clipper taxied in across Biscayne Bay, the four engines sending great plumes of white spray against the darkening sky. She was moored at the dock and I again pressed my human chain into service, unloading her in twenty minutes (northbound cargo loads were light – mostly baggage and mail). The maintenance crews now had a couple of hours to clear the snags, check the engines and prepare for the next flight. Two hours before departure I called the loading crew together and advised them

The M-130

that we were going to handle the loading the same as last night, and that I expected an on time departure. We chose up the below decks crew and the dock crew and walked out to start loading. We were finished in less than an hour and made a timely departure.

In the months that followed, the China Clipper completed six round trips a week between Miami and Panama with seldom a delay or mechanical interruption. Utilization was an unheard of 400 hours per month, 16 hours a day, 25 trips a month. After almost a year we were ready to launch the Leopoldville, Congo service and the Panama flights were taken over by our three Boeing B-307s.

The key to making the China Clipper loading work was not only to set up the human chain, but also to station myself in the key position at the top of the hatch and use my position to urge the two groups of loaders, neither of whom could see the other, to move faster. Not wanting to be outdone by the other group, each did.

Gold to Caracas

In 1944 the U.S. Government was shipping gold to the Venezuelan government in Caracas in payment for oil and for other assistance for the war effort. Pan Am was designated to move the gold shipments. Twice a week armored cars arrived at the airport in Miami loaded with twenty 100-kilo (220 pounds) kegs of gold bricks. The kegs were quite small, about 15 inches high by 12 inches in diameter, but very stout and bound with steel bands. Pan Am had committed to carrying them in special cargo flights, but since we had no spare freighters, the kegs were supposed to be loaded into the passenger seats and tied down with safety belts, one keg to each seat with an extra seat for the armed guard. Our DC-3s were equipped with twenty one seats at that time and, at war overload of 26,900 pounds gross takeoff weight, could carry the 20 kegs of gold and the guard. An en route stop was scheduled at Ciudad Trujillio (now Santo Domingo) in the Dominican Republic for fuel.

Carrying gold with a log carrier

But at departure time a problem arose. How would we get the kegs into the aircraft and onto the seats? The floor of the DC-3 slants upwards at about 15° due to the then-conventional tail wheel landing gear design. The kegs were too heavy for one man to carry and too small for two to get hold of. The loaders tried rolling them up the aisle but one got away, rolling back down the length of the cabin and crashing through the rear bulkhead, destroying the control cables. That put the aircraft out of commission and a substitute had to be dragged up. Finally, after four hours of effort, the aircraft was loaded, barely ahead of the night deadline for arrival in Caracas. It was obvious we had to find a better way to load the gold.

That afternoon I went down to a hardware and supply store in Miami and bought two log carriers. These woodsman's implements consisted of a five-foot pole with a pair of hooks mounted in the middle, much like the old-fashioned ice tongs used to carry fifty pound blocks of ice. The next morning I showed up at the airport with my log carriers just as the armored cars arrived with the day's gold shipment. We drove out onto the ramp and I asked one of the loaders to help me.

The first gold keg was rolled to the door of the truck. We stuck one tine of the log hook in each end of the keg and grabbed the ends of the pole. The two of us carried the keg to the plane, up the aisle, and then gently lowered it into the first seat in about thirty seconds. Within fifteen minutes the aircraft was completely loaded and the kegs were tied down. That flight, and subsequent trips, departed on time. We sent one of the log carriers along for use on the other end.

Thus was added another to a lengthening list of legends. As my mentor, Johnny Donahue, said, "Look at that Mort Beyer, he's one smart guy." To me the solution had seemed sort of obvious.

Flying Boats

Flying Boats were inherently unstable and dangerous. In the eighteen years the Clippers flew in Latin America we lost seventeen of them in landing and takeoff accidents on the water. The aircraft had a tendency to porpoise on takeoff, with the bow rising and falling in rapidly accelerating oscillations in the waves. As a result, the aircraft would become airborne much too soon, fall back into the water, and break up. Other hazards included sunken logs floating in the harbors, cross winds, and under-trained inexperienced pilots during the war.

The S-42 Sikorsky flying boat was particularly unforgiving, and a total of six were lost over a period of ten years. Eddie Musick and his crew died in a fiery explosion in the harbor of Samoa. There were several fatalities in an accident at San Juan in 1941. We lost one at Cienfuegos, Cuba in 1944 on a choppy takeoff with a green crew, killing all onboard. We sent a rescue mission

Fokker F-7

down with another aircraft, including a supply of coffins, and boxed up the remains of the dead passengers. When we flew them back to Miami, our beaching crew, a half-dozen Blacks, refused to unload the coffins and slipped away into the darkness. So I and a couple of mechanics undertook the task.

The high mortality rate in seaplane operations, regardless of the romance and glamour of the flying boat, soon doomed them and forced the airline to turn its energies to land planes, the DC-3/C-47 and the Boeing 307.

But while it lasted, the romance of the flying boats was awesome. In my first weeks at Pan Am, I used to go down to a seawall where a canal entered Coral Gables, a few hundred yards below where the Clippers taxied out, one by one each morning, to take off for their varied destinations in the Caribbean and South America. They would cast off, slowly maneuver into position in the early dawn light, and then, with a great blast of power and a long plume of silver spray as they gathered speed, take off toward the sun rising over the Gulf Stream to the east. One by one they would lift off the black waters of Biscayne Bay and rise into the golden sunlight of the new day. It was a spectacular sight. It was a romance of aviation that no land plane or jet can even begin to replicate today.

For night operations we were required to take battery-powered floating lights out to illuminate the floating runway for the boats. Each light was on a small platform, with an anchor to hold it in place. The lights were supposed to be laid in line with the wind, but the wind would change, and often we would have to pick up the lights and put them down several times before a plane could take off or land due to changes in wind direction.

This was very frustrating. The Germans, operating in South America on the Amazon and Orinoco Rivers, put all their lights on small floating rafts, tied them together with fishing line, and put an anchor at one end and a sail at the other. When the wind changed the sail simply swung all the lights to a new bearing. Pan Am's crews were out there picking up the lights and trying to reposition them again, while the Germans were long gone, having taken off using their wind-directed lights.

One night we were out struggling with the lights and a contrary wind. Captain George Snow taxied out with the Clipper headed to San Juan and queried us over the radio. We told him to "hold." The next thing we knew, he was roaring by us, disregarding our carefully repositioned lights and disappearing into the darkness. A few minutes later he called the Dinner Key Tower.

"Dinner Key, Clipper 822, off at 2245, climbing to level zero eight en route San Juan. Over and out. Good night."

He had taxied out and taken off down the path of light made by the moon's reflection on the water – far better than any FAA-approved takeoff procedure.

The Rehabilitation of Bob Fatt

Bob Fatt was one of Pan Am's first pilots, flying the Key West-Havana route. He even had the dubious distinction of missing Key West's landfall one evening and having to ditch his Fokker Tri-Motor in the sea. But Bob was a strong leader, and played an important part in the subsequent development of Pan Am's Eastern Division.

In late 1944 Bob was appointed Chief Pilot, a position which carried a lot of responsibility in terms of disciplining the pilot group and passing on their qualifications (or lack thereof). As a tough and not overly diplomatic taskmaster, Bob Fatt was increasingly the object of the collective hatred of the pilot group.

One night Johnny Donahue (who was then temporarily seconded to Havana as station manager), myself and two overnighting pilots were sitting in the courtyard of a lovely Havana bar drinking our usual *Cuba Libres*, a concoction of Ron Anjeo and Coke, when the subject of Bob Fatt came up. The pilots immediately chimed in with "He's a bastard, and he's unfair."

"Now, wait a minit yez guys," Johnny responded. "What's he ever done to yez?"

"Well, well, but…but, everybody says he's a bastard…"

"Yeah, but what's he ever done to yez?"

"Weeeelll…nothing …"

"OK," said Johnny. "Bob Fatt's been getting a bum deal from the pilots. He is trying to do a good job. He needs your help. Let's all agree that every time we hear Bob Fatt's name, we will immediately say real loud, 'Bob Fatt's doing a good job. He's all for the boys!'"

We all solemnly swore to uphold this pact, and when we went back to Miami we began to "talk up" Bob Fatt. When his name was mentioned at

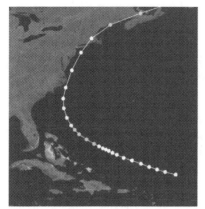

North Arlantic Hurricane Map

Tommy Hand's Bar we would immediately respond, "Bob's doing a great job, he's all for the boys..." Other voices began to take up the chorus and it spread quickly through the ranks. Within weeks all you had to do was mention Bob Fatt's name and somebody would respond, "Bob's a great guy. He's doing a good job. He's all for the boys."

The image building held for many years. Bob Fatt was eventually appointed Vice President of Labor Relations when he could no longer fly.

The Hurricane Manual

The Caribbean is known as the spawning ground of hurricanes. In the mid-1940s Miami was the target of a dozen major storms, often two or three a year, which swept up out of the island archipelago to the south and east of us and threatened our operations. Miami had experienced the great storm of 1926 which had all but destroyed Miami Beach, sweeping across it with twenty foot tides, and the more recent 1935 storm which had obliterated the Florida Keys with winds of over 200 mph. The 1935 storm was probably the most intense ever to hit the American mainland and is today classified as a Force 5 (maximum intensity) storm, even exceeding the power of 1992's Andrew which devastated the fortunately narrow area between South Miami and Homestead, and Katrina which devastated the Gulf Coast.

Hurricanes were a major problem for Pan Am's operations, particularly in the days of flying boats. Meteorological forecasting techniques were primitive, communications were inadequate, and all too often these vast storms seemed to arrive unheralded on our doorsteps to wreak their vengeance. Pan Am employed a veteran and respected meteorologist, Bob Bush, whose primary job was to forecast hurricanes and attend the international atmospheric and meteorological conferences. Hurricanes in the Caribbean kept him busy from July through November every year, and Bob was by all odds the most listened to executive in the Latin American division during those days. Bob Bush was a nice quiet scientific man, always humble and muted in his response to the urgent hurricane questions: Where is it? Is it growing in power? Where will it go? Will it hit Miami (or any of the rest of our Pan Am ports)?

The horror stories of storms past were legion. The cities laid waste by previous storms, the aircraft destroyed at anchor or ashore. Like the story of the S-42 flying boat, caught in a hurricane at Cienfuegos, Cuba. The captain taxied out into the harbor in the teeth of the storm and rode it out, keeping the nose of the aircraft into the wind and the engines running and the spoilers deployed to prevent lift off until the storm finally passed. Pan Am hurricane SOP (Standard Operating Policy) in the mid-1940s when I got to Miami was to flee before the storm. When it became apparent that the hurricane might hit Miami (about twenty-four hours before the eye would pass), Bob Bush would issue the final "red alert," and arrangements would be made to move all flyable aircraft north, out of the storm's path. A massive panic then ensued as aircraft were made ready and ferried north. Inbound planes landing in Miami could still do so for twelve hours or so, before the winds got too high. They were immediately unloaded and flown north, too, to Jacksonville, Charleston, Atlanta. Non-flyable planes were secured inside the hangars and all movable equipment moved inside. In a 150 mph wind almost any item of ramp equipment, not to mention an aircraft parked outside, would become airborne.

Eastern Airlines, National, the U.S. Navy based at Dinner Key, and the Army Air Force all joined the exodus, until there were literally no aircraft left in Miami. The hurricanes roared in, with winds of 125 to 150 miles per hour, doing relatively minor damage but downing power lines, ripping off roofs, and driving the sea up into Coconut Grove and other low lying areas.

Hurricanes generally move fast. Within 12 hours of reaching hurricane intensity (75 mph), the eye had passed, the storm subsided, and the sun was out bright and clear. Unfortunately, all the aircraft had fled north, so we had no planes with which to operate. Our routes to the south, to the Caribbean, and to Central and South America could not be served because all of our aircraft had gone north before the storm.

A strange thing occurs with these storms. The typical Caribbean hurricane "re-curves" to the northeast and speeds up as it reaches the U.S. mainland. The aircraft that Pan Am and everyone else had flown north out of harm's way the night before were now menaced by the threat of the hurricane chasing them north – moving fast and still vicious. So the aircraft that had found safe haven in Jacksonville and Charleston had to be moved again, fleeing still further north before the advancing storm to Wilmington, Norfolk, Washington and Philadelphia. Often the storm pursued them for three days before veering out to sea and dissipating in the vastness of the North Atlantic, and at last the Pan Am fleet would come dribbling home. We lost days of operations and millions in revenues.

Every year the U.S. Weather Bureau published charts showing past historic hurricane tracks. I studied these with great interest and compared them to my own experience. The answer seemed obvious: Pan Am was doing the wrong thing in fleeing north in front of the storms. History indicated that hurricanes seldom turned back on their own tracks but moved invariably northward. Instead of fleeing north before the storms, Pan Am should be flying south around behind them. Instead of wasting days and days and flying a thousand miles to the north, we could fly two hundred and fifty miles to Havana, Camaguey (Cuba) or Nassau and wait for the storm to blow itself out at Miami. Hurricanes were usually only a few hundred miles in diameter and their counter-clockwise winds gave a powerful boost to aircraft escaping them to the south.

Apparently nobody had ever thought of this before. I talked to Bob Bush, our hurricane forecaster, and he readily agreed that I was right. Together, we collaborated on Pan Am's first Hurricane Manual which laid out the strategy of flying behind the storms rather than fleeing before them. We did not have long to wait. In 1944, a violent hurricane hit Miami on September 14th. Pan Am flew its aircraft to Camaguey, in Central Cuba and held them there. Everybody else fled north. The storm hit about sundown and by the next morning it was gone – north. We gave the signal to bring the planes in from Camaguey and by 0900 had our full fleet on the ramp in Miami, ready to resume a normal day's operations. It was days before Eastern's and National's operations were back on schedule.

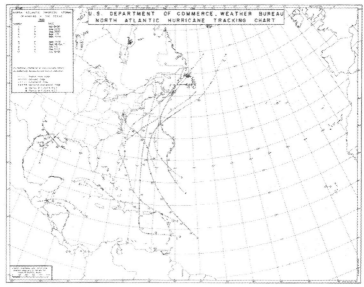

1943 Hurricane Map

WWW.PANAMAIR.ORG

Boeing 307 Stratoliner

The Boeing 307 Stratoliner

The Boeing 307 was the world's first pressurized, wide body aircraft. It was designed based on the B-17 wing and tail platform and, like the B-17, powered by four Curtis Wright R-1820 engines. Grossing 54,000 pounds at takeoff, it had a full payload range of some twelve hundred miles with forty passengers seated in three spacious compartments. Cruise speed was in excess of 200 miles per hour, the fastest of any commercial transport of the time. There were only eight B-307s built, entering service with TWA and Pan Am in 1940. TWA's five were commandeered by the U.S. Army Air Force when World War II broke out but Pan Am was permitted to keep its three due to the defense role played by Pan Am.

I first flew in the B-307s by cadging rides on the ex-TWA planes flying military flights nonstop from Washington to Miami en route to the United Kingdom, North Africa and China. These flights were vastly superior to the multi-stop flights via Eastern or National to Miami where you had to fight priorities and risk getting bumped – and had to pay.

Our B-307s were highly unreliable and we had great difficulty finding a role for them. For a while they flew from Miami to San Juan, and later from New Orleans to Guatemala. Finally, in 1944, when the Martin M-130 was taken off the Miami-Cristóbal route, I was tasked with operating the New Orleans, Merida (Mexico), Guatemala, Panama, Miami route with the aircraft. I set up a schedule which most operations staff felt was well beyond the capabilities of these troubled aircraft, a daily round trip Miami-Panama-Guatemala-Merida-New Orleans and return. A total of some thirty-two hours round trip.

In one of my studies of the Company operations I determined that 80% of all mechanical delays occurred on the outbound flights from a crew base. On the flights returning to home base, pilots seemed capable of completing the trip without delay. Therefore, I closed the crew base in New Orleans and moved all B-307 crews into Miami. This resulted in an immediate improvement in on-time operations and revenues.

The B-307s continued to serve the Latin American Division of Pan Am for a year or two after the war, and then were sold to airlines in South America and Africa. One was lost in Ecuador, another was scrapped in North Africa. The last, N19903, eventually was bought by "Baby Doc" Duvalier, Dictator of Haiti, and was used as his executive aircraft. After he was deposed, a number of retired Pan Am pilots discovered the aircraft, bought it, and flew it to Oakland, California where it was gradually restored to its original Pan Am configuration. Many old Pan Am mechanics gave time and effort while other employees contributed cash to the restoration. The aircraft has now been donated to the National Air and Space Museum, and is exhibited at Dulles Airport.

Flying the M-130

The last of the Martin M-130 flying boats had been taken off the Panama route and we were readying her to open a new route from Miami to Leopoldville in the Belgian Congo, an area virtually inaccessible due to the German submarine activity off the coast of West Africa and in the Gulf of Biafra. There was no land airport at Leopoldville, but the Martin flying boat could land in the Congo River.

The planned route ran from Miami to San Juan, Port of Spain, Belem and Recife in Brazil, and then to Monrovia, Liberia in West Africa and on to the final destination in the Congo. The aircraft would overnight along the way, taking almost a week to complete the trip and another week to return.

The CAA insisted we operate a proving flight to demonstrate Pan Am's capability to conduct the planned operation safely. I went along on the first leg of this operation, conducted in the summer of 1944.

Passengers entered the M-130 through a hatch in the top rear fuselage that opened to a stairway down into the cabin. The hatch had a windscreen that could be cranked open in flight, and served as a navigator's station. The navigator raised the windscreen and then sat on the top step to take his sightings. It was a superb observation post, and I took advantage of it on my flights.

I particularly recall a night flight from Miami to San Juan as we were setting up the Leopoldville run. We taxied out from Dinner Key Marine Terminal and took off across Biscayne Bay toward the moon rising before us.

The China Clipper Martin M-130

As we climbed out over the Gulf Stream I went back, opened the rear hatch windscreen, and sat on the top step. Before me was the black outline of the aircraft's hull and wings, with the four great propellers cutting shining arcs against the sky. The moon laid a silver track across the sea and, as we flew southeast, the dark outlines of the Bahamas Islands appeared one by one on the horizon – Andros, Exuma, Inagua. Over each towered a giant thunderhead, reaching up twenty-five to thirty thousand feet. These clouds formed over the islands due to differential land and water temperatures. White and gleaming on the moonlit side, black and forbidding in the shadows, they were constantly illuminated from within by lightning flashes – changing patterns of light and dark that were eerie to watch. Hour after hour we cruised southeast, at some 10,000 feet altitude, as the Bahamas finally disappeared behind us and we flew the last three hours over the open ocean. Just after dawn we landed at San Juan's harbor terminal.

The last of the China Clippers crashed on its next flight, hitting a sunken log on takeoff from Port of Spain at night. This ended our efforts to serve Leopoldville and destroyed a magnificent aircraft which had pioneered many of Pan Am's early air routes.

Let 'Em Burn!

Following World War II and the demobilization, many Air Force veterans aspired to get into the airline business. The military surplussed C-54 (DC-4), C-46 and DC-3s by the hundreds. The veterans, using their "procurement preferences," bought and leased them by the score. CAA (now FAA) rules were lax and largely unenforced against the vets and their new airlines. But what the Government made easy on the one hand, the Civil Aeronautics Board made hard on the other. There was no way these hopeful new airlines could become legitimate because the door was barred by the CAB. A few made it as cargo airlines: Flying Tiger, Slick, Seaboard and Riddle. But out of all the hundreds of new airlines spawned in the wake of the war, only Trans Caribbean Airlines made it to fully certified status. The rest tried to operate on the fringes of the law as "non-skeds" (non-scheduled), as they were contemptuously called by the regular airlines. Long involved hearings were held – "The Large Irregular Case" and others – but nobody was issued a license.

But the non-skeds offered one thing people wanted – low fares. A $49 fare was charged for San Juan-New York and $99 coast-to-coast. With changed political status for Puerto Rico, a huge wave of immigrants moved from Puerto Rico to New York to find a better life, and the non-skeds carried them. The most popular non-sked aircraft was the C-46, which could carry fifty people. It was a twin-engine military transport converted at war's end to a passenger aircraft. It did not have the range to operate San Juan-New York nonstop and, therefore, used the longer route San Juan-Miami-New York. At Miami passengers cleared customs and immigration formalities as they were then applicable.

At Pan Am we viewed the growth of the non-skeds with hostility. They were growing in our backyard and stealing passengers who never would have dreamed of riding on a Pan Am flight. But nonetheless, they appeared to be a threat. Our lobbyists joined the other airlines to fight them in Washington, and we on the flight line in Miami watched the growing number of flights night after night landing in Miami, refueling and clearing government formalities as they headed for New York and San Juan, filled with "our" passengers.

The non-sked airlines had no facilities and no equipment except their aircraft. Thus, when they arrived in Miami they "borrowed" what they needed to handle their aircraft: boarding stairs, loading stands, baggage carts, and fire bottles to extinguish possible engine fires. This equipment all belonged to Pan Am. We resented it when the non-skeds simply helped themselves to it, and told us "where to go and what to do when we got there" when challenged.

At the time I was Assistant Superintendent of Stations for the Division. I ordered the Miami station to padlock all equipment when not in use, thus preventing its use by the non-skeds. At the same time I sent word to the non-sked managers that we would be glad to rent them equipment and provide services for a reasonable fee should they so desire. They didn't, so we locked up the ramp equipment. For a few nights the non-sked flights rolled up. No equipment was available so the passengers had to climb down the Jacobs Ladder and carry their own luggage into customs. Non-sked flight crews had to start the aircraft on ship's batteries (no more free battery carts or generators) and without the protection of a fire guard armed with a 100 cubic foot carbon dioxide fire bottle. The cabin crew had to reload the baggage when the passengers came struggling out from Customs. Finally, the last crew member would crawl up the Jacobs Ladder, pull it up after him, start the aircraft and taxi away into the night for takeoff.

But then the inevitable occurred. After loading up again, a C-46 began to start engines. The number one engine started fine, but the number two "torched" on ignition. Surplus gas was often pumped out of the carburetor prior to ignition, and would light up when the first cylinder fired. Normally there would be only a brief puff of flame, but sometimes flames engulfed the whole engine nacelle and threatened a major fire. This one was a big fire and it did not go out when the crew shut down the engine. Seeing the flames, our Pan Am mechanics ran for the fire bottles, locked up by the wall, and started for the aircraft. I intervened. "Stop, don't go out there!"

"But he's on fire!"

"Let 'em burn."

The crew leaped from the cockpit eight feet to the tarmac carrying their portable fire extinguishers and sprayed the flaming engine frantically. The emergency doors burst open and passengers began pouring out of the aircraft onto the ramp. The fire slowly flickered and died out. Once the engine was shut down, and the fuel pumps turned off, the fire was soon starved for fuel and died. The engine was designed to cope with this problem and, while the pyrotechnics were spectacular, the real danger was relatively slight.

The next day the Feds (the CAA Inspectors) arrived to investigate the fire. They determined that the non-sked operators were in the wrong for not providing adequate fire protection at departure times, and that it was not Pan Am's responsibility to provide it for free.

A few days later we signed agreements with the non-sked operators permitting them to use our equipment and services – for a fee.

The Schedule Section

When I arrived in Miami to work for Pan Am, the Company was divided into four Divisions: The Atlantic, Pacific, Eastern and Western. The Eastern Division covered the routes to Cuba, Panama, and the Caribbean, as well as the long flights to Rio and Buenos Aires and all of the varied intermediate points. Pan Am used the Sikorsky S-38, S-40 and S-42 flying boats, a dozen DC-3s and our three pressurized Boeing 307 Stratoliners. The Western Division, based in Brownsville, flew a half-dozen DC-3s through Mexico and Central America to Panama.

Each division was under the jurisdiction of a division manager reporting directly to Juan Trippe in New

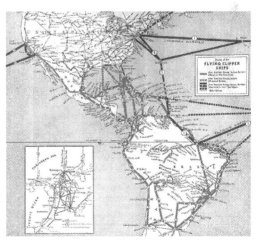

Route of the Flying Clipper Ships (circa 1940's)

York. They each had managers of Operations, Maintenance and Sales. Day-to-day operations were under the control of section superintendents covering the Caribbean, South America and the Antilles. Most operations were conducted in daylight only due to a lack of proper airfield lighting and radio and navigation facilities. Operations to Rio and Buenos Aires were still conducted with the S-42 flying boats on a five-day flight each way. The first day was from Miami to San Juan via Cuba, Haiti and Santo Domingo, then on to Port of Spain for an overnight layover. The second day we flew from Port of Spain to Belem via the Guyanas, Georgetown, Surinam and Cayenne. The third day took our flights east to Forteleza, Natal and San Salvador. The fourth day took us to Rio with a stop at Victoria along the way. The last day we flew from Rio to Buenos Aires via Puerto Allegre and Montevideo. Landings took place in the rivers and harbors of these cities, with the S-42s tying up at floating docks. The passengers – brought ashore in speedboats – overnighted in Pan Am-owned staff houses. Total flying time was on the order of 50 hours each way over five days – but far faster than the infrequent ocean liners that required weeks.

The Rio route had been pioneered in 1929 by New York Rio Buenos Aires Airlines using Consolidated Commodore flying boats. However, in a brilliant political move in 1933, Juan Trippe had deprived NYRBA of its mail contract to Rio that subsidized and supported the company. He then took over the unfortunate company, transforming Pan Am's Key West to Cuba operation into the intercontinental "empire of air" which it became.

The autonomous Section Superintendents controlled aircraft movements. They handed off control to the next Section as the aircraft flew to their destinations. Communications were by "Charlie Whiskey" radio using Morse code, or via primitive landline teletypes from station to station. High frequency radio telephones between the aircraft and the ground did not become practical until the late 1940s, permitting the replacement of the radio operators on the aircraft and the ground. Trippe fired them all on Christmas Eve, 1945.

Needless to say, operational control by the Section Superintendents was clumsy, and ultimately recognized as inadequate. As the war wore on, Pan Am was allocated more DC-3s and we were able to retire all of our remaining flying boats by 1945. We also bought every DC-3 we could find that crashed but was not destroyed totally. We rebuilt them with pieces of other crashed aircraft and added them to our fleet. As the war ended we eagerly bought military C-54s – a Douglas-designed four-engine long-range passenger and cargo liner – and converted them as DC-4s to replace our DC-3s.

In 1944 I had been promoted to Assistant Superintendent of Seaplane

Service, helping Captain Jim Crane, an original Pan Am "boat" pilot relegated to this position. I was asked to get the most out of what was left of the boats, and did so by improving reliability and concentrating utilization on routes where their 40-passenger capabilities were most useful. Unfortunately, not a single one of Pan Am's flying boats survived in retirement, and all were broken up or wrecked so that we have none in the air museums of the world.

With the Seaplane Section winding down, I proposed to the Division Manager, now Wilbur Morrison, that the Section Superintendents be retired, and all daily division operations be placed under the control of a Schedule Section which I would head. This section would consolidate all of the scheduling and control functions of the Division into one office, manned around the clock by controllers and tied to headquarters, aircraft and downline stations by radio, telephone and teletype. The Section would also have responsibility for all crew scheduling of pilots, engineers and flight attendants, the scheduling of all aircraft through maintenance and assignment to flights, and coordination with reservations and marketing. Whenever breakdowns occurred (which in those days was frequent), the Section Coordinator was responsible for rerouting and consolidating flights, finding and assigning new crews, and getting operations back on time.

By 1947 the Pan Am Latin American Division – a consolidation of the former Eastern and Western Divisions in 1944 – had a total of thirty DC-3s and twenty DC-4s – an immense fleet in those days. The DC-4s flew the long-haul routes while the DC-3s flew the shorter sectors between the islands of the Caribbean and local service in Central and South America. Ten new Convair 240s had also been added to our fleet, a step backward because, if filled with passengers, they could no longer carry the baggage and cargo on over-water flights between Florida and the Islands. The Schedule Section devoted a lot of effort to working its way out of mechanical programs.

It is hard to imagine today how unreliable the old DC-3s, and particularly the DC-4s, were. One night we had eight premature engine failures in flight on our fleet of 20 DC-4s. Fresh engines had to be found, failed engines repaired, aircraft ferried to Miami on three engines, and disrupted passengers accommodated and re-routed. The teletype address for our section was "OXMIA" (Operation Control – Miami), and we were responsible for everything that went wrong. However, our centralized control operation was a pioneering effort in the growing airline industry, and attracted the attention of Wayne Parrish, editor of American Aviation, then the only airline industry publication. Parrish came to Miami to write an extensive article featuring OXMIA.

I resigned from Pan Am in mid-1947 to found Dispatch Services in

Miami, an ill-starred effort (more about this later), but returned at the invitation of Captain Horace Brock, Division Manager of the Atlantic, to establish a schedule section for him in New York.

The Havana Shuttle

The war was over and once again tourism in Florida began to prosper. The Miami Beach hotels, which had served as training barracks for the young men being prepared for overseas shipment to the war zones, were turned back to their civilian owners and were feverishly being renovated for the coming winter season. World War II transport aircraft were being sold or leased to the airlines, and the DC-3s, conscripted during the hostilities, were also returned, somewhat worse for the wear. Ex-service mechanics were rushed through training and put to work refurbishing these aircraft, and once again the airlines began to dream of expansion.

In the winter of 1946, one of the first routes to feel the pressure of the growing tourism was Miami-Havana. During the war Pan Am served this route much of the time with old S-40 Sikorsky flying boats of 40-passenger capacity. They made the run from the Miami Dinner Key Marine Base to Havana's inner harbor in about one-and-a-half hours, flying low and slow. As the war wore on, we began to find occasional DC-3s available to serve the route, usually enroute to Mexico or Guatemala. Space was at a premium and tourists of either nation were few indeed. But now things were opening up and we were under constant pressure for more and more service.

By this time I had been appointed Superintendent of Schedules, responsible for virtually everything to do with the movement of aircraft:

> *Schedule planning and fleet planning*
> *Scheduling of pilots, crew and flight attendants*
> *Maintenance scheduling and planning*
> *Daily operational control of the airline, aircraft routing, and passenger load control*

My Scheduling Section planned the schedules in cooperation with marketing, deciding what new and old routes to fly, how often, and with what aircraft. We managed the day- to-day and hour-to-hour operations of the airline on a round-the-clock basis. When airplanes broke, we devised and implemented the emergency plan to get us out of whatever problem we were in. And when accidents happened, which was all too often, we served as the emergency control office for the airline.

Thus, as our Havana loads grew and pressure increased for more and more lift, that was my problem too. The seaplanes had now been retired. The long range four-engine DC-4s were committed immediately to routes to Rio when they became available. Havana had to be served with our old, reliable DC-3s.

I foresaw a major increase in business to Cuba. The rest of the Caribbean had not even begun to develop as a tourist destination. The Bahamas were still a sleepy backwater of the Empire. But Havana gleamed and glistened with bright lights, gambling, girls, and other forbidden pleasures not to be found on U.S. soil.

I prepared a plan to deal with the situation and took it to Wilbur Morrison, crusty and cantankerous vice president of the Latin American Division of Pan Am, as it was then known. Mr. Morrison ushered me into his vast office crowded with memorabilia of his days in the Mexican Sierra Madre.

"Goddammit, Beyer, waddyawant?"

"I would like to talk to you about the Havana service."

"Well, what about it?"

So, for thirty minutes or so I outlined my idea. Havana was a swiftly growing market. Other U.S. carriers were already snapping at Pan Am's heels, wanting "in" to all of our historic markets. We needed to make a pre-emptive strike to take this market out of play. Mr. Morrison heard me out, then said "Well, waddyawanta do?"

"Mr. Morrison, I think we should begin a high frequency service from Miami to Havana, with a DC-3 every fifteen minutes from 7 A.M. to 10 P.M. This means sixty flights a day in each direction, seven days a week. It requires eight aircraft, with liberal ground times and back up and it certainly will pre-empt the market."

Morrison was a decisive executive. "OK, Beyer, you can do it and if it doesn't work, you're fired!"

The schedule was quickly drawn up and filed. Depart Miami every 15 minutes. One hour fifteen minutes flight time to Havana; thirty minutes ground time in Havana; one hour and fifteen minutes back to Miami; forty-five minutes ground time in Miami for catch up, cleaning and servicing. Traffic responded instantly. Flights were completely full. The fare was some $19, which made it attractive to even day-trippers, not to speak of the hordes of tourists from New York. The Havana Shuttle was a big marketing success but the operational reliability was an unmitigated disaster. Planes piled up on the ramp in Havana, one after the other, and the station staff could not get them turned around and back out. In Miami the results were even worse. As delays in Havana mounted, we did not have aircraft to meet our outbound schedule.

In Miami, too, the congestion was appalling. Four, five, six aircraft all sitting on the ramp together. Staff members were running from one to the other. Unload this one, cater that one, where is the damned fuel truck? Call the mechanic to change a tire. We need two more flight crews because the assigned pilots ran out of time waiting for the inbound plane. Everybody complained about "Beyer's Folly," and word reached Mr. Morrison.

I was summoned to his office. "Goddammit, Beyer, I told you that if this didn't work you were fired!"

"Yessir, it's sure not working."

"Well, waddya gonna do about it . .?"

"Mr. Morrison, give me three days to fix it."

"OK, but if you don't, you're still fired!"

I returned to the airport and ordered drastic revision of the Havana Shuttle schedule.

Turnaround ground times were cut to five minutes in Havana and fifteen minutes in Miami.

Flight times were cut five minutes in each direction, to remove any leeway.

All spare aircraft were withdrawn from the schedule.

An on-time contest was set up between the station staffs at Miami and Havana, with a prize for the winners – the losers had to work the winners' station for a day.

These changes were effective immediately. They did not have to appear in the timetable, it only affected the operational side of the service.

By cutting the flight times we encouraged the pilots to make the extra effort to leave on time and expedite their en route procedures. There was no longer any slack here. Pilots usually want to be on time, and this encouraged them to smarten up their procedures.

Cutting the turn time in Havana to five minutes meant that they had only one aircraft at a time to worry about. With the previous schedule they had three, which quickly grew to four or five, dividing the ground crew's efforts and confusing traffic, operations, and everybody involved. Now they had only one aircraft to unload, reload and dispatch. Everybody concentrated on it. We eliminated fueling in Havana, instead performing this service in Miami for the round trip. Catering was similarly done in Miami for the return flight.

Again, the fifteen minute ground time in Miami was adequate for unloading, reloading, refueling, and catering. Usually one aircraft was leaving as the next taxied in. The staff could concentrate on one aircraft at a time.

The on-time contest produced wonderful results. We kept score hourly by teletype. On time operations increased from 10% the first day to 70% the third, and 90% within the week. Both Miami and Havana battled to a draw, so we rewarded both staffs with a trip to the other station to watch and participate.

To this day, the Pan Am Havana-Miami shuttle is the highest frequency operation ever conducted between two cities by a single airline.

Vanquishing the "Non-Skeds"

We now turned our attention to the pesky problem of the "non-skeds", which you will remember was the opprobrious name disdainfully applied to the hordes of unscheduled charter airlines that sprang up after the end of World War II.

As the war veterans streamed back, the U.S. Government urged ex-pilots to start entrepreneurial new airlines using surplus transport aircraft from the War. Planes were made available to veterans for a few thousand dollars each, and dozens of small cargo and passenger airlines sprang up, founded by groups of pilots and eager investors. These airlines, while not well organized, began to offer the first low cost services in mass markets such as the Trans Continental routes and the New York-Miami-San Juan routes.

However, not all sectors of the Government cooperated with the new airlines. The Civil Aeronautics Board controlled the allocation of operating rights and routes and they adopted stringent regulations prohibiting the new upstarts from operating scheduled passenger services. A few new airlines were awarded Cargo Only certificates, including the fabled Flying Tigers, Seaboard World Airlines, Slick Airlines and Riddle Airlines. But the new passenger carriers were left floundering in a regulatory purgatory. A series of CAB investigations culminated in the Large Irregular Air Carrier Case, which handed out a number of charter (called Supplemental) certificates, but banned other "irregular" activities.

Many small would-be airlines struggled on in this limbo, selling tickets through bootleg travel agencies for low prices, while the regular scheduled airlines such as Pan Am tried to shut them down through the CAB and the Civil Aviation Administration's (CAA) safety regulations. The struggle grew increasingly bitter, as illustrated earlier in this chapter when Pan Am faced up to the non-skeds "stealing" our ramp equipment.

By 1947 a number of the non-skeds were well established in Pan Am's New York and Miami to San Juan markets. Several had acquired World War II C-54s and had converted them to passenger liners, capable of carrying 66 passengers.

Pan Am operated the San Juan markets as a certified monopoly except for the increasing non-sked competition. We flew four or five DC-4s a day in the San Juan markets, equipped with 40 sumptuous First Class seats, and at high fares. But the non-skeds were eating into our markets. Pan Am was forced to cut flights in half and watch average passenger loads fall to a dozen high fare passengers as the Puerto Ricans opted for the low cost non-skeds.

Conventional wisdom was that all scheduled services should be full-service and high class. No self-respecting passenger would opt for the crowded, cheap non-sked flights with no meals. But we were finding out that this was not the case.

Wilbur Morrison, Latin American Division Vice President, called me to his office. He was worried about the non-sked inroads into Pan Am's historic markets.

"Godammit, Beyer, what are you going to do about this?" I was in charge of day-to-day operations and scheduling and planning. Evidently Wilbur expected a solution from me.

"Mr. Morrison, let me think about it for a couple of days, and I will get back to you next week with my suggestions."

"OK, soon!"

I went back to my office to think about Pan Am's problems. We had the reputation and public image as the world's premier airline, and here a bunch of non-skeds were literally eating our lunch in major Caribbean markets.

It seemed to me that Pan Am was attempting to sell not only basic transportation, but also luxury and comfort as well, without seeing the difference. Carried further, this line of thought took me back to my Atlantic crossings on the USS Washington before the War. My parents were traveling First Class, in luxury, with a few dozen other passengers while I was among hundreds packed into the crowded cabins of Tourist Class. There were ten times more Tourist Class passengers than First Class, but we were all going to get to New York together. And why was it that there was only one Pullman and ten crowded Coach cars on the trains from Miami to New York? And why did five million Americans buy a new Chevy or Ford every year, but only fifty thousand a Lincoln or Cadillac? How many more bought used cars instead?

The comparisons came together in one inescapable conclusion: When people buy cars, or rail tickets, or sail on ships to Europe (there were few trans-Atlantic planes in those days) they are buying transportation. A few elect to pay more and also buy comfort. Is not air travel the same? Weren't the masses cramming into the non-skeds DC-4s to Puerto Rico telling us the same thing? Most people can only afford basic transportation, and yet the established scheduled airlines did not seem to recognize this (many still don't to this day).

Suddenly the answer to Pan Am's problem was obvious; change our "First Class Only" strategy and meet the mass-market challenge head on.

"Mr. Morrison, I believe I have the solution to the problem in the San Juan markets."

"Yeah, what?"

"I recommend we take six of our DC-4s, remove all of the first class seats and install 66 high density seats. Charge the same fares as the non-skeds. The lower fares will raise the load factors, and we will make more money carrying planes full of low fare passengers than we do now carrying a few First Class passengers on almost empty flights."

"Beyer, you're crazy!"

"Wilbur, you've told me that before. I think we should try it because it stands a good chance of succeeding. We know if we keep on as we are now, we will go on failing and the cancer will spread."

"All right, Beyer, I'll approve it, but if it don't work, you are fired!"

We ordered the new high density seats and scheduled the shop work to reconfigure the aircraft. Six DC-4s were scheduled for conversion and allocated to the San Juan markets. New schedules were filed and advertising for the new low fares begun. In June 1947 the new low cost Pan Am services to San Juan were started.

A remarkable thing occurred. The aircraft filled up immediately and we could not handle the overflow passengers. More and more flights were added and more aircraft converted. The New York service grew from two flights a day to eight – all full – and utilization rose to sixteen hours a day.

One by one the non-skeds dropped away. Some cut fares to as low as $5 one-way for last minute passengers. As winter approached, some bought the overcoats of southbound passengers and sold them to those going north from San Juan in order to raise revenues. Pan Am held the line with basic low fares. By year-end, only Trans Caribbean Airlines, owned by O. Roy Chalk, remained in the market. Chalk owned the Spanish-speaking newspapers in New York as well as papers in San Juan and, thus, had an advantage in reaching the Puerto Rican ethnic market – enough to keep a profitable operation. All of the rest failed. A dozen years later Chalk sold his airline to American Airlines, starting their Latin American Division.

I had proved the basic truth of air transportation. It is not "something special in the air." The same economic laws as all other transportation govern it. Air travel is not a luxury market, it is a mass market in which a few people will pay a premium for added comfort. However, the masses won't.

It was a principle that I would apply again and again in the future, and which, until recently, Southwest Airlines alone understood.

Cattle to Montevideo

At Pan Am in the summer of 1947 we had one DC-4 cargo aircraft that we used for freight flights, utility purposes and training. An enterprising cargo salesman contracted what proved to be the first in a new market for air freight; moving premium livestock from Canada to South America. Our initial contract called for carrying twenty four cows and two handlers from Toronto to Montevideo, Uruguay.

The request came to my department at Pan Am and I directed the modification of the aircraft, NC90010, for cattle carriage. Strong tarpaulins were spread on the floor and a series of iron stanchions were constructed out of two-inch pipe, separating the aircraft into six stalls. Maximum payload was limited to eighteen thousand pounds to allow for the carriage of fuel for the longest sector, Belem, Brazil to Rio.

The flight was dispatched from Miami to Toronto to pick up the beasts. The contractor had weighed the animals three days before and found that they weighed twenty two thousand four hundred pounds. He would have to off-load four cows. But, he had a better idea. Unbeknownst to us at Pan Am, he simply stopped feeding and watering the cattle, bringing their weight down to the eighteen thousand pound limit by departure time. The cattle, two German handlers and several bales of hay and barrels of water were loaded in Toronto and the plane left for Miami, where I joined the flight as extra crew.

Departure from Miami was without incident, except that more bales of hay were added along with more barrels of water – not included on the weight and balance papers. Between Miami and San Juan the cows happily ate most of the hay, stamping the rest into the tarps on the floor. The water, too, disappeared only to reappear a little later on in both liquid and semi-solid form. At San Juan the process was repeated – more hay and water and fuel for the next leg to Port of Spain.

By the time we reached Piarco Airport in Port of Spain it was clear that we had a problem: the aircraft was getting heavier as the cows ate, drank and defecated in the hay. They were rapidly gaining back their original weight. To make matters worse, three calves had been born on the last leg of the trip, keeping the handlers busy.

Our next stop was Belem, Brazil, at the mouth of the Amazon River, thirteen hundred miles and six and a half hours away. What with the fuel, the restored cows, the offal on the floor, the three calves, another few bales of hay and several more barrels of water I calculated the gross weight of the aircraft at seventy five thousand pounds for takeoff. This was over our max takeoff gross of seventy three thousand pounds, but we had a long runway and a brisk wind so the aircraft should not have any difficulty. As we taxied out to takeoff all of the station staff came out on the ramp to watch.

"Look at those bastards," the Captain said. "They don't worry about us, but only about their asses if we crack this thing up."

We took off without incident for the long flight over the jungles of the three Guyanas to Belem.

We arrived in Belem at 8 P.M. There was a ceiling of two hundred feet, a light rain, fog, no wind and an oppressive 90° temperature with humidity to match. The jungle was flat and after a long, slow and low approach the lights of Belem's airport flashed through the murk. The Belem airport had been built by Pan Am engineers, like so many others in South America and Africa, to accommodate the Army Air Corps flights in support of Montgomery's offensive in North Africa and the operations against the Japanese in India, China and Burma. Its five thousand foot runway was adequate for military operations, but not for the flight of Pan Am's NC90010 tonight.

As we taxied up to the ramp and slowed down, the tail of the DC-4 began to sag toward the runway. The load of cattle and manure had gotten too heavy, and the aircraft was about to "squat" with its tail on the runway. I ordered the Captain to lock brakes, put the wheel full forward to depress the stabilizers and give it full power to hold the tail up. He did so while I rushed aft to find the tail post, hand it to the ground crew and order them to install it to keep the tail from drooping to the ground. After some confusion the task was accomplished and we shut down the engines. It was evident that we had a problem.

Now the aircraft was even more overweight. The next leg to Rio was more than eight hours, requiring even more fuel. The runway was too short and the heat and humidity reduced engine power and efficiency significantly. We were scheduled to have a crew change here in Belem and it would be the first flight for the new crew. While used to flying the DC-3, they had only been checked out a week before on the DC-4 and they were worried! What to do?

We had to lighten the aircraft and restore the center of gravity to mid-point so we could remove the tail stand and take off. I ordered pitchforks to shovel out the excess hay and manure – now a foot deep on the aircraft's floor. There were no pitchforks to be found at Belem Airport, only a hoe, a rake and a short-handled shovel. Shoveling manure was not part of the job description of the local ramp handlers, or our flight crew. So the two German handlers and I tackled the chore. Hour after hour we shoveled, raked and hoed tons of manure to the rear door and out onto the ramp. The cows were herded forward until we had gotten rid of all we could. Dripping sweat and reeking of manure I finally went back into the operations shack to calculate the gross weight and take-off possibilities.

With the cows now at full gross weight and full of hay and water, the remaining manure and the fuel were grossed out at about seventy three thousand pounds. However, the effects of the high humidity and temperature increased our gross to the equivalent of seventy eight thousand pounds. With all engines at full power I calculated that we could take off, and I advised the Captain of our situation. We could either go or offload half the cows and leave them behind to an uncertain future. The Captain decided to go.

We taxied out to the end of the runway and turned as close to the fence as we dared. Ahead in the mist and rain lay the shortest five thousand foot runway in the world. We set flaps for maximum lift, locked the brakes and checked the magnetos, fuel pressures, and temperatures, then gave the engines full power. As the engines screamed at 100% throttle, the Captain tripped the brakes and NC90010 lurched forward, slowly gathering speed – 60 ... 80 ... 100 ... 120 ... 140 knots. Huge red lights marked the end of the runway and beyond lay the blackness of the Amazon jungle night. As we rolled ever faster the lights rushed at us. We now had no choice. With the Captain and copilot both gripping the yokes I was expected to respond to the "Gear Up" command and, at the last second, did so. The plane sagged slightly and then began to climb as the gear disappeared into the nacelles. A great noise and crashing shook the plane as we took the top branches off a tree and slowly, ever so slowly, climbed out over the Amazon and turned south to Rio – seventeen hundred miles away.

Due to weight and temperature our rate of climb was not what it should have been. After an hour we had only reached six thousand feet. Fuel consumption was enormous – way over normal flight plan – and we had none to spare. Four hours out we passed over Barrerias, a giant eight-runway, lighted airport gleaming like a wheel in the darkness of the plateau below us. So near, so inviting... But Barrerias was unusable, unpaved, a sea of mud in the rain forest. More than half our fuel was now gone, and we were only halfway to Rio. I assured the Captain that our fuel burn would decrease sharply now that we had burned off so much excess weight and were in cooler air. We climbed higher and fuel consumption dropped hour by hour.

Unfortunately we now had a new problem. Rio's airports closed in front of us. Both were zero-zero in fog and the radio told us the forecast was for no improvement. The only problem was, we no longer had fuel to hold or to go anywhere else. We had to attempt a near zero-zero landing on the radio range. The Captain was Rio-based and knew the airport well, so we had reasonable confidence in his ability to make the landing.

We approached the Rio radio range, passed over it to determine its exact location, made a timed procedure turn and proceeded to let down on the final approach, knowing that the first ground we'd better see was the end of the runway. And we did. The young Captain made a perfect landing and started to taxi in when, one after the other, the engines died from lack of fuel. We sat on the taxiway until a tug came out with a tow-bar, hitched up and dragged us to the terminal.

A new crew awaited us. The cows would get no more water or hay. After refueling, and as the weather cleared, we took off on the final leg to Puerto Allegre and Montevideo, easy flights with no problems. In Montevideo we were greeted by the Consignees who were happy to get their cows but unmindful of the perils of our flight.

I went to the hotel with the crew, drank a glass of the local equivalent of aquavit, the most horrible stuff I ever drank, and ate a three-pound steak fresh from the Pampas. Then it was off to bed for twelve hours of dead sleep – preparation for the return flight to Miami the next day.

A few weeks later I left Pan Am to found Dispatch Services, which is the subject of the next chapter. ✈

CHAPTER IV

Dispatch Service

In September 1947 I left Pan Am to form a company providing ground handling services for the many new international airlines coming to Miami from South America. My partner was Tom Green, who had been a Pan Am Operations Agent. We called our new venture Dispatch Services, Inc. and offered all manner of services on a contract basis - loading, unloading and cleaning aircraft; passenger ticketing, handling, and immigration clearances; customs clearance for cargo and baggage; towing and parking aircraft; and finally dispatching, flight following, communications and weather.

Our first client was Peruvian International Airlines, whose President, Dick Mitchell, gave us his facilities, ticket counter and ground equipment in trade for free handling. Then came KLM, TACA, VIASA, BWIA and others. Our business built up slowly, payments were always late, and we struggled to stay afloat.

Our big break came when National's pilots went out on the first of many strikes. National's President, G.T. Baker, was a tough, autocratic executive who did not suffer fools graciously. When the pilots' demands became too extreme he invited them to "paint signs and pound salt," and they did. Baker immediately began hiring new pilots to replace the strikers. The ground unions joined the pilots in a sympathy strike, thus starting one of the most bitter and protracted strikes in the airline industry. Baker dressed his new pilots in Confederate grey, replacing the dark blue of the strikers' uniforms, and thus the strike became known as the "battle between the Blue and the Grey."

Baker's Vice President of Marketing was Herb Dobbs, formerly of Pan Am. On the first day of the strike I called him to offer Dispatch Services to provide ground handling, loading and other ramp services for National, replacing the strikers at Miami. He and Baker agreed immediately and, thus began a contract that lasted for 32 years - from 1947 until 1979 when Pan Am bought and swallowed up National. National turned over all of its ramp facilities and equipment to Dispatch Services. We hired eager young replacement ramp agents and were on our way as a major force at Miami International Airport, eventually with hundreds of employees and millions in revenue.

But early on there were major and minor disasters that threatened to terminate our little company on the spot. A shipment of golden kinkajoos arrived destined for a northern zoo, and promptly escaped into the rafters of our warehouse where they swung from beams and wires, screamed epithets and hurled handfuls of offal down on us. Finally they were enticed with bananas and returned to their cages for shipment north.

A Venezuelan had a valuable Tennessee coonhound shipped to him through Dispatch Services. The huge beast arrived – C.O.D. – and we had to write out a $2,000 check to pay for the dog. We held him in the warehouse until the Venezuelan paid us – no money, no dog. The dog escaped and raced out on the runway, with Tom Green in hot pursuit in our Jeep. When we finally caught the dog we decided not to take any more chances. I took him home and chained him on the wire clothesline in the backyard. The next morning he was gone – the chain had been cut with bolt cutters. Now we were really in the soup, no money and no dog.

I put an ad in the Miami Herald stating "One lost coonhound – REWARD!" A few days later I received a phone call from a man who asked:

"You de man wid de lost coonhoun?"

"Yes," I said, hopefully.

"Well, I was out huntin' down in de Glades wid Judge Oliver, and we seed this coon dog in the convict camp down there. He just walked in and they put him up."

"What do we do?" I asked.

"You go down and see the sergeant and tell him Judge Oliver sent you, an' identify the dog an' dey'll give him to you. Reward, no, de Judge said he don't want nuttin."

Without delay we piled into our truck and set off for the convict camp on the edge of the Everglades. As we neared the gate we could hear the lugubrious howling of a coonhound. "Tom, I don't know if that's him, but if not we got ourselves a ringer."

It was our dog. He rushed up to us like an old friend, tail wagging. The Sergeant said the dog had walked into camp a few days earlier dragging a broken chain after having escaped from thieves. We gratefully paid $10 to the Convicts' Fund, crammed the dog into his cage and set off for the airport. The money had come from Venezuela, so the next morning the hound was dispatched on the first flight to Caracas.

A DC-3 arrived from Central America loaded with 5,000 pounds of gold bars – each weighing 100 kilos – tied down on the floor in the back of the aircraft. A hundred kilo gold bar was worth about $180,000 in those days, and we had 23 of them. The consignee could not come for them until the next day and refused to pay us to have an armed guard watch the plane overnight. We dragged the aircraft to a parking area, locked it with a "100 key," and left it. The bars were too heavy for anybody to steal anyhow. The next morning they were still there.

Joe Silverthorn, President of SAHASA, a local airline in Honduras, arrived one day with a DC-3 loaded with silver bars. When our ramp personnel tried to cut the tangled ropes tying them down, Joe burst through the cockpit door yelling: "Don't you bastards cut my fucking rope – it's valuable! Untie it." We meekly untied the silver bars, loaded them on baggage carts and stored them in the warehouse for the night. Joe demanded that I pick him up at 3 A.M. and take him to the Miami Produce Market in our stake truck so that he could buy produce to take back to Honduras. At 3:30 A.M. we arrived at the market, which was ablaze with lights and bustling with restaurant and hotel buyers laying in the day's supplies. The vendors each had sections of the market set aside to display their wares. One huge sign announced "Hymie is here!" and there we stopped. Joe and Hymie entered into a furious bargaining session while warehousemen rushed crates of lettuce, fruits, eggs, frozen produce and other goodies to our truck. When Joe complained about the freshness of one carton of produce, Hymie delivered a brutal kick to the backside of the hapless Black carrying it, and in a torrent of expletives and racial slurs ordered him to bring a carton that was fresh. By 5 A.M. we had some 10,000 pounds of produce piled high on the truck and headed back to the airport to load Joe's waiting DC-3.

It was just getting light when we finished loading, tying everything down with Joe's precious rope saved from the night before. The DC-3 was loaded with ten thousand pounds of produce and eight hundred and twenty gallons of gas (it was cheaper in Miami and Joe wanted to carry back all he could to Honduras). The DC-3 grossed in excess of thirty thousand pounds – a good bit over the certificated limits, but Joe made sure the paperwork was OK. He taxied out and took off down the long left runway Number Nine. We went outside to watch the takeoff. Joe cleared the Jai Lai Fronton on 36th Street by a hundred feet and climbed ever so slowly into the sunrise.

This was only one of many similar incidents. Joe Silverthorn went on to a distinguished career in the dirty undercover war in Viet Nam's Laos and Cambodian operations.

In December Tom Green wanted to bring two of his associates into

Dispatch Services on an equal footing, with each of us having a 25% share. I objected to this dilution of my interest. About the same time a friend and mentor from Pan Am days, Captain Horace Brock, was appointed Manager of the Atlantic Division of Pan Am in New York. He offered me a job running Operations Control, the same job I had held in Miami, at a 50% increase in salary. Since it seemed to offer a good opportunity to solve my problem with Green, I took Brock up on the offer. I sold my shares in Dispatch Services to Green for a few hundred dollars and went back to Pan Am.

Dispatch went on to become a major handling company in Miami. Tom and his new partners eventually sold it to Greyhound Financial Corp. for $5 million.

Airline Start-Up Dreams

Tom Green and I had dreams of starting our own new airline using aircraft that could be acquired cheaply since Tom was a war veteran. Our first plan was for Trans Gulf Airlines that would operate from Tampa, FL to Havana, Cuba. In late 1947 nobody had yet applied for this route and Tampa had a large Cuban and tourist market that promised success. Since inquiries to the CAB indicated that they had no intention of awarding certificated authority to any new airlines we reluctantly dropped this idea. The following year National Airlines inaugurated service.

Our next plan was far more grandiose and was perhaps more politically possible. It was based on the synthesis of several facts:

1. The highest position an African American could attain in the airlines at the time was that of cleaner, loader or porter. [1]
2. During World War II an all-Negro squadron of fighter pilots had been formed and had served with some distinction, actually shooting down one or two Axis aircraft. These pilots now had no opportunity in aviation.
3. President Truman had just eliminated segregation in the Armed Forces, lending impetus to the integration movement.
4. Black voters were increasingly favoring the Democratic Party and abandoning the GOP.

Tom and I thought that there might be an opportunity to found an all-Black airline, giving Blacks full opportunities as pilots, agents and executives.

---

[1] *Until 1945 National Airlines, for one, placed any black passenger behind a curtain in the forward right hand seats of their aircraft.*

President Truman would surely favor granting a certificate to such an all-Black airline serving the major metropolitan centers populated by Blacks: New York, Detroit, Chicago, Washington, D.C., Atlanta, Dallas, Los Angeles, etc. Tom and I would provide aircraft and top management direction, but Blacks would provide financial and political capital and would get the opportunity to prove their competence in aviation. We even had a name for our airline: Afro American Airlines (adopting the name used 50 years later for the race as a whole).

Filled with enthusiasm, we went to Black media, business and political leaders to solicit their support. We were rejected out of hand.

"Look, sonny, we don't put up none of our money for things like that. Whitey pays for our developments."

"We don't want to have our own airline – we want to get jobs in Whitey's airlines."

It was obviously apparent that our idea was DOA.

Many years later a young Black entrepreneur actually founded an airline along the lines we envisioned, providing high class service over major routes. It was called Air Atlanta, and he raised some $60,000,000 in capital from major white investors including General Electric and Pratt & Whitney. Air Atlanta went bankrupt in 36 months despite this massive influx of capital.

Pan Am, New York – 1948

I returned to Pan Am on January 2, 1948, reporting for duty at what is now the Delta Shuttle terminal at LaGuardia. Then it was the terminal and headquarters of Pan Am's Atlantic Division. The last Boeing 314 Flying Boats had been withdrawn and all operations over the Atlantic were conducted with Pan Am's new Lockheed L-049 Constellations – a curvaceous aerodynamic design with three tails and a 40 passenger capacity.

The Division had 15 Lockheeds, but services had been cut way back for the winter so that 12 were on the apron behind the hangar and the remaining three were en route to or from Europe. After checking in at my new office where I would be taking over duties as Schedule Superintendent of the Atlantic Division, I went out on the ramp to survey the situation. Maintenance had advised us that they did not have a flyable aircraft for the evening departure to London – but there sat 12 aircraft on the tarmac!

It was cold and snowing. The Connies stood in a long semicircle as half a dozen mechanics with ladders, heaters, generators, start carts and tugs went from one to another. They would pull up, place the entry stairs at the nose, hook up the support equipment, climb up in the cockpit and try to start the aircraft. Slowly #1, #2 and maybe engines #3 and #4 would be coaxed into operation, blowing long plumes of fresh snow out over the blast fence. But sometimes, despite all efforts, one or more engines refused to start. So the mechanics shut down the engines, removed their equipment and went on to the next aircraft, only to repeat the same futile process.

The London flight eventually departed – many hours late. A check of the records showed this was a common occurrence – it was unusual when an on-time departure was made despite having a dozen aircraft from which to choose.

This was, in fact, the problem. Given a dozen planes to choose from, there was no incentive or seeming necessity to have a particular aircraft airworthy and ready to go. So, inevitably, none were. As long as the mechanics had what they believed to be alternatives they failed to have any aircraft ready.

The remedy proved simple: each shift I and my Superintendents met with the Maintenance Foreman and jointly selected a designated aircraft for each flight. It was then the foreman's job to see that his men had that aircraft ready on time. Since I worked directly for the Division Manager, Capt. Horace Brock, I had sufficient influence to see that our agreements were understood and complied with. On time performance improved sharply and we were in a position to plan our summer schedule, designed to meet the maximum traffic requirements of the coming peak season.

Full Throttle Over the Atlantic

The initial Atlantic schedule for the summer of 1948 contemplated the use of eight of our 15 Lockheed Constellations, with seven held in reserve for spares and maintenance. While traffic demand was known to be greater, Pan Am's chief pilot assured me that he did not have enough crews to man any additional aircraft. A bit of homework disclosed why. The flight time from London to New York was 15 hours – too long for a "single crew" (one captain, co-pilot, radio operator, flight engineer and navigator) to be on continuous duty. Therefore, Pan Am carried a "double crew" – two captains, co-pilots, etc. – so that one could fly and the other rest and supply relief. We also carried a double crew of flight attendants, making 16 crewmembers on each flight. The only trouble with this was that the Connie did not have enough range or fuel capacity to fly non-stop over the Atlantic, so we made an obligatory fuel stop in Gander, Newfoundland. Sometimes weather was below minimums in Gander in which case the flight stopped in Goose Bay, Stephensville or even Halifax.

In winter we often carried more crewmembers on each flight than we did passengers, a phenomenon I observed with interest and dismay. I ordered a study of the actual summer weather in Gander and found the conditions were far better than represented by the Chief Pilot, with below minimum weather conditions existing less than two percent of the time, and then generally for short, often predictable periods of time. This meant that we had sufficient reliability to establish a crew layover point in Gander. We could fly the Atlantic with a single crew of eight rather than a double crew of 16, and effectively double our crew capability with the personnel we had on the payroll.

Flight Operations put up a major battle to prevent having to lay over crews in Gander, citing all the weather uncertainties (which I proved did not exist) and the effects on pilot "morale" – a risk I felt we could take in view of the enormous gains in schedule capability. In the end Management sided with me, and we scheduled twelve of our fifteen Connies over the Atlantic in the summer of 1948, extending our service to several new points in Europe and carrying a record number of passengers. During this summer we seldom had a problem with the weather in Gander. A superb airfield with first class navigation and landing aids, Gander always seemed to be open when we arrived.

Farewell to Pan Am – 1948

During a visit home to the farm in Virginia in the summer of 1948 my father introduced me to Jim Franklin, who had just been made Vice President, Operations, Maintenance and Engineering at Capital Airlines. Capital was

based in Washington, DC, and was an amalgam of Pennsylvania Airlines and Central Airlines. Recent over-expansion had led to financial difficulties and the Board had just ousted the founder, C. Bedell Munroe. A new management team headed by "Slim" Carmichael had just been appointed and Jim was designated to his position as vice president, as part of the reorganization.

I listened with great interest as Jim Franklin outlined his problems and his plans for Capital. Overstaffed, equipped with old war surplus aircraft, and hobbled by an uncompetitive route system, Capital was slowly starving to death economically. Drastic surgery was necessary.

Passengers disembarking   Far into the evening we talked about what had to be done, and how to do it. At the end of the night Jim offered me a position as his assistant. It sounded like a real challenge.

I went back to New York the next day, thinking over Jim's proposition. While we were making great progress at Pan Am I felt constrained by the growing bureaucracy of the company. In Miami we had been relatively free of the interference of headquarters which were located in the Chrysler Building in downtown New York, but at LaGuardia we were right under their noses and they were sniffing around all the time.

I decided to accept Jim Franklin's offer to join Capital and went to Captain Brock's office to tell him of my decision. He was very understanding: "Mort, you have to decide if you want to be a little fish in a big pond, or a big fish in a smaller pond. Good luck . . ."

We soon moved to my parents' farm in Virginia and were immediately involved in the effort to save Capital.

Years later I worked for Pan Am as a consultant devising a plan to rescue them from their downward slide in the 1980s. A decade later I was Advisor to the Creditors' Committee of Pan Am in its bankruptcy – a frustrating and poignant assignment. I was so often reminded of the glory days of Pan Am. Our routes girdled the globe and penetrated almost every country. In many we owned the local domestic airlines as well. European competitors were just starting up again after the ruin of World War II, and the new US. carriers now permitted to compete internationally with Pan Am, had not gotten their wings yet. I have often wondered what would have happened if I had elected to stay with Pan Am – to me and to the airline.

Pan Am in Retrospect

I left Pan Am in 1948, but never lost my interest in Juan Trippe's "Empire of the Air" as one author called it. In the days I worked with Pan Am it was America's chosen instrument. In many countries the Pan Am station manager had more influence than the American Ambassador. Pan Am's routes extended to every continent and the Company owned many of the domestic routes as well. Pan Am built many of the airports on the islands of the Pacific and the jungles of South America used by our armed forces to reach and supply the war effort in Asia and Africa.

But Pan Am was arrogant, from Juan Trippe on down. This attitude permeated to the employees at the lowest level. Competitors, both U.S. and overseas, played on this arrogance to Pan Am's detriment. The CAB during its forty year history never awarded Pan Am a domestic route, while permitting the large US airlines more and more international routes: American and TWA penetrated the Atlantic and, to a lesser extent, the Pacific. The Caribbean became an Eastern lake. Northwest became predominant in Japan and the Far East. In its final agony Pan Am sold its last routes to the U.S. Majors. United got the Pacific and morsels of the Atlantic. American took principal London routes, and Delta got the remains of the carcass in the bankruptcy.

One wonders how the most powerful airline in the world could have come to such an ignominious fate. The disintegration of Pan Am's Empire of the Air began under Trippe and Pan Am passed its apex even before it ordered the 25 Boeing 747s in 1965.

Foreign governments acted to take over the domestic routes Pan Am had built in their countries. Among them were Mexicana, Varig, AVIANCA, Aviateca, Lanica, and Avensa. At its high point Pan Am and its satellites served over a hundred cities worldwide.

Juan Trippe relinquished the reins at Pan Am in May 1968 and was followed by five other presidents of increasing incompetence, ending with the pitiful Tom Plasket who presided over its bankruptcy and final humiliating liquidation.

My consulting firm AVMARK was retained in 1982 at the insistence of the Pan Am unions, led by the Teamsters. We were asked to recommend changes which the management could make to improve operations, revenues and finances, and to verify that the labor parties had to make wage concessions to keep the Company afloat. We worked for six months and developed a Draconian plan to save Pan Am through restructuring of routes, fleets and marketing, reconfiguration of aircraft, and resultant increases in efficiency and productivity. President Ed Acker and his management rejected all of them.

Finally, I participated in the Pan Am bankruptcy proceedings as Advisor to the Unsecured Creditors' Committee and helplessly watched Tom Plasket and his toadies repeatedly snatch defeat from the jaws of victory as restructuring options were rejected. At one point, we presented a carefully crafted plan to eliminate uneconomic short-range B-727s and costly A-310s from the fleet. Pan Am's pilot union leader promptly flung the plan to the floor and jumped up and down on the fluttering pages shouting "This is garbage, this is shit!" A few months later Pan Am was gone. ✈

✈

CHAPTER V

Capital Days

Joining Capital

ost reduction and cost control were major challenges at Capital, hampered as we were by old, non-competitive aircraft and a weak route structure where our competitors had all the advantages. And with all of this, we also had to get employee morale to a fever pitch to overcome the obstacles we faced.

Franklin's first action was to put most of the maintenance supervisors and engineers back on the hangar floor where they could again use their skills to fix broken aircraft. Hundreds of inexperienced new hires were furloughed causing productivity to soar.

Every year we awarded one station a "Best Station of the Year" citation and all executives from "Mahogany Row" went to the chosen station for a day to run the operation while the bemused employees looked on. President "Slim" Carmichael loaded baggage, VP Jim Franklin drove a tractor, and I sorted baggage in the baggage room. It gave a great boost to staff morale – and gave the executives a taste of what the "real operation" was like.

However, the Mechanics' Union, the IAM and the Pilots, represented by ALPA were a different matter. When I first joined Capital in 1948 the IAM put out a bulletin to all employees: "Efficiency Expert Joins Capital" and went on to explain my alleged technique: "Lay off 50 employees, and when they complain, hire back 20 and they will treat you like a hero." Bob Quick, the IAM President, didn't know it, but he was right!

The pilots were even more oblivious to the Company's need for efficiency, with incessant demands for higher pay, more rules and less flying hours. Capital's economic history was a roller coaster of good times and bad times. The management faced a continuous dilemma. They could not take a strike in bad times because they could not afford it. And they would not face a strike in good times because they were making so much money. So Capital lurched on, year after year, becoming less and less efficient in spite of our best efforts – new aircraft, and the expansion of our route system.

By the late 1950s, Capital was the fifth largest airline in the United States, with a system covering most of the U.S. east of the Mississippi. Our fleet grew to over a hundred aircraft, including seventy five British-built jet-prop Viscounts that gave us a major competitive advantage for the first time. But the management squandered its opportunity. Half of the Viscounts were deployed in the Company's historic east-west routes against American, United and TWA, where they ran at a 70% load factor and made money. The other half were wasted in the new north-south markets against Delta, Eastern and National where load factors seldom exceeded 40%. We lost all the money we made in the east-west routes. For some reason the management could never understand the stupidity of their aircraft allocation policy.

Another management decision that eventually proved fatal to the airline was the election to operate the Viscount with only 44 seats in an essentially first class configuration. The Viscount was capable of carrying fifty-five passengers in a three across and two across seating configuration. Had Capital done this, its seat miles costs would have been 20% lower and revenue potential 20% higher, especially in our east-west markets where we operated at turn-away

load factors. The management of Capital, having become somewhat successful, were desperate to upscale the Company's image and simply could not understand that we were still in the business of providing basic air transportation – a lesson that should have been learned with the success of the Night Hawk five years before.

Thirty years after the demise of the airline, Capital employees still gathered for a picnic. Mort on the left, with Ron Davies.

Ultimately, these two decisions led to the ouster of Slim Carmichael and his management. General David Hodges Baker III, USAF Retired, was brought in to right the sinking ship, but instead hastened and presided over its demise. As one associate said of the General, "Never had so much stupidity been crammed into the head of one man."

Capital became insolvent in 1960, with all of its bills paid except its obligation to Vickers Armstrong, the British company which had built and financed the seventy-five Viscounts.

The British wanted desperately to work things out and refinance Capital, but General Baker sold it to United for a few million dollars. Capital was swallowed up and vanished from the airlines of the world.

It is now almost fifty years since Capital disappeared, but until recently the former employees held a reunion in a park in Alexandria, VA. Over thirteen hundred former employees gathered for an afternoon of remembrances. Many traveled from all over the U.S. using their life-time passes from successor United Airlines. All remember the pride, the enthusiasm and the camaraderie of Capital Airlines, one of the truly great pioneer airlines of the world.

At Capital as Jim Franklin's assistant I had an extraordinary freedom to develop and implement new ideas, many of which were instrumental in building Capital. Some of them are still standard airline practice today.

The Night Hawk

When I joined Capital in September of 1948, the Company was teetering on the brink of insolvency. Capital lost a DC-4 with some fifty passengers and crew on Lookout Rock Mountain, west of Washington, the previous Memorial Day weekend, the same day United and Eastern also lost DC-4s in unrelated accidents. The crashes cast a pall over the industry, loads fell precipitously and, in Capital's case, it was almost fatal.

The Company was frantically pursuing an application to the CAB to get back on subsidy, then disguised as "mail pay," and the application dragged on slowly through the uncaring bureaucracy of the Civil Aeronautics Board. When granted, our application would be retroactive. But for now we lived on hope.

Capital owned 20 slow, underpressurized, ex-military DC-4s. Eight of them were out of service due to excessive wing-tank fuel leaks and an inability to keep pace with repeated engine failures. Utilization of the flyable DC-4s was a pitiful five hours per day, between 8 A.M. to 8 P.M. Our rivals were already adding scores of fast, modern pressurized DC-6s and L-749 Constellations to their fleets, crushing Capital in a veritable competitive vise.

In the spring of 1948 "Slim" Carmichael replaced C. Bedell Monroe, the

Capital Route System in 1957

founder of Pennsylvania Airlines, who had merged it with Central Airlines in 1946 to form Penn Central, "The Capital Airline." By 1948 the Penn Central had dropped away and we were now Capital. Slim cleaned house, placing Jim Franklin in charge of Operations, Maintenance and Engineering; Jim Austin as head of Marketing; and Ray Locheil as director of Finance.

These and a half-dozen secondary executives, Bob Wilson, Hayers Deever, Pamela O'Hanlon, Ted Hardesty, Ralph Reed, and others, directed Capital's fortunes for the next decade. A roller coaster ride perhaps unparalleled by other airlines.

Under Monroe, Capital had too many chiefs and not enough qualified Indians. In Maintenance, Franklin wiped out virtually the entire supervisory structure, putting the old timers who had been promoted to non-productive desk jobs, back on the floor, and furloughing the untrained new hires. Job One: get the DC-4s flying. In a few weeks they were. The fuel leaks were cured, engine overhaul standards tightened up and inspections were rigorous and demanding. In the evenings we would walk the hangar floors talking with the men and showing our real interest in how things were coming. It made a difference.

Our Engineering Department had grown to 73 men, many of them drawn from the floor, where they had been good mechanics, to be put at drawing tables where they were lost. Franklin and I reviewed the roster and Jim invited 60 of the engineering group to the boardroom. I remained in his office with the remaining 13, whose long drawn faces clearly showed their fears as to their futures. Shortly, the Boardroom doors opened and the large group filed by, quiet and with faces averted. My group of thirteen, all of whom were fairly junior members of the staff, literally trembled with apprehension as Jim came into the room and we closed the door. "Gentlemen," he said, "you are now the Capital Engineering Department."

However, our major problem was revenue, or rather the lack of it. Our better-equipped competitors were expanding at our expense. In 1948 the CAB rigidly controlled routes and fares. Capital, for example, was allowed to fly from New York to Chicago, but our flights had to stop at Pittsburgh in order to protect American, United and TWA, all of whom had nonstop rights to New York-Chicago. All fares were the same. All fares were first class, $70 one way. As a result, Capital was an insignificant competitor in the New York-Chicago market. On the ground, the New York Central's 20th Century Limited provided premier rail service between the two cities at $29.70 for coach, carrying hundreds of passengers. The Interstate (started under Eisenhower in the late 1950s) was not yet a factor.

Thinking of our predicament one night, I remembered my experience with Pan Am and the non-skeds in the San Juan market. There we had added seats to DC-4s and cut fares drastically to match the low cost charter and non-sked airlines. It had worked, with our business growing ten fold and the non-sked being forced from the market. Perhaps ...

Jim and I went down Mahogany Row to Jim Austin's office. The Vice President of Marketing, Austin was an aggressive and innovative marketeer and, in the twelve years I was with the company, played a strong if not always positive role in its development.

I outlined my plan to Austin. Take two DC-4s which overnighted in Chicago and New York and cross them over, flying a trip in each direction departing at 10 P.M. Charge $29.70, the fare on the 20th Century Limited's 24 hour coach trip between the two cities. Jim agreed, and the next day we filed for authority to conduct the flights with the CAB.

CAB approval was needed not only for the new low "off peak" fare, but also for the nonstop routing we wanted. Capital was required to stop all current flights in Pittsburgh in order to protect American, TWA and United, all with nonstop flights between Chicago and New York. And we wanted to remove the required stop. The CAB approved the low fares and required us to take on-board surveys to see how many passengers were diverted from the "Big Three" carriers. But they refused to let Capital overfly Pittsburgh, and so our "Night Hawk," as we christened it, had to operate Chicago-Pittsburgh-New York and return

Capital Airlines Douglas DC-4

regardless of the fact that relatively few passengers wanted on or off, even when the service was offered.

The first flight was November 7th, 1948. Winter was already upon us and traffic was down system wide. Our advertising was confined to puny 4"x4" plugs on Page 2 of the New York and Chicago tabloids. No rich man's newspapers could be afforded. Surprisingly to many, the first flight was full and, in the weeks building up to Thanksgiving, the load factors were over 80%. For the holidays we added extra sections, putting more overnight aircraft into the air between the two cities. On Christmas Eve we ran an unheard-of total of eight extra sections in each direction, all full. The Night Hawk was a success.

The CAB's on-board surveys revealed that only three percent of the passengers had been "diverted" (stolen) from the Big Three's high priced airline flights. The rest were people off the 20th Century Limited, or out of their autos and, most importantly, people who otherwise would have stayed home.

In the months to come, the Night Hawk spread its wings. Washington, Detroit, Minneapolis, Milwaukee, and Cleveland were all added. Our nighttime utilization of DC-4s increased until it equalled the daylight flying. The Big Three airlines watched in contemptuous disbelief and it was more than a year before anyone began to duplicate Capital's services. By that time we had won CAB approval to fly an "Interchange" flight from Washington to Florida in cooperation with National Airlines. With this began the Day Coach using high density DC-4s in competition with other airlines' more modern first class DC-6s and Connies. Thus began the concept of "Coach" or "Economy" flights in the United States. Prior to this all flights (except the non-skeds) were first class, with big seats and low capacity. DC-6s, which later carried eighty passengers in two classes, carried only fifty in a single first class. Finally, in the early '50s, all the airlines came to recognize the merit of Capital's Night Hawk, and low fares proliferated over all the major routes, followed by the Day Coach as well at a slightly higher price.

The Night Hawk brought an immediate and sharp increase in Capital's revenues. The CAB finally ruled in favor of Capital's mail contract. We received several million in retroactive mail pay, as well as a generous allowance for the future. Capital was on the way!

Square Windows

As 1953 opened, Capital was doing well, but not well enough. Our new (second hand) L-049 Connies had regained market share in our principal markets but five aircraft were not enough. The bulk of our routes were served by our twenty five World War II DC-4s which were slow, unpressurized, dingy and at a distinct disadvantage compared to the shiny new pressurized, high-speed DC-6s being delivered in increasing numbers to our major competitors, American and United.

My boss, Jim Franklin, and I were standing at the windows of Mahogany Row, the office corridor that ran the length of Hangars 3, 4 and 5 at Washington National, our base. Outside our mechanics were swarming over a DC-4 while Jim and I discussed our competitive disadvantages. We concluded many of them were image and perception. Capital's fleet was seen as old and outmoded by our colleagues in the industry. Flying times were actually not too much different, maybe fifteen or twenty minutes a segment. Our reliability was better because the Capital team was highly motivated and put out the extra effort to make quick turns, take advantage of breaks in the weather, and make schedule.

As we mused, I had an idea, first dimly and then more clearly. The major distinguishing feature between the DC-4 and the DC-6 to the layman was that the DC-6 had square windows while the old DC-4s were round, like portholes on a ship. Ergo, why not paint square windows on our DC-4s and make them look like DC-6s?

Franklin went for the idea immediately, and the next morning the Engineering Department laid out the new livery. A 16" black border would surround each window, with white paint up to the glass. Within a day the paint shop had the pounce patterns laid out, and by morning the first "Capital DC-6" rolled out with painted square windows.

Our idea gained instant attention and howls of derision from airline people (ours included) all up and down the line. The effect of the black frame, white paint and small dark round window was startling. The aircraft looked like the USS Constitution with its gun ports. We obviously had it wrong.

Jim and I worked late that night and ate at the National Terminal, after a few of the inevitable martinis. Colleagues stopped by our table to kid us about our aberration with the windows.

Back at the hangar we again stood at the window looking out at our creation on the hangar floor and ruminating about what to do. Change it back? Press on? What are our alternatives?

"Jim, why don't we paint the area around the windows gray instead of white?"

We thought about it for a while and, at a short meeting the next morning, Engineering was directed to find the right shade of neutral gray which would closely approximate the appearance of and blend with the plexiglass windows. In a few hours we had it right. By the end of the month the entire DC-4 fleet had "square" windows – black frames outlining gray windows.

Marketing was still agnostic. "You can't fool the passengers, you make us look dumb." So we took on-board surveys, asking the passengers some twenty-five questions concerning service, dependability, personnel, schedules, and other things. Imbedded in the questionnaire was this:

What kind of airplane are you flying in?
❏ DC-4　　　❏ Constellation
❏ DC-6　　　❏ Don't Know

The results were surprising. Over 80% answered "DC-6." The rest were split between DC-4, "Connie," and Don't Know.

Capital's DC-4s flew with square windows until they were retired a decade later. Load factors improved by several points concurrently with the cosmetic change. As our Constellation fleet grew to a dozen planes, industry wags claimed that "Those aren't Connies, they are DC-4s! That Franklin painted three tails on them."

At Capital we also pioneered in-flight television in 1949, cutting a hole in the forward bulkhead of the cabin and installing a twenty Inch black-and-white unit in the hole. Color had not yet been developed, and we rigged a 110-volt converter off the ship's electrical system. The installation worked okay, but one had to continually change stations as we flew along due to the limited range of the transmitters. Unfortunately, not all stations were carrying the same programs, so it was impossible to receive the hometown football games in their entirety. We terminated the effort to have in-flight TV until better technology was invented.

In Flight Booze

In the late 1940s, liquor was forbidden on scheduled airline flights. It was sort of a rule, nobody really knew where it came from or why it existed. Capital was suffering from the competitive inroads in its major markets from the superior equipment of American, Northwest, TWA and United. Therefore, I began to wonder if some way could be found to serve, or better yet, sell booze on our aircraft, just as was being done in Europe.

State liquor laws were paramount and for some reason extended to the stratosphere over each State's domain. Virginia was "dry," so no liquor could be served until outside its borders. Other states demanded each aircraft have a state liquor license.

We made an initial breakthrough, advising passengers to "bring your own bottle," and we sold them setups in flight. That avoided all the messy state laws, and people loved it.

For several years we chipped away at the restrictions and finally arrived at a compromise with state liquor authorities which permitted sales of in flight booze almost everywhere. Virginia hung on until well into the '60s with its prohibition, but eventually it too capitulated to the 20th century.

In the meantime, Capital pioneered in flight booze and, for a few precious years, had another small edge over its bigger and stodgier competitors.

Korean Air Lift

On June 25, 1950, the North Korean Army struck across the 38th parallel and invaded South Korea. The U.S. had indicated over the past year or so that it was not much interested in the fate of South Korea under our protege Singhman Rhee, but when the North invaded there was an instantaneous change of heart. MacArthur was ordered to move his small forces from Japan to Korea and President Truman called on the U.S. airline industry to contribute cargo aircraft to move ammunition and supplies to the battlefront some seventy five hundred miles away.

At Capital we had four DC-4 freighters, all of them short-range aircraft incapable of even reaching Hawaii from the West Coast. During the recent war these aircraft had been fitted with auxiliary fuel tanks in the cabin and long range tanks in the wings, which had been removed in peacetime. To use these aircraft in the Korean airlift we would have to recommission the wing tanks and find and install cabin tanks and plumbing. I undertook to find the hardware while the Engineering Department tackled the plumbing and installation job.

For 15 hours a day, three days in a row, I sat at my telephone armed with a list of the part numbers I needed. The tanks were easy to find and were soon on their way to Washington for installation. The piping to rig them into the fuel system, including shut off valves, gauges, brackets, elbows, baffles, pumps and other hardware had to be dug out of Air Force military depots, part by part. I established liaison with virtually all USAF C-54 depots and air bases, contacted senior supply officers and gave them my "wish list." Hour after hour I wheedled, pleaded and demanded parts I needed. I found that assuming a commanding tone of voice was always effective. They didn't know who I was but I came from Washington and I did know what I wanted, so the officers evidently thought that compliance and cooperation were their preferred courses of action. By the end of the third night, I had the equipment and parts needed.

Meanwhile, down on the hangar floor work was going forward on the first installations. Within a week of commencement of hostilities our first

Capital aircraft was ready to go. We had already asked for volunteer crews to fly to Korea and a half dozen were en route to San Francisco, where they would join a pilot pool organized by Pan Am to fly the airlift to save Korea.

Contacting our Air Force liaison, we were ordered to take our aircraft to a base in the Carolinas to load up with rockets and mortar shells for Korea. Twenty thousand pounds were loaded and the plane proceeded to a refueling stop at Midway Airport in Chicago where I joined it. The next stop was McCord Field near Seattle where we would transfer our load to military aircraft and ferry our DC-4 to San Francisco to join Pan Am's pool at Travis A.F.B.

We were fully grossed out of Chicago's short obstructed Midway field on the two thousand mile flight to McCord. The cabin tanks, newly installed, were full to the brim and ten tons of live ammunition covered the cargo floor to a depth of several feet. It was a hot August night with no wind to speak of. The takeoff performance charts showed no margin for error. We were on military over gross and any engine malfunction at a critical point in the takeoff flight path would have unfavorable consequences. But our boys in Korea needed the ammo and we went. I sat on the jump seat between the captain and copilot, the better to observe. We taxied out all the way to the last few feet of available runway, turned, locked the brakes, and slowly pushed the engines up to power for the critical magneto checks. One by one, the engines checked out within limits. With brakes fully locked, we ran the engines to full takeoff power, dropped the flaps to maximum lift, and released the brakes to begin the takeoff roll. Aircraft performance is poorer in hot air than in cold. Without any headwind to provide added lift, the takeoff roll is extended. Acceleration seemed ever so slow on the short five thousand foot runway. Midway was surrounded by houses and small business buildings and, therefore, there was no extra safety margin.

On and on we rolled, slowly gathering speed – 80, 100, 120 knots. Still far short of the 150 knots we needed for lift off. We passed the "point of no return" where we could have aborted the takeoff and stopped. Now there was no alternative . . . it was GO or else! Within a few hundred feet of the runway's end we reached "VR," the rotation or lift off speed. The Captain pulled back on the yoke and ever so slowly our DC-4 staggered into the air. A roof flashed by a few feet below our wing. An apartment loomed in the dark, to be avoided by a slight bank. After two or three minutes of slow climb we were finally in the clear and eased up into the low cloud cover above us.

The hours droned by as we climbed slowly to our initial cruising altitude of eight thousand feet. We drained our cabin tanks and switched to the newly re-activated outer wing tanks. Routine instrument checks showed all in order. Over eastern Montana we climbed higher to clear the 14,000 foot peaks of the Rockies. The number three engine instruments began to show signs of trouble – increased temperature, erratic RPM, falling oil pressure. The captain shut it down and we proceeded on the remaining three engines. As dawn broke we lined up at McCord's main runway and came in for a normal landing. Taxiing to the parking area, we turned the aircraft over to the sergeant on duty for unloading and servicing, while we all trooped to the BOQ for a few hours of sleep before our final leg to San Francisco.

It is legal to ferry a four-engine aircraft with one engine inoperative to the nearest maintenance base and we elected to do this. The next morning we departed early, flying down the magnificent Cascade Range over Mount Rainier, Mount Hood, Crater Lake and the others, over the wine country of northern California to the Pan Am base at San Francisco. There I checked in with the Operations Manager, Captain Brick Maxwell, to assure that Capital crews were being phased in and that a spare engine would be supplied for our DC-4. This was done during the night and, in the morning, our plane was ready to depart on its first flight to Korea.

At 7 A.M. we ferried from San Francisco to Travis Air Force Base some fifty miles away and northeast of San Francisco. This huge facility was the jumping off place for flights to and from Korea and dozens of military aircraft lined the parking pads. Ours was the first "volunteer" aircraft. Pan Am was the established Pacific carrier and already in business on the airlift. But American, United, Eastern and others still were getting organized. Capital was ready to go. On the parking pad we were loaded to the maximum with weapons and ammunition. Destination: Tachikawa, Japan. First stop Hawaii's Hickam A.F.B. on Oahu, target of the Japanese at Pearl Harbor less than ten years before.

Pan Am, in operational control, assigned our aircraft to a Pan Am crew. I called Brick Maxwell. "Brick, this ain't right. We brought this plane out here. Our guys are here to fly and I would appreciate it if you would let them have the first flight with our aircraft." He agreed.

Loaded and ready to go, the crew boarded. A brisk wind was blowing and, as the last crewman entered the cabin, the main door was blown from his hands and slammed back against the fuselage. The door handle broke a cabin window. A "no go" problem. We did not have a spare window and a search of the Travis Supply Depot failed to locate one as well. I noted an Air Force C-54 parked a few spots away, not going anywhere, and promptly went to the Colonel in Operations. "I would like to borrow a window from that C-54," I said.

"You can't do that!"

"Why not?"

"That's a United States Air Force plane."

"When is it due out?"

"Maybe tomorrow ..."

"I can get you a replacement window in a couple of hours from San Francisco, but if we don't go now we'll miss our deadline. Look Colonel, I can remove that window in fifteen minutes with a screwdriver and get our plane going. I want your permission, or do we have to go see the General?"

"OK, you can have it"

The window was removed and the broken one replaced in the Capital aircraft. Thirty minutes later she was airborne, the first civilian airliner to join the Korean Airlift. Later that day Pan Am sent over a replacement window for the Air Force plane and we installed it.

For four years Capital served in the Korean Airlift, flying hundreds of missions from the West Coast to Tachikawa and Pusan via Honolulu, Midway, Wake and Guam. We were proud of the role we played.

Pentagon Days

In late 1951 the Korean War was dragging on, a stalemate on the ground despite American air superiority. The Air Force was finding it difficult to keep fighters and bombers airborne in the Korean theater. With a large number of civilians from the airlines now doing staff work, the question constantly came up. Why could the airlines fly their airplanes twelve to fourteen hours a day while the military could barely get one mission a day? How could 90% of the airline fleets be operational every day, while 80% of the military aircraft were grounded? It was not battle damage. That barely affected 10% of the military jets, bombers and transports. It was just that the military maintenance system did not work.

After each B-29 mission it took three days to do a daily check on an aircraft. After twenty-five hours of flying a B-25 light bomber was flown back from Korea to Japan for a check which took a month to perform. The airlines did a similar service in a few hours. And so it went. Despite hundreds of men and millions of dollars in parts, the Air Force could not get more than a tiny fraction of its aircraft airborne in any one day.

So, somebody in the Pentagon's Operations Research Center said, "Why don't we see how the airlines do it?" An Air Force analyst was assigned who contacted the Air Transport Association (ATA), the airlines' Washington trade group, and the ATA suggested they talk to me. Capital was the only airline headquartered in Washington. So one day, a delegation from the Pentagon showed up on my doorstep anxious to learn how the airlines achieved their amazing in-service rates.

One thing led to another and, in a few weeks, I was assigned to the Air

Force as a consultant. Our mission was to "find out how the airlines do it." I believed that the most effective research technique would be for an Air Force expert and myself to visit each of the major airlines' maintenance and overhaul bases around the country. We would interview the senior executives, and obtain statistical data as to the work content of various maintenance operations, the frequency with which they were conducted, the manpower skills and man-hours required, and the organization and scheduling of the work. This plan was accepted.

A few weeks later I had scheduled interviews and appointments with many of the major airlines maintenance management executives of the day – Eastern in Miami, American at Tulsa, United at San Francisco, and Western in Los Angeles. Northwest was also included. We traveled from base to base, usually spending a week at each one. Our reception was invariably cordial, if somewhat bemused. Each airline opened up its books and records to us and executives spent many hours explaining how they managed their maintenance functions to produce high utilization and in-commission rates with near perfect reliability and at acceptable cost. Some of the nuggets which fell out included Ambrose Chabbott (VP, Maintenance at Eastern) when asked how he determined manning levels. "It takes as many people as you have as long as you give 'em to do any job."

"Our job is to maintain airplanes when people don't want to fly in them, so we do most of our work overnight." This from George Warde of American Airlines.

"We have 30% of all our maintenance problems in the first hundred hours after we finish a major overhaul." (United official)

After two months of on-site visits, we sat down to synthesize our findings and to try to explain to the Air Force what we had learned. Our major findings included:

➤ The Air Force attempted to grossly over-maintain their aircraft, performing hundreds of operations that were totally unnecessary, on a frequency that was excessive.
➤ Every time an aircraft was "opened up" for maintenance, the opportunity to make mistakes far exceeded the corrective actions required.
➤ Air Force training was utterly inadequate, due in large part to the infusion of thousands of unqualified personnel.
➤ Parts and components were a major problem. Any component suspected of causing trouble was removed and sent back to Depot Maintenance in the USA. Replacement parts were slow in coming and often mismatched to the aircraft.

➤ There were no firm schedules to finish anything. Aircraft poured into the rear echelon bases in Japan and just piled up there. The more aircraft, the greater the confusion. No one could decide which aircraft to work on next and, as a result, none flew.

We finally filed our report. I returned to full-time responsibilities at Capital, having learned how every other airline in the industry ran its maintenance, production, planning and stores. I made some extra income and got a priceless education. I am not sure that the Air Force boys in blue ever understood what we were talking about in our report.

The Viscount

By 1951 Capital was doing well. The CAB and the United States Postal Service had restored our subsidy mail pay in 1948, saving us from bankruptcy. The night coach concept – the Night Hawk – had caught on and now covered all of our major stations, almost doubling aircraft utilization. We purchased five Lockheed L-749 pressurized, high speed transports from KLM and then traded them to British Overseas Airways Corp. (BOAC) for five older, but still adequate L-049s and five million dollars. The Company was in the black for the first time ever.

In England the British had developed the Comet, the first jet passenger aircraft. This pioneer aircraft was an immediate commercial success, but a technical disaster. Three aircraft disintegrated in midair and the rest were grounded until the problem could be identified and corrected. It was discovered that stress cracks developed at the corners of the square windows when the aircraft was pressurized, causing the airframe to rupture. The British corrected the problem by installing oval windows and ever since all windows have been rounded on passenger jets. But despite the Comet problem, the British were well ahead of the Americans in aircraft design. In the early 1950s they announced the Vickers Viscount 700, a forty-four to fifty- five passenger turboprop. Again it was the first of its kind.

Vickers Viscount 800 N7450 of Capital Airlines 1959

I read about the Viscount in a British trade publication and wrote to Vickers for further information which they obligingly sent. I prepared a comparison of the Viscount, our existing aircraft and the competitive DC-6s, DC-7s and Lockheed Constellations.

The Viscount offered some startling features, fifty miles an hour greater speed than any competitive aircraft, much greater fuel economy because it burned kerosene rather than high octane gasoline, a two-man crew and an all-new jet engine replacing

Viscount 700, N7446

the complex high cost, unreliable piston engines. The big twin row piston engines became more unreliable and expensive to operate the bigger they got – hardly progress in aviation.

Franklin and a group of engineers flew to England to visit the Vickers plant at Weybridge and fly the aircraft. A skeptical old mechanic commented after his return, "I can't believe we let this idea sit on the shelf all these years while we wasted our time on piston engines." But that is exactly what the U.S. manufacturers had done, and now the English were five years ahead of the United States and we didn't even have anything on the drawing boards to match the Viscount.

Vickers was anxious to break into the American market and offered Capital three aircraft on consignment. If we liked them, we kept them. If we didn't like them, we simply gave them back. Vickers and Rolls Royce (who made the engines) even set up a complete warehouse of spare parts for Capital's use. When we needed parts, we bought them. We didn't have to go to the expense of inventorying the spares – a major saving.

Imagined perils of operating the higher speed new technology Viscounts proved illusory. They did not disrupt the airways or airport traffic patterns, they did not run out of fuel, they were quiet and comfortable on the inside and not overly noisy on the outside.

But then Capital's marketing department made a major strategic mistake, one that they steadfastly continued even as successive orders were placed and the Viscount fleet grew to 75 aircraft. Marketing was afraid to use the Viscount head-to-head against the major carriers' DC-7s and Connies. In the final analysis it was a fatal error which contributed greatly to the demise of Capital.

So instead of scheduling the Viscounts non-stop in Capital's major market – Washington-Chicago – where American, United and TWA were out-scheduling us with their big piston aircraft, marketing scheduled the faster, more comfortable Viscounts in the short haul markets – Norfolk- Pittsburgh-Cleveland-Detroit-Chicago. They carried well and passengers loved them, but

The Lockheed 049 Constellation, "The Connie"

these were Capital monopoly markets where we could carry all the passengers going in DC-3s and DC-4s.

As the years dragged on, marketing continued to deploy the Viscounts on the short haul markets. They retired the DC-3s and DC-4s and added more Connies – aerial manifestations of the laws of diminishing returns – to the major long haul routes. Then marketing made their second strategic miscalculation.

The CAB was gradually expanding Capital's route system to the South, adding Atlanta, Birmingham, Mobile, New Orleans and cities in Florida. Our Viscounts were operating at load factors of 70 to 80% in the Northeast, but only 35 to 50% in the South against the aggressive competition of Delta and Eastern. Common sense dictated reducing the low load factor (and therefore, low revenue) flights in the South and adding capacity to the high load factor routes in the Northeast and Midwest. Experience showed us that adding more flights to routes operating with turn-away load factors resulted in even more passengers and revenue.

Only in the final years of Capital's existence were Viscounts operated extensively in major long haul, non-stop markets. Washington and Newark to Chicago were increased to hourly non-stops in both directions. Four flights a day flew Washington-Minneapolis, a segment which marketing said we could not fly non-stop due to fuel limitations. The operations department said we could fly non-stop, but marketing controlled scheduling. So that was that.

The Viscount was designed to carry fifty-five passengers in a five-abreast configuration. From the inception marketing insisted on a forty four, four-abreast seating configuration in order to provide maximum seating comfort to our passengers. Since the CAB set the fares based on the SIFL (Standard Industry Fare Level) which was based on the operating costs of our major competitors there was nothing we could do about fares. But by having only 44 seats we cut our revenue 20% from what it would have been at 55 seats, and potentially eleven more passengers. Experience had again shown that on major routes load factors were a constant. If you have 80% seat utilization with 44 seats, you will have the same load factor with 55 seats. This is due to the effects of peak hour and peak day travel, no shows, and seasonality.

In the Viscount, Capital had an enormous advantage over its competitors. We had a faster, quieter, more comfortable and more reliable aircraft with a much greater passenger appeal. The marketing department squandered this advantage by scheduling the aircraft in short haul monopolistic markets, allocating a disproportionate share of capacity in low load factor Southern markets, and configuring the aircraft with only 80% of the seats they were capable of carrying. They recognized these strategic errors too late. By that time our competitors had their larger and even faster Lockheed Electra turboprops and the first Boeing 707 and DC-8 jets.

The Caravelles

In 1954 Capital pioneered the introduction of the Vickers Viscount four-engine forty-four seat turboprop in the United States, ordering three and eventually expanding the fleet to seventy-five. By 1958 American, Eastern, and others had gotten their first Lockheed Electra turboprops, bigger, faster and more efficient than the Viscount. The Brits had the Jet Comet, and Boeing and Douglas were about to enter the stage with the 707 and DC-8 big jet transports.

In my capacity as assistant to the senior vice president of Operations, Maintenance and Engineering I was responsible for fleet planning and aircraft selections for our department. Aviation magazines were beginning to carry articles about a radical new French design, the Caravelle jet. Patterned on the Comet fuselage and wing, it carried sixty passengers but its other design features were highly unconventional by then-current standards. The two jet engines were mounted on the tail. At this time conventional wisdom held that transport aircraft should have four engines mounted on the wing, as the Viscount and Electra turboprops had (along with the Comet, Britannia, the piston DC-6/7 and the Lockheed L-1049s), and as the DC-8 and B-707 now being developed by Douglas and Boeing would also have.

Thus, there was considerable skepticism concerning the new twin-engine Caravelle with its only two engines on the rear.

United Airlines Sud SE-210 Caravelle VI-R

Designed and built by Aerospatiale, the French jet with its Rolls Royce engines was bought only by the French airlines, Air France and Air Inter. The aircraft entered service in March 1959 and reportedly did well. There was no string of horrible accidents such as those that plagued the British Comet. The rear engines made for a quiet ride for passengers, and the twin-engine configuration made for outstanding low fuel consumption and economy of operation.

I was intrigued and talked the Caravelle up among my colleagues at Capital. They were not impressed. But VP Jim Franklin, remembering the Viscount's success, quietly encouraged me to continue my research.

In due time this led to a visit from Mr. Ford Studebaker, a middle aged somewhat unsuccessful manufacturer's representative, who had been appointed U.S. Representative for Aerospatiale. We discussed the aircraft and the brochures and specifications he brought along and, early in the afternoon, repaired to a small French restaurant on the corner of Wisconsin Avenue and M Street in Washington. Greeted by Camille, the ebullient owner, we were treated to an exotic French lunch of salad, mushroom soup, fish du jour, flan, and bottle after bottle of red and white wine.

A long laundry list of questions concerning routes, schedules, performance, fuel consumption and operating costs over Capital's system was teletyped back to France that night. I was hot on the trail of Capital's next aircraft, a road that would prove more difficult, more exciting, and eventually more frustrating than one could imagine.

Two weeks later, Bob Blanchet appeared on the scene. Senior international sales representative for Aerospatiale, he brought the answers to our early questions. They were positive. The Caravelle, being a jet, was 150 miles an hour faster than the Electras and DC-7s of our major competitors, giving us again the "leap frog" advantage Capital enjoyed when we first got the Viscount. The smooth, quiet ride was something American passengers had yet to experience, still being subjected to the noise and vibration of the big propeller aircraft. Capital should once again be able to win back the key routes being lost to American, United, Northwest, and others – Chicago-New York, Washington-Chicago, New York-Atlanta.

Economics looked good. With its high speed the Caravelle would cover four thousand miles a day as compared to three thousand with a fast prop plane. We knew from the Viscount that the Rolls Royce engines would be a vast improvement over the 18-cylinder Curtis Wright 3350s and the Allison turboprops. Fuel costs would be low as the Caravelle's jets burned kerosene, while the DC-7's needed high-octane gasoline. Safety would be enhanced by the rear engines and the less flammable fuel in event of accidents.

So, week after week stretching into months, Ford Studebaker, Bob Blanchet and I continued with our planning, much of it conducted during long afternoons in the Rive Gauche where our jolly host Camille kept our thirst slaked. Camille was a real French restaurateur, taking vast pride in his place. He wore his medals from World War II on his jacket, along with a few Nazi and German ones acquired from fallen foes. Attention was the name of his game, and he made sure his guests were happy. We were.

In France, Aerospatiale's production lines were beginning to turn out Caravelles in large numbers. But orders did not live up to expectations. A recession cut demand and a surplus threatened. Once rolling, it was virtually impossible to stop the French production lines. Unlike the U.S.A, it was impossible to lay off workers and cut back production.

My studies at Capital had convinced me we needed an initial fleet of twenty Caravelles, capable of blanketing our principal markets with a superior level of service. The schedule planners in Marketing and Finance agreed, although still not convinced of the Caravelle's merit.

In the meantime, Capital's fortunes were slipping. A dissatisfied Board fired President Slim Carmichael and replaced him with a retired U.S. Air Force Major General, David Hodges Baker III. Losses were mounting and Capital was sliding toward insolvency.

I made full disclosure of this to my friends at Aerospatiale, pointing out that we did not have the cash to purchase either aircraft or spares, nor even enough for substantial down payments. We were confident, however, that the inauguration of the Caravelle services would result in a significant improvement of our position. The French shared our conviction based on the good results which were being achieved with the aircraft at Air France in Europe.

Out of mutual necessity was born a plan under which the initial aircraft, along with spares, would be delivered on a "consignment" basis, to be paid for when Capital could afford it. The aircraft were already being built and delivery could be made within a matter of months after contract signing. All that now remained was to get the approval of Capital's management and directors.

I prepared a complete report of the Caravelle project, outlining its advantages and opportunities and explaining its current status. Jim Franklin thought it worthwhile and, perhaps with a Machiavellian motive, suggested I ask the General for an opportunity to present my program. I asked for an appointment and was granted a few minutes at 9:15 the next morning.

Filled with pride and enthusiasm for the project I believed would bring salvation to Capital, I went to General Baker's office down Mahogany Row and was ushered in.

"Good morning, General."

"Good morning, Mr. Beyer. What do you want?"

"General, for the last several months I have been working on a study involving acquiring Caravelles for Capital, giving us a five-year head start over our competitors."

"Mr. Beyer, don't waste my time. I am not interested."

"But General, why? I've got all the financing worked out too"

"Look, Beyer, there are three things wrong with that airplane. First, it has two engines. Second, the engines are on the back. And third, and worst of all, it is FRENCH!" he sneered.

I turned and left, disappointed and dejected. Shocked that what seemed such a good idea was given such a swift and brutal shrift.

Ford Studebaker, Bob Blanchet and I had a last lunch at the Rive Gauche. A wake to mourn the demise of our project.

This story has an epilogue. Several months later, United Airlines bought insolvent Capital Airlines and merged it into their system, strengthening United in the northeast and south and making United the largest U.S. airline. A few months after the merger was accomplished United bought the twenty Caravelles which I had programmed for Capital, and for the next dozen years used them very successfully over the self-same routes for which I had intended them. A few weeks after the merger General Baker was also fired.

Why I Believe in Fortune Cookies

Lunch among Capital's junior executives was normally a period of social relaxation and planning away from the phones and intrusions of the office. No company cafeteria on most days, when two or three of us would head across the river to the waterfront restaurants, or perhaps a different and more exotic place further uptown.

It was mid-April, 1960 and to break up the frustration of another day "fighting the battle at Capital," my colleague C.P. "Pate" Hutchens and I headed over the 14th Street bridge to Washington's small Chinatown for lunch. A couple of martinis put us in good appetite for fried rice and mushi pork. We talked of the increasing financial difficulties of our company and the hopes of the employees to find new investors to take over Capital before it collapsed. I was among those most critical of the General's new management and their failing policies, and was actively organizing for change. With twelve years of service I was confident of my future and the rightness of our cause.

Chinese tea came along with the inevitable fortune cookies. I opened mine to read the little slip of paper concealed inside: "Great changes are in store for you."

We laughed, paid our checks, and drove back to the office. A few minutes later I was called into the office of the new senior Vice President of Operations and Maintenance, Marvin Whitlock, and was fired.

Epilogue

Capital became technically insolvent in 1960, but with only its major payments to the British in arrears. Major General Baker, the new President, hated the Viscounts and made a deal to turn half of them over to United Airlines and sell Capital to United for its liquidated value. The other half of the Viscount fleet was returned to Vickers.

United all too quickly found it had made a mistake in letting Baker return the Viscounts to Vickers and hastily agreed to take back all which had not already been reclaimed and sold. United also opened negotiations with Aerospatiale and ordered the 20 Caravelles that Baker had spurned.

The acquisition of Capital greatly strengthened United's position in the eastern United States and established it as the largest airline in the United States - a position which it only recently lost to American. ✈

CHAPTER VI

Riddle Airlines

Joining Riddle Airlines

It was in May 1960 that the new management of Capital Airlines fired me. After twelve years of service I received a generous two weeks' severance pay. By now, I was married with four kids, fifteen Black Angus cows and a farm to support. I had to find a new job fast.

I had become acquainted with Bob Hewitt, a Ridgewood, New Jersey entrepreneur, who was in the process of acquiring Riddle Airlines, a down-at-the-heels all cargo airline with scheduled routes on the East Coast and the Midwest to Puerto Rico. Riddle was also a time-to-time operator of the USAF Logair and the Navy's Quicktrans Airlift contracts, which supported the domestic military bases of the two services. Hewitt had just made a deal with Hawker Siddley, a British aircraft manufacturer, to acquire three Argosy airfreighters for operation in Logair. These aircraft had three features the military liked:

➤ A level floor, truck-bed height fuselage for easy loading.
➤ Large clam-shell doors at each end which permitted handling of out-sized military cargo.
➤ Modern turboprop engines as opposed to the old, unreliable piston engines used on the World War II C-46s which operated the existing Logair services.

Riddle Airlines was one of the original all cargo airlines founded after World War II by former military aces, in this case John Paul Riddle. He had recently sold the airline to Arthur Vining Davis, heir to the ALCOA fortune who, in his dotage, wanted to be in the airline business. After losses of millions in the late 1950s, Davis' handlers were now trying to sell the airline. Hewitt made a deal to acquire the majority stock with the help of the stock brokering Price brothers, one of whom ran a bucket shop in Miami that made the market in Riddle stock. The deal was largely done with smoke and mirrors, involving very little Hewitt and Price cash, with continued infusions from the Davis estate as the price for getting rid of this turkey.

Hewitt had just been made President of Riddle and hired me as his assistant, with the specific task of getting Riddle into the Military Airlift Command (MAC) overseas contract airlift business. Until 1960 the USAF.s overseas contracts were let annually on a "sudden death" bidding procedure under which the low bidder got all the business he could handle and the next lower bidder took the rest. This low-bidder-take-all procedure had produced disastrous results for the winning airlines, most of whom had been bankrupted in the process. On the other hand, the military were getting shoddy service with the oldest and cheapest aircraft the operators could find. At this point, the USAF's MAC and the then Civil Aeronautics Board got together to regulate the MAC business with the objective of securing bids only from financially and operationally responsible carriers, providing reasonable controls on MAC rates to prevent low-balling of contracts, and modernizing the MAC fleet through acquisition of new, more efficient aircraft

Hewitt and I saw an opportunity in the new rules for Riddle to participate in what could now be a profitable business. Therefore, my job was threefold:

➤ Figure out which aircraft would be best for Riddle to acquire based on cost, availability and mission-capability.
➤ Negotiate their acquisition and modification to Riddle's and the USAF's requirements.
➤ Get the military contracts and put the aircraft to work.

Step One involved an evaluation of both new and used aircraft. The USAF was anxious to acquire jet-powered turboprop aircraft to speed their modernization program. Riddle's chief competitors already had on order the Canadian built CL-44, a four-engine long-range turboprop. The British built the Britannia, an even larger passenger turboprop which could be modified to the military cargo/ convertible configuration, and which they were

Armstrong Whitworth Argosy
Riddle Airlines

anxious to sell. Douglas and Lockheed were still building the passenger/cargo-convertible DC-7C and the L-1049H that they were also anxious to sell on favorable terms.

On the bottom of the scale were used DC-6s and DC-7s and the Lockheed aircraft, which Flying Tigers, Slick Airways, Seaboard World and the major civilian/military cargo airlines were phasing out as their new CL-44s were delivered.

The dilemma was a classic one in aviation: to favor the newest designs with their greater appeal to the military, fuel efficiency, greater speed and performance but with vastly higher capital costs, or the in-betweens, or the older aircraft which were widely available and cheap to buy, but less efficient to operate.

I immediately began preparing a spreadsheet, listing the characteristics of each aircraft in great detail – weights, payload, speed, range, fuel consumption, maintenance cost, and capital investment. This clearly showed that, considering Riddle's limited capital resources, when aircraft could be made available and considering their operating costs, an aircraft known as the Douglas DC-7C was the obvious choice. A fleet of ten passenger models, fresh from overhaul, were being offered with good financing by General Dynamics and Douglas, who had taken them as trade-ins from SAS and Swissair on their soon- to-be-delivered Convair 990 jets.

But there was a problem. The DC-7C had a terrible reputation among many of its operators. Its Curtis Wright R3350 twin-row super charged engines with 18 cylinders, dual ignition systems, and PRTs (power return turbines) were simply a nightmare to keep in service. In-flight fires were common, shut downs were frequent, and engine overhaul expenses exorbitant. Obviously, unless the problem was corrected, the aircraft was unsuitable.

Nevertheless, I was impressed by the potentially low cost of the DC-7C and its long range and high payload capacity. I was determined to find out why its maintenance performance was so poor, and immediately visited the maintenance bases of current operators – Braniff, Northwest, Pan Am and Swissair - to learn what we could of the operation of these aircraft. At the three American carriers the flight operations and management staff cursed the DC-7C for its unreliability, while the maintenance engineers faulted the operating techniques employed as causing the problem. Swissair had not had any major problems.

As always, the airlines were in a race to see whose planes could cross the Continent the fastest and, as a result, DC-7C operations were conducted at maximum power in the U.S. This resulted in high fuel consumption and a mismatch between the operating temperatures of the cylinder heads and the

PRTs. Crews sought the maximum climb rate and highest possible cruise altitude, further exacerbating the overheating. The results were cracked cylinders, burned through PRT shrouds, engine fires, in-flight failures and plenty of delays.

The experience at Swissair was entirely different. They "babied" the engines using long slow climbs, low altitude cruise, slower flight times, and lower engine temperatures. As a result, the problems experienced by the American carriers were seldom, if ever, encountered by the more prudent Swiss. Riddle's potential deal included the acquisition of four DC-7s from Swissair, three from SAS and three from Northwest.

I returned to Miami to recommend the acquisition of the DC-7Cs and a deal was structured under which seven aircraft would be traded in to General Dynamics by SAS and Swissair with fresh major overhauls and zero time since overhauls of the engines.

Douglas would take the aircraft, strip out the passenger interiors and convert them to all cargo configuration, including the installation of a large aft cargo door, and the converted aircraft would be financed by General Dynamics and delivered to Riddle as pure freighters.

Riddle would develop and install our own convertible passenger interior which could be removed and re-installed in a matter of hours, making the aircraft truly cargo/passenger convertibles meeting the military specifications.

The total transaction with General Dynamics (GD) was for $1 million per aircraft. I appeared at their 29 Broadway, New York office in late July, 1960 with the signed contracts on behalf of Riddle in hand. The only thing missing was agreement on the amount of the down payment, which at that point stood at 10 %, or $700,000 for the seven aircraft. I had two checks in my pocket, one for $25,000 and the other for $50,000, and was authorized to give GD one or both depending on how negotiations went. GD was aware of our financial situation and impressed by our purchase of the airline from Arthur Vining Davis. They wanted the deal – bad. I pulled out the check for $25,000 and carefully explained that Riddle needed to husband its resources to complete the cargo to passenger/cargo convertible conversion that was the final step. The General Dynamics executives huddled among themselves and accepted the $25,000.

I returned to Miami with the signed contract, and with the unused $50,000 second check. We used the funds to meet the payroll that week.

We later concluded a contract with Douglas for three more DC-7Cs from Northwest on similar terms.

On to Tokyo

As our newly converted DC-7Cs rolled off the production line at Douglas' Santa Monica factory, we were frantically preparing to bid and operate the military contracts we hoped to win.

I was Riddle's chief contracting officer on this project and spent several weeks at Santa Monica getting the program going from our side. Douglas's business was slow at the time, DC-6/7 orders had fallen sharply and, therefore, our DC-7C cargo conversion line was being run down the main production line for new aircraft. Douglas had already converted ten DC-7Cs to cargo for Pan Am and was well experienced in this task. They had absolutely no idea of what we were talking about in designing a convertible cargo-to-passenger and back again aircraft. Normally such a conversion would take weeks, if not months, to re-install the galleys, seats, overhead lights and baggage bins, lavatories, and other such amenities. These were considered permanent fixtures in conventional aircraft, but we needed interiors that were quick change, that could be assembled and disassembled in a matter of hours.

Therefore, we told Douglas to leave all the wiring, plumbing, and fixtures for passenger operations under the cargo sidewalls in place. Ceiling lights and air vents were also left in place. When we got the aircraft back to Miami, we would design and install our own certificated convertible interior with removable seats, overhead bins and galleys.

At Douglas I had the opportunity to meet Donald Douglas, Sr., the founder of the famous firm, who was now about to retire. We spent several relaxing long lunches, with more than a bit of libation, listening to his reminiscences of the past; the birth of the first Douglas transports, the difficulties of the '20s and '30s, the design of the DC-3 and DC-4, and his visions for the future of his DC-8, now approaching delivery at their new Long Beach plant.

Ironically, across the Santa Monica airport was the headquarters of Howard Hughes' aviation enterprises. On the ramp sat a DC-6A that had been delivered to Riddle Airlines ten years before. Riddle was in one of its frequent low spells at the time, and sold the aircraft to Hughes, who ferried it back to Santa Monica and parked it. It had not been flown in ten years. Its paint was now badly faded and the fuselage corroded. But one could still read "RIDDLE" on its side. Typical of the strange ways of Howard Hughes, it was under twenty four hour armed guard and no consideration whatsoever was given to selling it or putting it back to work. I believe that ultimately it was scrapped for junk.

The DC-7C re-conversion program at Riddle, making the aircraft into quick change planes that could carry a load of cargo outbound and bring returning GIs back, was under the direction of a young engineer, Jim Ireland.

Jim designed galleys, partitions, storage bins, seats and other passenger facilities that could be removed quickly and collapsed for storage in the bellies of the aircraft. Seats could be unsnapped from the tracks in the floor and also folded up and stored in the bellies, each pre-marked to facilitate re-installation. Within ten days of delivery to Riddle, the aircraft conversion was completed and the aircraft ready to enter service, worldwide, as either a cargo or a passenger aircraft.

The first plane was christened by Arthur Vining Davis himself, who was still putting money into the airline. His wheelchair was secured to a pallet and a forklift raised him and Bob Hewitt to cockpit height, where they poured a symbolic bottle of champagne over the nose.

Riddle bid in its first MAC contracts, promising to carry twenty tons of cargo per flight from Travis A.F.B. near Oakland, California to Tachikawa, Japan, near Tokyo. The route lay over Hawaii, Wake and then to Japan, a distance of some seven thousand miles. We were awarded business because our DC-7Cs could carry about five tons more freight than the Lockheed 1049Hs of our competitors. But Riddle's pilots were all newly trained on the DC-7C, upgrading from the twin-engine World War II C-46s. They had no over-ocean experience. They were scared of the vast distances and empty oceans, carrying far too much fuel, so they cut ten thousand pounds off the payload of each flight. Soon Riddle had a mountain of backlogged freight, some two hundred thousand pounds, piled up in Travis. Under MAC rules, Riddle had to move the excess freight at its own expense, an impossible feat.

Howard and I visited Travis to size up the problem and to find an answer now.

We persuaded Douglas to permit us to increase the payload capacity of our DC-7Cs by 10% through a paperwork change to the zero fuel weight. Then we conducted training courses for our pilots, showing them how to plan fuel loads more precisely, reduce reserves and planned consumption, and thereby increase payload to the maximum.

Riddle DC-7

We took advantage of a quirk in the MAC shipping rules. The DC-7C, with a long constant section fuselage, had about 20% more available cubic interior capacity than the whale-shaped L-1049. MAC cargo ranged from high-density freight such as armaments and machinery to "balloon freight" such as medical supplies, uniforms, tents and other low-density cargo. Often MAC loaders "bulked out" (i.e., filled up the cubic capacity of the aircraft) before the "grossed out" reaching the weight limits of the aircraft. In either case, they paid full price for the flight.

So Howard went to the USAF contract managers on site at Travis and persuaded them, in a series of after hours meetings at the Officers Club, that they could move a lot more cargo if they gave Riddle all the bulk freight, and gave Flying Tigers, Slick and the others the heavy freight. The Air Force agreed, and every day we offered our aircraft at forty-four thousand pounds ACL (allowable cabin load) and the MAC crews loaded thirty thousand pounds of low weight, bulky freight. We got credit for forty-four thousand pounds offered and in a few weeks worked off our backlog at no cost.

Cold Bay

In mid-1960 the CAB took control of the rates paid by the Military Airlift Command (MAC) to its civilian contractors. The initial rules specified a flat rate per ton between the origin and destination points regardless of flight itinerary. Thus, everybody got the same revenue per ton from Travis AFB in California to Tachikawa in Japan regardless of routing. Riddle was flying the central Pacific routing over Hawaii and Wake, while Flying Tigers and our other competitors generally preferred the shorter route via Anchorage and Adak, Alaska. Due to the greater payload of our DC-7Cs, Riddle was receiving the lion's share of awards and our fleet was fully utilized in the fall of 1960.

Tigers, Slick et al went to the CAB and demanded a change, alleging that they should be allowed to give the Air Force the benefit of their shorter routing via Alaska and the Aleutians (saving 984 miles). The CAB agreed and, in a matter of days, Riddle was underbid. All of our business via the central Pacific was taken away and given to our competitors with their shorter routes and lower rates. At best, we could match them and get a smaller share of the business. It was a major crisis, since we stood to lose between 60 and 100% of the military business on which Riddle depended to support its new fleet of DC-7Cs.

The Tigers' L-1049Hs flew Travis-Anchorage-Adak-Tachikawa, a total mileage of 4,846 nautical miles. Riddle's DC-7Cs could carry a full payload of over twenty tons nearly one thousand miles further than an L-1049H and, given the USAF's policy of utilizing the greater cubic capacity of our aircraft by "bulking us out," we often had less than 20 tons on board and could fly even farther. Given the CAB's new policy of permitting an airline to bid on the actual mileage flown, we had to find a way to undercut the miles flown by our competitors. I spread the aeronautical charts of Alaska and the Aleutians on the conference room table and began to look for alternative airports that might give Riddle back its edge.

Our objective was to find a point west of Anchorage that would reduce significantly our total miles flown to Tachikawa. During the recent war the Japanese had captured Attu and Kiska, at the far end of the Aleutians, the same week as the battle of Midway, threatening the entire Alaskan peninsula. U.S. forces built a string of facilities and airfields on the remaining islands of the Aleutian chain in order to protect Alaska and to prepare for retaking Attu and Kiska. We looked at Adak, Dutch Harbor, Umnak, Kodiak and numerous others. All were short airfields, often facing mountain ranges. The Aleutians have the foulest weather in the world: wind, rain, snow, cold, low ceilings and uniformly bad visibility. One airport struck our eyes, Cold Bay. The airport was used by Northwest as an alternate airport and refueling station on its Boeing 377 trans-Pacific passenger operations. It had a 7,000-foot runway, long enough for a fully grossed DC-7C. Fuel and services were available through Bob Reave's Reave Aleutian Airways that operated the length of the chain and was the only airline in Alaska to make money without subsidy. The secret of Reave's success was his frugal operation. In order to man his dozen stations on the Aleutian chain he persuaded the Alaskan prison authorities to furlough incarcerated criminals to him, and Reave put them to work at prison wages operating his isolated Aleutian airports.

Cold Bay was almost exactly equidistant from Travis AFB and Tachikawa. Our DC-7Cs could fly it in two hops instead of the three (Travis-Anchorage-Adak-Tachikawa) required by the shorter range Lockheeds. We avoided the weather problems of ice and fog at Anchorage and the low ceilings at Adak (the weather at Cold Bay was uniformly terrible, but seldom below minimum). Best of all, our route was 320 nautical miles shorter than that which could be flown by our competitors, permitting Riddle to underbid them on the next round of MAC contracts.

In mid-December Riddle was awarded the bulk of the MAC trans-Pacific commercial airlift. All of our DC-7Cs were fully committed and our revenues soared, permitting the Company at last to pay its past due obligations and get current. We thought we had it made.

The potentially serious sticking point of getting our pilots to fly the Cold Bay route turned out to be a problem – no problem. All of the pilots had just transitioned off the C-46s and had barely become acclimated to the easy mid-Pacific route. Suddenly, they were fully fueled and loaded, and ordered to fly 3,000 miles to Cold Bay, half way out in the Aleutian chain. It was midwinter, with nights 21-hours long. The weather was abominable, with snow, ice, high winds, and low ceilings and visibility. To pilots trained to fly the sunny climate and benign weather of the Caribbean, this was an awful shock. The first trip was almost aborted as the designated crews developed mysterious ills, chills and fevers at departure time. Fortunately, our chief pilot was in Travis and took the trip.

In preparing for the Cold Bay operation we contacted Bill Clark, who was Station Manager at Cold Bay for Canadian Pacific Airlines, which also used the airport for refueling of its trans-Pacific flights. Bill volunteered to act as our on-site manager as well, and said the only support he required from Riddle was a case of whiskey each week. This seemed a reasonable request, and it arrived on the first flight. The reason soon was obvious. When each crew arrived after the ten hour flight from Travis, Bill was in the control tower to talk them in on their first approach between the 6,000-foot peaks surrounding the airport. He guided them up the Cold Bay fjord and down onto a runway they could not see until the last minute. Once on the ground, he checked them in at Operations and then took the crew to the BOQ for a hearty meal, making them a present of a bottle of bourbon as he left. He met them the next day for a bit of sightseeing and briefing for the next leg to Tachikawa. The crews rested at Cold Bay overnight, taking out the next plane that came in. Bill Clark's calm and assured handling of Riddle's crews at Cold Bay made what might have been a very difficult exercise turn out to be very simple. A year later Bill moved to Miami, joining Riddle full time. He subsequently worked with me at Saudi Arabian Airlines, Modern Air Transport, Capitol, and Johnson (later Evergreen) from which he retired in 1992.

In Tachikawa, Riddle hired a young Japanese meteorologist as our local manager. This young man was an expert on a weather phenomenon called the "Jet Stream" which none of us had ever heard of, but which was a river of fast moving air flowing at higher altitudes through the slower, more stable air currents. It flowed West to East at upwards of 200 miles per hour at altitudes above 20,000 feet and its path and location varied from day to day.

Our Japanese meteorologist studied these upper air currents and prepared a flight plan for our 5,200 mile trip back to Travis from Tachikawa. By taking advantage of the Jet Stream the DC-7C could make the return flight nonstop. There was no return cargo and, thus, we could carry a full fuel load. The dispatcher located the Jet Stream and plotted its course to North America. Sometimes it swung far south over the Wake-Hawaii route, and at other times it was as far north as the Aleutians. Wherever it was we found it, and stayed in it. One could tell its presence by temperature changes (it was colder), the rough air on its fringes and the incredible increase in ground speed.

On takeoff from Tachikawa we would climb slowly, in low blower configuration and at lower power, until we reached the lower limits of the Jet Stream. We would climb a few thousand feet into the stream and then throttle back to the most economical cruise configuration in terms of fuel consumption. This also babied the engines that were temperature sensitive, and vastly improved reliability and longevity. We routinely made the nonstop return flight across the Pacific in eleven to twelve hours, to the amazement and consternation of our competitors, who had not yet mastered the art of cruising the Jet Stream. Controllers and pilots alike could not believe our enroute speeds of over five hundred miles an hour with an old piston-powered DC-7C. At this point, the Pacific was Riddle's oyster.

But not for long.

The Body Snatcher

The Jewish faith requires that the deceased be buried by sunset of the day following their demise. Miami had many old retired Jewish couples who wanted to be buried in their home soil of New York. Riddle Airlines operated the DC-7, the only aircraft that could transport a coffin between Miami and New York. The belly pit doors of the passenger aircraft of Eastern and National were too small to fit a normal sized coffin inside.

At Riddle we had a cargo sales representative named Frank Bine who himself was one of the faithful, and who made a career of catering to the movement of remains from Miami to New York for burial. We called him "the body snatcher," and every day he would visit the major hospitals, Mount Sinai, Jackson Memorial and others, talking to the interns and nurses to see how many elderly patients were expected to die that day. Learning the identities of the dying, he contacted the families and the funeral homes to make sure that they were aware of Riddle's services transporting coffins from Miami to New York. Bine further made arrangements for the hearses to gain access to the cargo area and made "reservations" for the deceased on the 10 P.M. northbound freighter. We had plenty of commercial cargo southbound but northbound freight was scarce and, at $100 a casket, the revenues were good. On a peak night we might have as many as fifty caskets neatly stacked in the cargo bays. One night the plane was fully loaded with coffins The Engineer went back to check the cargo, and was about to return to the flight deck, when he heard some tapping from within one of the caskets. Deeply agitated, he went forward to get the Captain. When the Captain arrived in the hold, he heard the tapping too, and was afraid one of the dead was living. A hasty inspection disclosed a small monkey, who could reach out of his cage, and was rapping on the nearest coffin.

With the coming of the B-720 jets, with their big belly cargo hold doors to the fleets of our scheduled competitors we lost our monopoly on the coffin carriage, but it was good while it lasted.

Bay of Pigs

For a long period, Riddle dominated the trans-Pacific military cargo airlift contracts. Using our shorter routing via Cold Bay, we had a considerable price advantage over our competitors, all forced to use the Anchorage-Adak or Central Pacific route. As a result, they only hauled what we could not. But they protested mightily to the CAB, and once again this august body changed the rules. Where previously all carriers had to charge the same rate per aircraft mile, the CAB now permitted all carriers to charge the same rate to MAC between the origin and destination points regardless of how far they had to fly. Once again the shoe was on the other foot. Due to Riddle's heavy flying in the winter, we had built up a big surplus of flying credits. So MAC now proceeded to give almost all of their business to the other airlines who had been famished for business during the winter. Riddle's surplus aircraft were ferried back to Miami where most of them sat idle, and Riddle once again faced financial ruin.

Riddle's so called "common carriage," or scheduled airfreight business, had always been a marginal operation, more often a loser. Our routes included New York to Miami and San Juan via Philadelphia and Orlando, Chicago and Detroit to Atlanta and Miami to San Juan, and other short hops. Large station staffs and a seventy man sales organization were unable to stand against the competition of the passenger airlines, all of whom had freight divisions, as well as larger, stronger cargo competitors Flying Tigers, Slick and Seaboard.

In January 1961 Miami was seething with agitation against Fidel Castro and his revolution in Cuba. Tens of thousands of refugees, most from the Cuban upper classes, had fled to Miami and taken over the "Calle Ocho" enclave north of Coral Gables. Plans and plots to return to Cuba and overthrow the hated Castro were abundant in the media, reportedly aided by our CIA.

One day three gentlemen arrived in Riddle's executive offices at the west end of Miami International Airport and identified themselves as "business men" wishing to arrange an extensive airlift to Central America. Our top executives were soon made privy to the real nature of their business and affiliations. Howard Donaldson, head of Riddle's station operations, had evidently been their contact man with Riddle. After ascertaining that complete secrecy would be maintained by all Riddle personnel involved, our operation to support the forthcoming invasion of Cuba was set up.

Each night one or two of our DC-7Cs was flown the few miles from Miami International to Opa-Locka Airport, an idle U.S. Naval Air Station ten miles north. There the planes landed without lights on a darkened runway. They taxied slowly in the wake of a "follow me" jeep to the grove of trees at one side of the airport and shut down. Out from the Australian pines came a hundred or so men, carrying their field packs and light arms. They boarded the aircraft using the aluminum emergency ladders and all sat on the floor or on their duffle bags. The excited but low-decibel conversation in Spanish filled the plane. We pulled the ladder, closed the doors, started the four great engines, taxied out onto the darkened runway and took off into the night, all without lights.

The flights headed southwest, flying without flight plans, CAA center, or tower clearance. Those who needed to know no doubt knew we were there and where we were going, but few others did. The DC-7Cs flew westward over the Florida Keys and, keeping well north of the coast of Cuba, passing Bahia Honda until reaching the Yucatan Channel between Cabo San Antonio and Cozumel. Here we turned south, making landfall over Honduras before proceeding to the training bases in the jungles of Nicaragua.

All during February we ferried the Cuban volunteers from Miami to Central America, building up the invasion force which was being organized and whipped into fighting shape by former Cuban officers and the CIA. Later on, the airlift increased in intensity as we began to move the landing craft and the equipment and heavy arms the Cubans would need to establish and hold their beachhead and march on Havana.

Riddle kept a tight lid on security and, despite all the loose talk in the Miami press, there was never a whisper about our involvement. We were paid weekly through a seemingly legitimate business house for our charter activities, and the local CAA office was encouraged not to ask too many questions about the log books of our pilots and aircraft. The most sensitive missions involving the carrying of volunteers and live bombs and ammunition for the upcoming air attacks on Castro's Air Force was flown by a very small select group of Riddle's pilots headed by Fred Soucey, one of our chief pilots and instructors.

The planning and preparation for the Cuban Liberation continued under President Eisenhower. In late January, as Kennedy took office, the Cuban Freedom Fighters began to bomb Castro's Air Force using World War II B-26s bought on the surplus market. While old and obsolete, they were good enough for the job, which was to eliminate the thirty odd fighter bombers Castro had prior to the launching of the invasion at the Bay of Pigs. In the first several days, about one third of Castro's planes were destroyed on the ground at Rancho Boyeros and other Cuban fields. But one of the Freedom Fighters' planes was hit and limped into Meacham Field at Key West, where he was immediately pounced on by a pack of the press corps. The pilot was an American mercenary, which made him far more newsworthy. A great wave of publicity swept the media and, amid howls of indignation by some, Kennedy ordered the bombing of Cuba to stop. It was a disastrous thing to do. With two thirds of his air power left, Castro was in a much better position to defend himself, and to reconnoiter and bomb the Freedom Fighters when they attacked.

A few days later, they did. Twelve hundred volunteers filled with ardor, but thinly armed and poorly trained, climbed into the boats we had brought them and churned ashore into the mangrove swamps of the Bay of Pigs. Once there, they established a weak beachhead and began an advance toward Havana, hindered by bad roads, poor reconnaissance and no air support. A vast American armada cruised in plain sight offshore – a battleship, a carrier and scores of smaller ships.

Castro had not been unmindful of the pending operation, and his well-organized columns descended on the attackers in unexpected numbers and ferocity. It had been an article of faith in the CIA and Cuban Liberation camp that the Cuban people would rise in revolution once the landing took place. This did not happen, and the Freedom Fighters found themselves outnumbered and outgunned. Castro's planes raked the columns of hapless and largely defenseless Cuban Liberators without mercy. At the end of the week it was all over. With 200 killed and wounded, the remainder surrendered.

Castro treated prisoners with surprising compassion, realizing they were an asset. The prisoners were taken to the Isle of Pines, a desolate place where he kept political dissenters, south of Cuba itself. After two years, he traded them back to the U.S. for some $70 million in medicines and tractors. Kennedy greeted the returning fighters as heroes in the Orange Bowl Stadium in Miami.

To those of us who played a part – even a supporting one – in the Bay of Pigs, we would never understand President Kennedy's cowardice in committing Cuban Freedom Fighters to what proved to be a futile fight, denying them all support and then leaving them in the mangroves at the Bay of Pigs to be massacred or imprisoned by Castro. The might of the American Navy stood offshore in plain sight during the entire proceeding, and seldom has there been such a craven abuse of American power. A year later, Khruschev came within a whisker of pulling the trigger on an atomic war based on his perception of Kennedy's conduct at the Bay of Pigs. Thankfully, this time Khruschev blinked first.

Alaska Ho!

In the summer of 1961 I bid on a small military airlift contract flying diesel fuel from Fairbanks and Anchorage, Alaska into two remote points on the DEW Line (Defense Early Warning Line) high in the Alaskan interior ranges. Here radar stations scanned the skies for incoming Russian missiles and were totally dependent on airlift for the delivery of fuel oil and supplies. For years these Military Air Lift Contracts had been the private domain of the Alaskan carriers, who serviced these stations with DC-3 and C-46 aircraft.

The two stations on the DEW Line were Sparrevohn and White Alice some three hundred miles, respectively, from Anchorage and Fairbanks. The airports were extremely hazardous with very steep gradients. There were primitive runway lights and a minimal directional radio system to aid inbound navigation. Contractors were required to serve them three hundred and sixty-five days a year, night and day, almost in spite of weather conditions. No lower 48 contractor had ever bid these contracts due to danger and unfamiliarity.

I researched the contract provisions and found that the current Alaskan bidders were very inefficient. To carry the fuel, their aircraft used fixed tanks mounted on the floor which were heavy and slow to load and unload. The Alaskans' aircraft were the old basic C-46s with minimum payload.

Riddle had three C-46Rs, late model aircraft with more powerful engines and greater payload. We had heard of a manufacturer in Ohio who offered a three thousand gallon plastic "pillow tank" which rested on the cabin floor. It could be filled and emptied in a matter of minutes through a single hose and did

not require extensive tie downs and plumbing systems. Using these tanks Riddle could carry 30% more fuel each trip and could turn the aircraft in twenty minutes rather than an hour, permitting us to make one or two more trips each day.

I went to MAC Headquarters at Scott Field and bid the contracts. A few weeks later we were notified that we had

Riddle C-46R

been awarded the entire procurement and were expected to have our three C-46Rs in Alaska within two weeks. My associates at Riddle were horrified, not having expected we would be awarded the business. Bob Hewitt, the president, who had initially approved, sent H.K. Howard, VP of Operations, to

Scott Field AFB to talk the Air Force out of giving us the award. The USAF refused. So we had to fly it.

With a group of five pilots and copilots and four mechanics, we set out for Anchorage with our small fleet of C-46Rs. A stock of spare parts was carried along. We met a hostile reception. During the two years in Alaska the natives never warmed to our presence, remaining ever hostile to the interlopers from the lower 48. Nevertheless, we set up headquarters on the military side of Elmendorf and Wainwright airports and proceeded to fly our new contract.

Several times during the next two years I spent a couple of weeks visiting our Alaskan operation. In winter the days were only a few hours of half-light and the temperature a bitter -40° or so. The aircraft were always in the open and we kept three Herman Nelson heaters running on each one, a heater on each engine nacelle and another stuck in the fuselage. Only in this way could we keep the engine oil warm enough to start the motors and the cockpits warm enough to activate the instruments. We conducted operations night and day, on instruments in snow and ice and rain, flying through mountain ranges far higher than the minimum en route altitude capability of our C-46Rs.

Approaches to the runways were particularly interesting since they lay at the heads of the valleys. With positive gradients of 7° and 11°, respectively, the upper end of the runway was 500 feet higher than the lower end. The valley was too narrow to turn around; once you had committed you had to land. The trick was to fly up the runway to the top at full power, land on the last 200 feet and roll out on the small turnabout area at the base of the mountain above you. There we opened the rear door, took out the hose to empty the tank, and turned the valve. In five minutes we were empty and ready to go back for another load.

Going out, the technique was a full throttle takeoff down a slope that looked like a ski jump. If an engine quit, you feathered it and also reduced power on the remaining engine, letting gravity build up your speed until you reached minimum control velocity, at which point full throttle could again be applied for the trip back to base. Had full power been maintained after engine failure the aircraft would have jack-knifed into the forest beside the runway. Riddle flew some three thousand missions into these two airports in two years without an incident.

When our contract was renewed for the second year, the Alaskan carriers were outraged and went to Congress, who passed a new law specifying that military contracts in Alaska could be bid only by Alaskan airlines. So at the end of the second year, our contract was canceled and we were left with three unneeded aircraft sitting forlornly in Anchorage.

I was sitting in my office in Miami. We had not made the payroll for a month, but had been able to persuade our people to work anyhow. Into my office walked Bob Reeve, legendary pioneer of aviation in Alaska and president of Reeve Aleutian Airways. "Mort, I'd like to buy your three C-46Rs in Anchorage," he said.

"What will you offer me?"

"$250,000."

"Make it $300,000 and you have a deal."

He agreed and wrote out a check on the spot. The next day we met our overdue payroll.

Riddle made a profit of over $1 million dollars a year on our little Alaska operation. We hated to lose it. At several periods in the last two years the revenue from Alaska was our only source of cash. At one point in our desperate quest for cash we discounted all of our accounts receivable with Walter Heller Financial, and when we could not pay them back they impounded all of our incoming mail, removing the checks. But Heller did not know about our Alaskan operation and we managed to slip this income into our payroll accounts with wire transfers, thus keeping our staff paid.

The Engine Problem

In mid-1961 I was posted to a newly opened Washington, DC office for Riddle, responsible for relations with the Civil Aeronautics Board and the Military Airlift Command. Mr. Hewitt's idea was also to get me out of Miami and direct involvement in the day to day operations of the airline. The situation with the company continued to deteriorate, with efforts to gain access to passenger charter business over the Atlantic not working out well. Military revenues were

falling as competitors offered more sophisticated aircraft, and scheduled airfreight revenues hurt by competition from the major airlines that were getting their first jets.

In January 1962 I ended my exile in Washington and moved back to Miami and set up my office in the Riddle

Dog teams watch
the USO departure

executive building. Whatever the problem, I was going to be in the middle of the action. We bid in the annual military contract and were awarded a record level of contracts involving five of our ten DC-7Cs, to be effective July 1st.

At the same time, President Bob Hewitt hired A. J. Rome and gave him responsibility to put Riddle into the trans-Atlantic charter business. Mr. Rome pursued this objective enthusiastically. We had been exploring the possibility of increasing the seating capacity of the DC-7Cs from ninety-nine seats to 109, which required FAA approval for a higher density seating capacity. This approval was not forthcoming, but Rome assumed it would be and sold several hundred trans-Atlantic charters with 109 seats, offering lower prices to win the contracts due to having more available seats. As the summer season approached (July through September), Rome had committed five Riddle aircraft to this charter program with Hewitt's consent, but without consideration of the Company's total capabilities. We had only ten aircraft in our fleet, but thirteen committed to service – five to MAC and five to A.J. Rome's charter program, and three to the scheduled air cargo business. This was three more aircraft than we owned.

In the spring of 1962 Riddle ran out of cash – and credit. Curtis Wright, the manufacturer of the R-3350 engines that powered our DC-7C fleet, was performing our engine overhauls. We owed them several million dollars and they, not unreasonably, impounded all the spare engines which were in overhaul at their facility and refused to perform more overhauls for Riddle until they were paid.

At our rate of flying, we were using up one engine each week. When they ran out of time we removed them from the aircraft and used the remaining good engines on the plane to keep the remaining planes flying. This gradual attrition eliminated one plane after the other from our flying fleet and, by the end of April 1962, five of our ten aircraft were grounded for total lack of serviceable engines. An additional aircraft was due to be grounded in May and another in June as more engines ran out of time. With our source of overhauled engines cut off, Riddle was in desperate shape, slowly strangling to death.

The Curtis Wright TC-3350 engine was overhauled by several U.S. air carriers but, based on Riddle's credit problems, none would undertake Riddle's overhauls. It therefore remained for us to try to seek a foreign overhaul source. The DC-7C and the Lockheed Constellation L-1049 used the same type of engine but with significantly different nose sections containing the propeller reduction gears. Thus, an L-1049 Connie operator could overhaul the engines, but needed a source for the nose assemblies which were different.

I undertook to try to find an overhaul source for Riddle's engines, as well as an immediate source of spares to get our grounded fleet back in the air. We were getting by with five flying planes, using two on military contracts and three on airfreight schedules. But come July 1st, we needed thirteen aircraft, meaning all presently owned aircraft had to be airworthy. We also had to do something about the three-plane deficit.

On May 1st I flew to Amsterdam, setting up headquarters in a small hotel in Sandvort, a local seaside resort. Many European airlines operated the DC-7C or the L-1049 and I planned to contact them all. KLM, SAS, Sabena, Swissair, British Airways, and Alitalia were all DC-7C operators and the preferred candidates, since they had overhaul capabilities for the same model engine Riddle used. So every day I planned a visit to the Technical Sales office of a different airline. I prepared a paper outlining Riddle's requirements and our prospects for the future. It was necessary to be completely honest with these carriers since they were aware of our financial condition and there was no point in hiding it. I believed that by being frank we had our best chance to win their confidence.

The first visit was to Mr. Doppenberg, head of technical sales for KLM at Schipol Airport in Amsterdam. KLM had the capability to help Riddle, but wanted up-front cash deposits, letters of credit, and prompt payment for overhauls performed and interim engines leased. These demands were not unreasonable from their point of view, but were completely beyond Riddle's impoverished capabilities.

In later days, which stretched into weeks, cadging passes on the airlines targeted for that day, I successively visited Swissair in Zurich, SAS in Stockholm, British Airways in London, and Sabena in Brussels, until I had exhausted all DC-7C operators in Europe. The executives I met were universally cordial and sympathetic, but unwilling to take the chance of supporting the poor risk they believed Riddle represented.

By mid-May all the DC-7C operators had been contacted and had refused to help. I turned next to the operators of the L-1049 Constellations, which used the same basic engines with different nose cases. I visited Lufthansa in Hamburg and Iberia in Madrid, with the same results. Finally I arrived on the doorstep of Air France in Paris, where Mr. Maurice Pasquet headed their technical sales activities. I again outlined my well-rehearsed pitch about Riddle's needs and prospects, and the opportunity of doing business with us.

By this time we were down to the wire. There were less than six weeks until we had to have all aircraft in full operation. Between now and then we needed thirty overhauled engines, a seemingly impossible goal. But I laid out our requirements, including the need for credit terms. And Maurice said "Yes!"

Air France overhauled the TC-3350 engines for its own L-1049 Connies and also for the French Air Force. The Air Force aircraft used the same nose

Mort as President of Riddle Airlines

cases on their engines as the DC-7Cs. So Air France "borrowed" the needed units from the military, also drawing on their stocks of spares.

Air France operated an all cargo flight to New York and each night one or two freshly overhauled engines were transported to New York for Riddle. We took them to Miami for buildup in our shops, sending back our run out engines for overhaul.

Every few days we put another aircraft back in the air equipped with four new engines.

Thanks to the courage and imagination of Maurice Pasquet, a minor Air France official, Riddle was saved. I signed a contract guaranteeing Air France all of Riddle's engine overhauls for two years which was kept to the benefit of both carriers. We leased another DC-7C from SAS and off-spaced some of the charter flights (at great cost) in order to meet our obligations under the Air Force contracts. While A.J. Rome's passenger charter program was bleeding Riddle white, our engine contract with Air France had saved us, for the time being, and permitted us to continue operations.

Taking Over

In July 1962 Riddle's problems boiled over. The debacle on the north Atlantic charter program cost the company dearly. Not only did we not have the aircraft to cover the flights which A.J. Rome had sold, but we had ten too many passengers on every flight. Rome had banked on Riddle's ability to increase the seating capacity from ninety-nine certificated seats to a hundred and nine. We could not do it and so Rome had sold ten more seats that we could provide. His solution, buy the excess passengers seats on scheduled flights. The problem, most flights were full. So he had to buy First Class space, often paying more for the ten excess passengers than Riddle got for the whole charter flight. The charter program was a financial disaster.

In 1960 Bob Hewitt had purchased some 40% of Riddle Airlines' stock from Arthur Vining Davis. The Price brothers, Jim and Bill, controlled some 20% more through their personal holdings and Jim Price's Coral Gables stock brokering company which made the market in Riddle stock. Millions of penny shares were in the hands of the general public, with a fair number of major holders in the aviation field. These investors grew increasingly restive as the value of Riddle's stock gyrated violently from $5.00 to 25 cents, depending on our current fortunes and the manipulations of the market by the Price brothers. Our creditors, including General Dynamics, Douglas Aircraft, Vickers Armstrong (U.K.), Curtis Wright, and others, were also unhappy. These parties demanded that Hewitt strengthen his management, which had been characterized by his "one man" style of operation. Thus, in mid-1962 Hewitt recruited James "Slim" Carmichael and Jim Franklin, former officials of Capital Airlines recently acquired by United Airlines. These veterans of the airline business moved to Miami and took over nominal control of Riddle in cooperation with Hewitt. By this time my relationship with Hewitt had deteriorated over various matters. Hewitt supported A.J. Rome's disastrous trans-Atlantic charter program and refused to cut costs of the cash draining scheduled airfreight operations. Therefore, even though I had backed Carmichael's and Franklin's joining Riddle, I was effectively fired and relieved of all responsibilities.

I spent the next two months documenting my position with respect to Riddle. I had purchased a hundred thousand shares of stock in 1960 with the proceeds being used for the down payment on our fleet of ten DC-7Cs, and had just persuaded Air France to loan us thirty engines to get our fleet back in the air. Thus, I was not going to be fired outright, but was removed from the daily operation. In my two months "retirement" I laid out the history of Hewitt's promotions and failures and a program to put Riddle back on its feet, based on sound operating principles. In October I presented it to Carmichael and Franklin. Riddle's annual meeting of shareholders was held in November. Hewitt realized he had made a personnel mistake in appointing Carmichael and Franklin and was determined to take back control of the company. Slim and Jim were determined to get rid of Hewitt. I offered to run the shareholders election effort. We had to get 50% of all voting shares and, with Hewitt holding control of 40%, we faced a major uphill battle. He could win if we failed to equal his share or if he could win even a small amount of additional shareholders' support.

I obtained the shareholders' list and began a methodical telephone campaign, calling each holder of over ten thousand shares and explaining the necessity of getting their proxy. Day by day our total grew. The Price brothers threw their lot in with us and used their market position to reach the shareholders they controlled. When the day of the meeting finally came we were still short of the required majority of votes. The meeting was held in the DuPont Plaza Hotel in downtown Miami. The auditorium was crowded with some three hundred shareholders. The business of the meeting was soon completed and we began the count. We were still a few hundred thousand shares short of matching Hewitt's total, a few percentage points away from victory. Several major shareholders remained uncommitted holdouts. The Board announced that the voting was incomplete and held the polls open, while I returned to the telephone in the lobby to solicit the final needed shareholders. The last I needed was George Doole, owner of Air America, a legendary figure in covert aviation operations. George was a good friend of Bob Hewitt and so far had held out, declining to vote either way. I called him again for a final plea to vote his shares for the management. Finally, at approximately 10 P.M., Doole agreed to vote with us and sent a telegram giving management his proxy. I took the telegram into the meeting, we added George Doole's shares to our total and declared victory for the management slate.

Hewitt was ousted as Chairman and his influence on Riddle Airlines was effectively eliminated. He returned to his offices in Ridgewood, New Jersey to pursue other interests. Slim Carmichael became Chairman and Jim Franklin was named President. I was appointed Senior V.P. - Operations, Maintenance and Sales. I moved into my new office in the northwest corner of the Riddle Executive building to face an operation in hopeless disarray.

Labor Problems at Riddle

We had just ousted the Hewitt Board and Management at Riddle Airlines and were beginning to recover from the desperate situation that all but forced us over the brink. Our CAB operating certificate had been restored and reduced scheduled airfreight services resumed. Military Airlift contracts were again being awarded to us. Our little Alaskan operation threw off cash. As the warm winds of recovery fanned us, we began to think of bigger things, such as our plans for jets and expanding routes with profits hopefully on the horizon. But increasing demands from our unions, chiefly the pilots' ALPA, threatened to disrupt our plans.

President Jim Franklin turned to Fisher & Phillips, a prominent labor relations and law firm in Atlanta for assistance. Partners Earl Phillips and Bob Berghel were dispatched to Miami to talk with us. In November, 1962, they appeared and, after a few hours, were retained to handle Riddle's negotiations with its unions.

A day or two later I was sitting in my new corner office when my secretary Emily announced Captain Tom Jenkins, Chairman of the pilots' MEC. Tom burst through the door waving his cap. Ignoring the proffered seat, he began to shout, "Jesus Christ, Beyer, what the hell are you doing?"

"What do you mean, Tom?"

"I thought we had a good relationship with you!" Tom yelled.

"I hope we do, so what's wrong?"

"Goddammit, you've gone and hired Fisher & Phillips," he replied.

"That's right . . . we did."

"Mort, don't you know they are the most vicious anti-labor lawyers in the South?"

"Tom, that's why we hired them . . . ," I replied gently.

And, thus, we were introduced to Bob Berghel, who worked with me as Labor Counsel in all the airlines I ran for the next 20 years.

Ordering the DC-8s

Throughout the winter of 1962-1963 we fought a desperate battle to keep Riddle afloat. Following our victory at the Stockholders' Meeting, Slim Carmichael and Franklin were installed as chief executives of Riddle. I was appointed Senior Vice President – Operations, Maintenance and Sales, and was generally in charge of running the airline. The CAB canceled our airfreight operating certificates because we were failing to provide the service we scheduled. Lack of engines and spare parts again impacted our military contract reliability and we were losing the additional overflow "add on" contracts on which we depended for much of our business.

Finally, in mid-December 1962, we could no longer meet the payroll. I called the pilot union leaders into my office and laid out the situation, outlining the measures we planned to take to restore our cash flow. I asked them to fly without pay, joining the executives who also went unpaid. I promised to pay their per diem and expenses currently, which we did. The pilots agreed.

The Teamsters unionized the mechanics and they were another matter. We had been in negotiations for a new contract without much success for several months, and the Teamsters were holding a strike vote on the hangar floor when word came down that they would not be paid. Their leaders marched on my office and I invited them in for a frank discussion. I outlined our financial position and what I hoped to do about it, explaining that we needed money first for fuel, then for spare parts, expenses for the pilots, and other essentials. Several of the union leaders did not believe me. I had earlier briefed Teamsters' Headquarters in Washington and so I told them, "okay guys, call Jimmy Hoffa and ask him what you should do . . ."

The Teamsters' Committee trooped out of the office to a pay phone in the lobby. Fifteen minutes later they were back, looking somewhat surprised. "All right," their leader said, "Jimmy said to keep working, so we'll keep working." I thanked them and promised to keep them posted on developments.

Meanwhile, we took drastic action to get our operation back on track. Our commercial cargo operation in the U.S. covered some eight cities and we had several hundred cargo employees, including seventy salesmen. I closed all stations except New York, San Juan and Miami. The bulk of the ground staff and sixty-eight of the salesmen were terminated. We concentrated on the three routes linking these cities and contracted the entire capacity of our DC-7Cs –twenty tons per flight – to a handful of freight forwarders who bought the entire payload of the aircraft. This vastly streamlined operation resulted in an immediate improvement in cash flow and an increase in revenue as our costs fell.

Flight Operations was reorganized and the vice president, Joe Dillard, was replaced by Joe Freehill who took immediate action to improve on time operation of our military contracts, winning back our lost business. Within three months we resumed meeting our payroll, including back pay.

The final hurdle was to restructure our debt. Riddle had fallen some $6 million behind on repayment of its obligations to General Dynamics and Douglas Aircraft on our fleet of ten DC-7Cs. We were in default and our creditors served notice they were coming to Miami to impose a final solution to our financial problems.

On a longer term basis, Riddle's DC-7Cs were becoming outmoded for our military contracts. Our major competitors, such as Flying Tigers, Slick Airlines, World Airways and others, already had turboprop long range CL-44s. B-707-320C convertible cargo/ passenger jets would soon be delivered to these carriers. While Riddle had pioneered the design of the Boeing B-707-320C, we had been forced to forfeit our delivery positions. The Military Airlift Command contract officers at Scott Field (MO) advised us that we would lose many of our military contracts unless we, too, acquired jets.

In March, 1963, the General Dynamics and Douglas Aircraft officers and lawyers turned up at Miami to seize our aircraft and shut down Riddle's operations. We met in our boardroom at 8 P.M. for the showdown. They stated their position and I set forth ours. I acknowledged that Riddle was in default, but emphasized the steps we were taking to overcome our problems: reorganization of operations, new military contracts, the revised commercial airfreight operation, and operating costs reductions. I went on to talk about our competitive position and the fact that we needed jet aircraft. In conclusion, we emphasized the futility of the manufacturer's taking back the DC-7Cs and trying to find a market for them elsewhere.

Douglas had two DC-8-54F convertible passenger/cargo aircraft on the ramp in Long Beach, California. Capitol Airways, a major charter airline, had ordered them and then defaulted on the final payments. Douglas had no other customer in sight. I knew the aircraft were available. As our discussions wore on into the night, it was obvious that the General Dynamics and Douglas representatives were losing their get tough resolve and were beginning to worry about what they would do if they really did get the DC-7Cs back. Returning to headquarters with no money and a fleet of unsellable aircraft would not make them look good. We had also partially convinced them of the viability of the changes we were making in the airline and so when I proposed a solution to our mutual problems, they were receptive.

Riddle's stock was trading on the open market at around 50 cents a share. We had some 12 million shares outstanding and 25 million more authorized but unissued. There was an upside potential in this stock if and when Riddle's financial health was restored. I offered the manufacturers a three-part proposal:

> They accept 2 million shares of new Riddle stock for their $6 million debt, which would be canceled.
> Riddle would purchase the two DC-8s at Long Beach with Douglas providing financing.
> Douglas would provide necessary DC-8 spare parts and training on a financed basis.

About 2:30 in the morning Douglas and General Dynamics agreed. A brief memo of understanding was drafted and signed. We shook hands, dropped our guests off at the Miami Spring Villas, and went home for a good night's rest.

This chapter had a sequel. The DC-8s were delivered and entered service a few months later. Riddle swept the MAC procurement requirement with new jets and became extremely profitable in the mid-1960s. The value of Riddle's stock increased to a high of $11 a share, at which point Douglas and General Dynamics sold the shares we had given them two years before, quadrupling their money in the process.

Our poverty had turned out to be our greatest asset.

I Want My Money Back

In 1961 Bob Hewitt and I had visited Boeing and laid out our requirement for a cargo convertible version of Boeing's new long-range B-707-320 passenger jet. Using our experience from the DC-7C conversion, we outlined to Boeing's designers how to build a quick-change convertible interior. To seal the deal we placed a deposit of $250,000 cash for the first two

B-707-320Cs that would come off the line. Boeing commenced the design and construction of our aircraft.

In the summer of 1962, what with A.J. Rome's disastrous charter program and the shutdown of most of Riddle's commercial cargo operation, it became obvious that Riddle would not be able to take delivery of the two Boeing aircraft. Hewitt sent Boeing a notice that he was defaulting on the purchase and forfeiting the $250,000 deposit.

Following Hewitt's loss of control of Riddle, Jim Franklin's election as President – and my appointment as Senior Vice President, Operations, Maintenance and Sales – I found myself in a desperate position. The pilots and mechanics had agreed to continue working without pay and we were scrambling to find enough funds to buy fuel, pay for parts, keep the IRS off our backs and stave off creditors. I went to work every day not knowing how we would keep Riddle out of bankruptcy that day.

I remembered the $250,000 deposit at Boeing. Even though Hewitt had relinquished it to Boeing to avoid litigation over the cancellation of our order for two B-707-320Cs, and even though we had ordered two DC-8s, I felt it was worth a try. I called my friend Don Hardesty at Northwest and asked for a pass to Seattle, which he provided.

The next morning I walked into the office of William Allen at Boeing, sat down and explained Riddle's plight. He listened attentively as I told him that we understood the legal position and Boeing's right to the $250,000. Then I explained that the life of our airline literally hung in the balance.

"Mr. Allen, I would like to ask you to give us back our deposit."

"Mort, I understand your situation, and I will do that ..."

Allen phoned the Treasurer's office, drew a $250,000 check payable to Riddle Airlines, and gave it to me. I returned to Miami with enough funds to again get square with our employees.

It was a magnanimous gesture by a great company, and one that I will always remember.

Fired from Riddle

As the spring and summer of 1963 rolled on, Riddle's fortunes improved. Our newly restructured scheduled airfreight services from New York and Miami to San Juan began to show a profit. Military contracts continued to be cash cows and Riddle maintained a steady share based on the imminent introduction of our new DC-8 jets. Miami's Herald took notice of our success and began to write favorable stories about Riddle, featuring myself.

But, as is often the case, success bred rivalries. Jim Franklin, our

President and my former boss at Capital Airlines and I, fell out of favor over personal and policy questions. I was effectively running the day-to-day operations of Riddle. Jim had an increasing problem with alcoholism that impaired his effectiveness and perspective in my mind, and he in turn became jealous of my prominence in the press. Members of the Board were increasingly aware of our problems and Franklin struck decisively to preserve his position – he fired me! Given the circumstances he probably had no choice, but it was a bitter blow for me.

With a generous nest egg of two weeks severance pay, I retreated to my apartment to recoup and plan for the future. My friends at The Company (CIA) owned a small cargo airline called Aerovias Sud Americanas that was based in Miami and provided cover for their operations in South and Central America. They offered me a consulting contract – an offer I gladly accepted.

The Company also operated small airlines in Nepal in Asia and Katanga in the Congo. These enterprises were also "Company cover" but were operated by an ostensibly independent Board of Directors. I was elected to the Board of Air Ventures and became President. Air Ventures operated small fleets of Portus Pilatus single-engine transports capable of carrying eight passengers or two thousand pounds of cargo from short, unimproved airfields at high altitudes and, thus, were ideal for the aerial support missions that we ran for the Agency. I gave up my position with ASA and Air Ventures when I moved to Saudi Arabia to head TWA's technical assistance program for Saudia Airlines the next year – more about this later.

Roy Tonks ran an enormous engine overhaul company on the Miami Airport known as Aerodex. Shortly after leaving Riddle I approached Mr. Tonks seeking a consulting contract and promising to help him cure a major production problem he was experiencing.

"Mr. Beyer, what is your fee?"

"$200 a day, Mr. Tonks"

"That's outrageous!"

"Yes, but I'm worth it!"

"OK, you're hired."

Aerodex had a contract to overhaul all Pratt & Whitney R-4360 engines that powered the USAF's B-29 bombers, as well as the Curtis Wright R-3350s powering various military transports. The R-4360 was a monster engine with four rows of nine cylinders each, with eight ignition systems and four carburetors. Aerodex overhauled over twenty R-4360s per day, along with eight R-3350s - and turned out more engines every week than Pan Am and Eastern combined did in a month. But Aerodex had a problem. The R-4360s were torn down for overhaul by standing them on end and removing the cylinders and wiring. The front row of cylinders was some eight feet from the floor, and the bottom row only about three feet. So Tonks employed a tear down crew that consisted of an eight-foot giant of a mechanic, a smaller six-footer, a normal five-footer and a midget. The tallest mechanic attacked the top row of cylinders, while the midget removed the bottom row and the two normal-sized mechanics took care of the two middle rows. This unique division of labor was highly efficient and removed requirements for scaffolding or the need to lay the engine down and rotate it.

After tear down, the engine parts were distributed to the various support shops for processing and overhaul. The cylinder shop re-bored the cylinders, the piston shop ground pistons and replaced rings, the plating and grinding shops reworked the rods and crankshafts, new bearings were inserted and, finally, the overhauled parts were transported to the Assembly Line for re-assembly. From Assembly the engines went to the Test Cells, where 60% of them failed. The test failures were sent to what was called the Hospital Shop, where they were partially disassembled, repaired as required and sent back for further test – and often a second and third failure. The Hospital Shop had almost as many mechanics as the overhaul and assembly lines.

This procedure was not working. Further, even after engines finally passed testing, too many failed in flight, causing aborted missions and potential crashes. The Air Force maintained a massive quality control contingent at Aerodex that had been utterly unable to correct the situation and Military Headquarters was about to cancel Aerodex's lucrative contracts.

My job – fix it!

After several weeks of walking the production lines, talking to mechanics and supervisors, meeting with the Air Force Quality Control team and studying the test results and Hospital Shop reports, I had my solution.

"Mr. Tonks, I believe I have the answer to your production problems."

"Yes, what is it?"

"You should shut down your Hospital Shop and send all of the failed engines back to the initial Assembly Shop."

"Beyer, are you nuts?"

"No, Mr. Tonks, I'm not nuts."

"What do you mean then?"

"Mr. Tonks, have you ever house-trained a dog?"

"Well, yes ... but?"

"Mr. Tonks, when your dog shits on the rug, you grab him by the collar, take him back and rub his nose in it, right?"

"Well, yes but so what?"

"That is what you have to do with the Assembly Line. They produce lousy engines and push them out the door to the Test Cell. If they fail, it is the Hospital Shop's job to fix them. The Assembly Line has no responsibility to correct its own mistakes. You have to make them eat their own shit. When you do that you will achieve quality production and engines that are right the first time."

Tonks saw the merit of my suggestion. The Hospital Shop was shut down and the best mechanics merged into the beefed up Assembly Line. For several days chaos reigned as failed engines piled up in the tear down section and their carcasses streamed back down the Assembly Line. But then the new plan began to work. Engines coming off the line began to pass the test the first time. The pass rate increased 60, 70, then more than 80% passed as the reinforced Assembly Line got more proficient at "doing it right the first time." Finally, the rejected rated dropped below 10 % – an unheard of improvement even in an airline shop.

A few months later an Air Force officer reported to me that the in-flight failure rate of the Aerodex R-4360 overhauls had also fallen dramatically. The Aerodex contract was renewed by the USAF and the company reported record profits.

With my $200 a day salary I bought a cute little white Chevy convertible with a red interior, christened MAVIS I.

In March 1964 I received a call from Tony Peck, Assistant to the Vice President of Administration for TWA. They wanted to know if I was interested in going to Jeddah, Saudi Arabia to head their Technical Mission to Saudi Arabian Airlines, the Flag carrier of the Kingdom of Saudi Arabia.

At the same time my friends at The Company asked me if I would be interested in going to Lagos, Nigeria to head Pan African Airlines, an Agency-owned company providing airlift services for the American Government in West Africa.

Epilogue

Riddle Airlines overcame its difficulties of 1963 without me, took delivery of the two DC-8s I had negotiated, changed the company name to Airlift and merged with Slick Airways, another all-cargo airline. The value of its stock increased from 35¢ a share at the time I left to $11 by 1966 – by which time I was in Saudi Arabia. I sold my hundred thousand shares that had financed the down payment original DC-7C purchase to General Dynamics and put it in the bank. The day President Kennedy was assassinated I reinvested in airline stocks. Between then and 1967 I made a little less than what I would have made if I had stayed with Riddle.

But starting in the early '70s, Airlift encountered continued difficulties. The company was unable to straighten out its management problems and lost market share to Flying Tigers, the largest and sole surviving all-cargo airline. Airlift's pilots went out on strike, shutting down operations and forcing it into bankruptcy in 1980. The airline struggled on in bankruptcy for a decade, finally ending up with only a single run out DC-8-54F (NC301G), the aircraft which I had bought in 1963, almost thirty years before. In 1991 the Airline (NE Riddle) was finally liquidated. ✈

CHAPTER VII

Saudi Arabia

On to Arabia

In March of 1964 I was invited to come to New York for an interview with TWA. They were looking for a new manager from outside TWA for their technical management contract with Saudi Arabian Airlines. Ever since 1948, TWA had supplied a cadre of pilots and mechanics to the airline, known colloquially as Saudia, as well as oversight of the flight operations of the Company.

The operation was essentially a "Foreign Legion," with only the General Manager and a few top staff, actually veteran TWA employees. All of the pilots and most of the mechanics were hired by TWA for duty especially in Saudi Arabia. They did not hold TWA seniority or get paid TWA wages. To make matters worse, the TWA-designated managers were generally "culls", sent to Arabia to get rid of them

Ostensibly the TWA mission was to train the Saudi nationals as pilots, mechanics and supervisors. In actual practice the TWA managers, and the ex-patriot pilots, dragged their feet on any training, figuring that once trained the Saudis would not need them any more. The Chairman of the airline, a westernized Saudi sheikh and Jeddah merchant named Achmed Jamjoon, was acutely aware of this deficiency in TWA performance and advised TWA's New York headquarters that they wanted some new blood. They did not want any more managers from the "bad old TWA." Thus, TWA was looking for new outside management to head their contract operations in Arabia.

My interview with Tony Peck, who headed the Saudi Arabian program for TWA in New York, went well. He told me frankly of TWA's problems and the concerns of the airline's Saudi managers. It seemed a challenge too good to miss. While my consulting activities in Miami were lucrative and fun, there was always the compulsion to get my hands on the throttles of a "real" airline. Further, Peck held out the opportunity for a subsequent full-time career with TWA, one of America's premier airlines.

But first I had to pass an intensive psychological screening to determine my aptitude for the assignment. The next day I appeared at the offices of a shrink designated by TWA for a day of tests and interviews. These tests consisted of interpreting blots of ink on a page, supposedly designed to detect any Freudian or deviant tendencies in my personality. There were also SAT-type intelligence tests and multiple-choice questions of various sorts. Here are a few examples:

Would you rather work in your rose garden or attend a football game?
    ❏ rose garden   ❏ football game
Do you prefer to drink whiskey or Dubonnet?
    ❏ whiskey   ❏ Dubonnet
Would you rather read poetry or a Western novel?
    ❏ poetry   ❏ Western novel

And so it went. I answered each question exactly as I believed the questioner wanted it answered, giving the "correct" answer.

The next day I went back to Tony Peck at TWA. "Damn it, Beyer, you broke the bank with those tests!" A few days later TWA offered me a trip to Jeddah with Mr. Peck to survey the situation and to be interviewed by the Saudi Arabian Chairman and Directors, who would pass final judgment of my acceptability.

At the same time I had been offered the presidency of Pan African Airlines, based in Lagos, Nigeria and owned by the CIA. It seemed desirable to survey both opportunities, so I scheduled a stop at Lagos on my return from the planned trip to Jeddah.

The State Department gives briefing materials to executives planning to live abroad, so I requested briefings on both Jeddah and Lagos. Jeddah was depicted in the harshest terms – hot, arid, unhealthy and peopled by backward nomads ruled by a despotic king. Lagos, on the other hand, was the crown jewel of Nigeria – an enlightened Black African democracy shedding the last vestiges of empire and emerging into the dawn of a new era.

The long trip to Jeddah with Tony Peck was uneventful. The Arab executives met us expectantly and gave approval to my appointment. TWA staff under Ed Haney – a long-time Jeddah hand serving as Acting Technical Manager in place of the previous manager who had gone home – were politely bemused at my obvious enthusiasm for the assignment.

On our way back Tony and I stopped for a day in Beirut, staying at the luxurious Phoenicia Intercontinental Hotel which featured a basement bar where one could observe the Pan Am stewardesses disporting themselves through the glass wall of the swimming pool. Beirut at that time was the watering hole of the Middle East, where East met West and West prevailed.

Tony and I parted ways in Beirut. I flew to Accra and then to Lagos for my look-see at Pan African. Accra was closed by weather, so we ended up in the alternate airport in Duala, Cameroon. Put up in a "hotel" with a tin roof and only ceiling fans for ventilation, we waited for the crew to get their rest before continuing to Lagos. Duala was hot, humid, and fetid, with mud streets, open sewers, no western amenities and lots of beautiful, tall royal palm trees. We could not wait to get back on our Pan Am jet to Lagos.

Arriving in mid-afternoon at Lagos' chaotic airport, I was met by Ralph Rhea, then President of Pan African Airways and a former colleague from Pan Am days. He was not exactly glad to see me becausee he knew the purpose of my trip was to replace him. But he was polite enough, taking me to my hotel in downtown Lagos, a five-mile, one-hour drive on crowded roads through masses of vehicle, bicycle and foot traffic. The hotel was reasonably modern and air conditioned, but had a pervasive stench that I eventually identified – it smelled like the elephant house at the zoo!

I spent three days in Lagos visiting with Ralph at the airline and learning about its operations. Pan African had a DC-4, several Cessnas and a handful of helicopters that supported the oil patch down the coast off Biafra. Its mission was also to transport personnel and supplies between Lagos and American outposts in Togo, Dahomey and inland in Nigeria. Its pilots and mechanics were all Americans who lived in a secure compound on the airport. Travel outside the compound at night was not encouraged.

The U.S. Ambassador threw a small reception in my honor attended by the airline managers and the Embassy staff. It was a polite and somewhat stuffy affair, with everybody wanting to hear about things back home such as the assassination of Kennedy. As I left they all gathered on the porch of the Embassy to wave goodbye. I had a strong impression that the State Department's enthusiastic description of Lagos was not in accord with reality.

The choice was easy. Jeddah, here I come! Two weeks later my apartment in Miami was closed, MAVIS I was sold and the farm in Virginia rented for the duration. The renters even bought my herd of fifteen Black Angus cattle and adopted the family dog. My wife Jane, the four children and I were off to Arabia. We flew first class on TWA to Beirut, then transferred to Saudi Arabia's Boeing 720 jet for the final leg to Jeddah.

Arriving in Jeddah was a bit of a shock. The aircraft pulled up on the

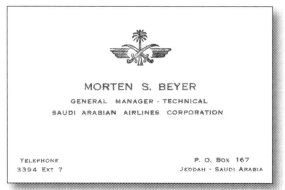

MORTEN S. BEYER

GENERAL MANAGER · TECHNICAL

SAUDI ARABIAN AIRLINES CORPORATION

TELEPHONE
3394 EXT 7

P. O. BOX 167
JEDDAH - SAUDI ARABIA

floodlit ramp, the doors were opened and the aircraft was immediately surrounded by dozens of Cadillac limousines, scores of Arabs in their long white galabiyas and burnoose native dress and a company of armed Saudi troops in battle dress. The Cadillacs were there to whisk the princes and members of the Royal Family to their destinations and the troops were there to protect them. TWA's Ed Haney and his assistant Duane Busch both were on hand to guide us through customs and immigration, a somewhat daunting process filled with shouting and gesticulation. Finally, we made it through and were transported to our new home – a villa in the Aramco Compound.

The Aramco Compound had once housed the chief executives of Aramco, the Arabian-American oil company, but all but one of them had moved to Dahran where all the oil was located. Now it was used to house people such as ourselves who were high-level guests of the Kingdom. The Compound was walled, gated and guarded – as much from roving herds of goats and packs of dogs as anything else. We had a tennis court and a swimming pool – a rarity in Jeddah in those days. Our villa was a four-bedroom affair raised on piers, with servants' quarters underneath and a garden on the roof. We lived there our entire four years in Jeddah.

We were furnished with a new Chevy station wagon and a driver of somewhat erratic behavior and unreliable habits, but I was encouraged to use him whenever possible. The Kingdom had very severe laws concerning automobile accidents – if a passenger or pedestrian was killed, the driver of the offending car was likely to be executed on the spot by the police. Thus, even though we felt the police would not kill a Westerner, all TWA personnel tended to use native drivers as a precautionary measure. Women were forbidden to drive at all by Moslem law – and still are to this day. We told our wives this was a safety measure – a joke they did not appreciate. The more daring women bought native Arab men's clothes and headdress and pretended to be men so they could drive. Fortunately, during my stay none were ever apprehended or involved in an accident.

Western food could only be bought at the Lebanese market down by the Souk – or marketplace – close to the sea. Selection was limited and fresh produce was unknown. All pork products were forbidden and other meats and fish were of unreliable freshness. As a result, most TWA families relied on shipments from the more modern and complete markets of Beirut. Supplies were brought in daily on Saudi flights from Beirut. Customs agents would go through our "care packages" with great diligence if they suspected they contained forbidden products or liquor, which was, of course, totally banned. But if you were honest with the Customs agents there was some leeway.

A large care package from Beirut is presented to the Customs Agent:
"Minn fadlack esch hadda?" – Please, what is in there?
"Mafish" – Nothing.
The result was bound to be a search, with your goodies strewn about.
"Minn fadlack esch hadda?" – Please, what is that?
"Khodar, khobz, laham, maya, khanzir ..." – Vegetables, bread, meat, water, pig meat.
"Shokran, ma salama ..." – Thank you, goodbye.

Our TWA contingent had no medical doctor or clinic so we had to rely on the local Lebanese Hospital, a small and somewhat primitive facility manned by a single qualified Lebanese doctor and several nurses from other Arab countries. Saudi women were not encouraged to work outside the home. Serious cases were flown out to Beirut. Fortunately, all in our community remained quite healthy.

The American Embassy

The Embassy was an oasis in Jeddah where one could enjoy extra-territorial privileges. The Embassy served liquor, bacon, ham and fresh produce that was not available outside. We in the TWA compound appreciated access to the Embassy at dinners and cocktail parties, and were often invited when TWA or the Embassy had guests from America.

I personally maintained close contact with the Ambassador, "Pete" Hart, and with his staff, particularly the Commercial Attaché, Herb Ferguson who represented The Company. They especially kept me informed as to political changes that were taking place in the Kingdom and the ones that were threatened. I, in turn, kept the Embassy informed as to activities at the airline that affected American interests. These contacts were to prove valuable to me in the future as the U.S. Government expressed its gratitude in unexpected ways.

Understandably, I did not share my contacts in the Embassy nor their results with my superiors in TWA's New York headquarters. I felt they would not understand or appreciate them.

The First Days

Early on the first morning of my assignment to Saudia I got up, woke my driver (sleeping in that station wagon) and asked him to drive me to the airport and the flight line. The sun had just come up and our two Boeing 720B jets, three DC-6s and a score of twin-engine Convairs and DC-3s were lined up on the tarmac awaiting departure. Two German mechanics and a single Saudi were going from plane to plane checking fuel, tire pressure, and oil quantities. At the same time they looked for leaks and signs of trouble. In addition to the TWA contract mechanics the airline hired European, Pakistani, Indian and Yemeni contractors to perform the actual labor. The two Germans, Judo Fritsch and Horst Wuttig, were members of this third national contingent, and both were to work for me again at Modern Air in Berlin and Air Berlin. Horst was also later a technician for AVMARK and MBA, my consulting firms.

All of the TWA maintenance staff came trooping in at 9 A.M., long after all of the aircraft had departed on the day's runs. The TWA Maintenance Manager and I had a few words about this and agreed that a number of TWA staff would turn up at 5 A.M. to man the dawn patrol – not leaving all the work to our third national contractors.

After having toured the facilities and met all TWA and Saudi staff, I went to the Bakashab Building to meet my new bosses, Sheikh Achmed Jamjoon and Sheikh Suliman Romaih, respectively the Chairman and Director General of the airline. Jamjoon was a small active and articulate Jeddah merchant. Suliman was a tall, taciturn desert Sheikh. I had met both of them on my initial visit to Jeddah. I also met Captain Greenstead and his contingent of British Advisors to the Chairman – more about them later.

Next on my agenda was a meeting with Sheikh Kamil Sindi, the Director General of the Civil Aviation Department (CAD) – the FAA of Saudi Arabia. Kamil was an American-educated executive with a strong influence on the airline and a member of the Board of Directors. He was also a critic of TWA's past failures to train the Saudi national pilots, technicians and staff.

Hamza Dabagh was head of the Airline's training department and reported directly to the Director General, not to the TWA Technical Management that I headed. He, too, was highly critical of TWA and its personnel.

Finally, I paid my respects to "Pete" Hart, the U.S. Ambassador to Saudi Arabia. A skilled professional, he briefed me extensively on American interests in the country, the politics of the Kingdom and his perceptions of TWA's role. We were to keep in close, if quiet contact during my stay in Jeddah.

My Arabic tutor began the Herculean task of teaching me rudimentary Arabic, including attempting to make me read the language, consisting entirely

Mort Beyer, Sheilkh Ahmed Jamjoon, Sheikh Suliman Tom Huntington, TWA VP

of different characters and read from right to left. After the first week I had enough confidence to address the staff in a meeting of some three hundred persons including the TWA staff of some one hundred souls. I included a halting introduction in Arabic.

"Sayyidati, Sadati..."

In my talk I outlined TWA's new direction and emphasized that our role was not only to operate a safe and reliable airline, but also to bring standards to the level of Western airlines and train our Saudi nationals in all phases of flying, maintaining and managing. The speech merited a front-page story in Jeddah's leading newspapers.

The British Advisors

The Chairman, Achmed Jamjoon, had hired a group of British advisors headed by Captain Greenstead. These gentlemen were aviation experts who involved themselves in all phases of the airline's operations, including "experting" TWA's technical operations, and had encouraged the Chairman to replace the "bad old TWA management" with new blood, hopefully British. Thus, they had been at least partially responsible for my assignment to Arabia.

In many respects the British advisors were helpful in bringing about needed reforms, including increasing wages of ex patriate employees, increasing procurement of spare parts, modernizing the fleet and bringing the airline's operations up to international standards. But as time went on their priorities became more focused: sell British airplanes, get rid of TWA and replace Mort Beyer – and not necessarily in that order.

A long turf battle took place over aircraft modernization with the Advisors pushing purchase of the BAC-1-11, a British-built small twin-engine

Saudi Airlines accepts first DC-9

jet. TWA's home office favored the Boeing B-727-100 tri-jet. I believed the Douglas DC-9-10 just entering production was the best suited to Saudia's requirements. In the end I won, and Saudia bought three DC-9s, but it was a long, drawn out battle.

Early in my assignment it became apparent that our expatriate pilots supplied by TWA were underpaid, making it more difficult to retain good pilots because they received alternative offers, and making it very difficult to replace them when they did leave. The TWA pilot group was a polyglot lot, and our cadre was a "French Foreign Legion," most of whom had worked as "scabs" and strike breakers at National Airlines, Eastern and other carriers. ALPA, the airline pilots union, blacklisted any airman who helped break strikes and denied him any future employment in the airlines they controlled – literally all of them in the U.S.A. A few pilots had had problems with the FAA or had difficulty passing proficiency checks. A job with Saudia was the last place on earth they could find a flying job.

A week or so after taking over, Captain Bill Boone – one of the leaders of the pilot group – burst into my office and flung a list of demands on my desk: more money, better living conditions, more time off and vacations, etc. Our pilots were not unionized per se, since the Saudi government considered unionism a crime against the State and the King, and punishable by beheading, the common form of execution in the Kingdom. I assured Capt. Boone that I understood the pilots' concerns but had to handle the problem with considerable delicacy since we were guests in the Kingdom and our job was to help train the Saudi Nationals as well as fly the airline. Patience and improved performance were required.

I appealed to the British Advisors who were trying to ingratiate themselves with the rank and file of the TWA pilots and wanted to seem to be doing things favorable to the airline. A better wage scale could also make it possible to attract expatriate pilots from the U.K. if they took over. In time, using the Advisors, we were able to greatly improve the pilots' wages, including the provision of generous overtime allowance for extra hours flown in peak periods such as the Hadj.

Sadekie Americaneekie

Liquor in all forms is banned in Saudi Arabia and the Religious Police, or Matawa, enforced the laws. Punishment of the natives was usually by whipping, with execution for traffickers. Foreigners were generally deported.

Ever since the early days of Aramco, American workers built small stills for themselves and produced a potion that we would call "white lightning" in the States, but that had a local name in Arabia. "Sadekie" is the Arabic word for "friend," and our local distilled product was known as "Sadekie Ameicaneekie" – Friend of the Americans.

The Arabian authorities were fully aware of the Americans' distilling activities and did not take action as long as we kept it to ourselves in the TWA Compound or in our separate villas. The various foreign embassies, including our own, also had liquor privileges since they were considered foreign territories, but were encouraged to keep it "in house."

Unfortunately, every so often a TWA employee would endeavor to enhance his income by selling some Sadekie to the locals, often using his Saudi houseboy as the mule. And every so often somebody would get caught:

Late at night, many times, the phone would ring at the Compound.

"Mort, this is Ed Haney."

"Yeah, Ed, what's going on?"

"Vic Brazowski is in jail . . ."

"Yeah, what did he do this time?"

"He was caught selling Sadekie again and they took him to jail. What are we going to do?"

"Leave him there."

"God, Mort, we can't do that . . . it's an awful place."

"Maybe he'll get wise and stop selling his Sadekie."

"Awww, Mort."

"No, Ed, let's leave him there and get him out in the morning."

"OK, good night."

"Good night."

Morning came and Ed got Brazowski out of jail. I was in my office at the Airport when the inevitable phone call came from the Chairman, Achmed Jamjoon.

""Good morning Mr. Beyer."

"Good morning, your Excellency."

"Mr. Beyer, come to my office immediately. I must talk to you."

"Yes, Sheikh Achmed."

I woke up my driver asleep on the floor outside my office door and ordered him to drive me to the Executive Offices located downtown in the Bakasheb Building. I went to Sheikh Achmed's office and was ushered in immediately, a sure sign of trouble. Usually it was an honor to be kept waiting while less important business was transacted. All of the others waiting in the office were thrown out and I faced an agitated Sheikh Achmed across his vast desk.

"Mr. Beyer, your Victor Brazowski was caught selling alcohol to our people again last night."

"Yes, Sheikh Achmed, I know, and I am sorry. We will punish him and send him home."

"Mr. Beyer, we know that you Americans must drink to stay happy, but please do not sell it to our people."

"Yes, Sheikh Achmed, I understand."

We did plan to send Vic home on the next flight, but he also worked for the Government's Civil Aviation Department keeping the Air Traffic Control system's radios and transmitters in good repair. The Director General of the CAD intervened to save Vic's job.

As a postscript, Vic later adopted the Muslim faith as a number of our TWA staff did, changing his name to Fouad and taking Saudi citizenship.

Sadekie was made by mixing a prescribed amount of sugar with water and adding malt to start the fermentation process. After about two weeks at room temperature the liquor was distilled at the exact temperature of 190°F. The distillate was a 99% pure alcohol that was cut by adding water. Good Sadekie had a rather pleasing taste, especially when mixed with Seven Up to create "Sadekie & Seven," the local alcoholic beverage of choice. Distilling Sadekie at the wrong temperature, or with the wrong ingredients, produced a vile mixture that could cause severe gastric disturbances and blindness. So you had to be careful to choose the right bootlegger.

Once one got to know the system there was also a plentiful supply of

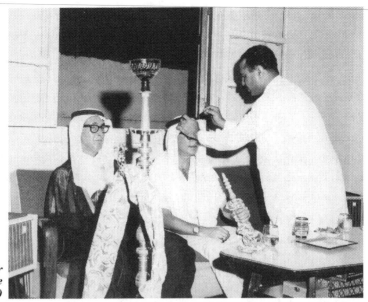

Fitting for
Arab robe
(galabiyas)

gin, vodka and Scotch to be had at reasonable prices of about $60 a case (270 Riyals – the exchange rate was 4.5 Saudi Riyals to the dollar, a rate still in effect today). An active supply system, reportedly administered by the Matawa itself, assured that one could always obtain supplies through the underground.

Many of our Arabic colleagues kept a good bar and we never hesitated to offer both Sadekie and the good stuff at our parties to Arabs and Westerners alike. Others, however, maintained strict abstinence. After I left Saudi Arabia one of my TWA successors attempted to impose a total ban on alcohol for all TWA employees.

Booze was a problem with the pilots, especially on long days off with little to do but fight with their equally bored wives. Early on while I was visiting Beirut for a day of negotiations with Lebanese International Airways which had leased one of our Boeing 720s, I received a call in my Phoenicia Hotel room from Lloyd Wilgus, our Chief Flight Engineer, that Captain Scott was drunk in his room. Scott was scheduled to fly our Boeing back to Jeddah that night. I thanked Lloyd and called our Chief Pilot in the next room, asking him to investigate. Scotty was rousted from his stupor, filled with coffee and sent to the steam room to work out and sober up. A slightly woozy Captain Scott showed up at departure time and was assigned to the jump seat while the Chief Pilot flew home. The next morning I called a very subdued but sober Captain Scott to my office. He had been with Saudia for some ten years and was a competent pilot. He readily admitted the stupidity of getting soused during his rest period in Beirut. I removed him from the prestigious assignment of flying the Boeing jets and sentenced him to dry out for thirty days in the desert flying the lowly DC-3s. Scotty got the message and so did the rest of the pilots. I could have terminated Scotty, but didn't. Good pilots were hard to recruit.

Saudi Training Accident

The Saudis had become disenchanted with TWA's lack of interest in training their nationals to fly. They had therefore removed the training department from TWA jurisdiction and placed it under the management of Sheikh Hamza Dabagh, a talented, well liked, well educated, English speaking Saudi national. He was to be assisted by Norm "Daddy" Doere, an American seconded by TWA.

In my opinion this was a necessary arrangement given the attitude of the TWA management and pilots sent to Arabia in the past. However, it had its problems and the training department marched to its own drum.

Around a month after I arrived the training department permitted three young Saudi pilots to take one of our DC-3s on a self-taught training flight. None of these young pilots had more than a few hundred hours of experience of any type. They took off with four hours' fuel and disappeared ...

Their flight plan called for them to fly south from Jeddah and perform practice maneuvers over the Red Sea. The flight was planned for two hours. When it did not return on time the training department called me and

Saudi pilots in training

explained the situation. I immediately called out two crews and activated two DC-3s that were sitting on the ramp.

The day was waning when, an hour before sunset, one of the search planes manned by our regular pilots called to say that they had sighted debris floating on the water - a wheel, insulation, some seats. The location was some 90 miles south of Jeddah and five miles off the coast. The Saudi Coast Guard was notified immediately and two diesel-powered cutters were dispatched to the scene. Unfortunately, it would be late at night when they arrived and they would have to wait until daylight to begin their search.

The accident site was off a point called El Shaja where the Saudis maintained a Coast Guard Station with whom we could talk by radio. They had not observed anything that afternoon, but were on the alert. Several of our Saudi technicians went south on the Coast Guard Cutters to help in the search.

At the same time I called a meeting of our senior staff. While the accident involved the training department, TWA was still in general command of the situation, and we had to act decisively to determine whatever facts there were. The Saudi system worked on the basis of personal responsibility, and the managers of the autonomous training department had gone to ground as soon as it was obvious an accident had occurred. We had to take command – and did.

There were no roads between Jeddah and El Shaja – only a hundred miles of empty desert. Camel paths and jeep trails existed, but there were no maps. We had to get a ground party to the El Shaja Coast Guard station by daybreak. It was decided that I would use my new Chevrolet station wagon. A local Saudi was designated "navigator," and four more TWA maintenance and flight operations managers piled in to complete the party. Boxes of sandwiches were prepared and stored in the back of the wagon along with coolers of ice water. Our route was traced out on an Air Force chart for the benefit of our staff in Jeddah should it become necessary to send out a rescue party.

Starting at 2 P.M. we headed out, leaving the lights of Jeddah behind and entering the virtually trackless desert. Our Arab guide had a general idea of where we wanted to go and how to get there. Much of the time we could drive in low gear at twenty-five miles an hour over flat, hard desert valleys. Sometimes there were stone cairns that marked an indefinite truck route through the valleys and between the dunes that towered above us. All through the Arabian desert giant sand dunes, hundreds of feet high, marched relentlessly across the landscape, driven by the constant winds. Thus, landmarks changed and disappeared, routes changed, and paths once open were often closed with mountains of sand.

Every few minutes we would come to another sand dune. We would stop and survey the situation. Did it block our path completely? Could we work around it? Could we just charge up over a small sandspur? Or did we need to go down the valley seeking a whole new passage to the south?

All night long we plowed south, feeling our way and charging small sand dunes or seeking new routes. We had packed shovels so that all of us could pitch in if we had to. Fortunately, we made it without getting stuck. As dawn broke over the Red Sea we rolled up to the El Shaja Coast Guard Station. A half dozen Arab Coast Guardsmen came out dressed in their gray galabiyas to greet us and offer the traditional cups of gahwa (Arabic coffee), along with a breakfast of meats, rice and other native foods.

The two Coast Guard cutters were bobbing offshore just outside the surf. Their crews and our staff aboard came ashore. After breakfast we planned our strategy for the day. We boarded the boats and went out to the presumed crash site where we found and recovered a single landing gear wheel and struts. The gear evidently had been in the down position when the aircraft crashed. The remaining flotsam and jetsam were all of no material consequence. The aircraft had evidently gone in at a steep angle and been destroyed on impact, sinking in ten thousand feet of water. There seemed little point in searching for bodies. A few predatory sharks ravenously devoured lunch boxes containing meat sandwiches almost as soon as they hit the water.

We returned to the station by noon, drank farewell ceremonial cups of gahwa with the Coast Guardsmen, and headed back across the desert to Jeddah in my station wagon. The trip back was much less eventful as, aided by better visibility, we made much better time.

A Saudi Royal Court of Inquiry was eventually convened to investigate this unfortunate incident and concluded that the accident was the "Will of Allah." But a few days later the Saudi Board of Directors transferred full responsibility for the entire Saudi flight training program back to TWA and my control. We had no more incidents.

Reinforcements

Our TWA management cadre was pitifully thin. It included me, my Deputy Ed Haney, Duane Busch (in charge of station and passenger service), Phil Passeti (managing Disptach), our Chief Pilot Sam Bigler, Russ Smedly in charge of Stores, and the maintenance contingent. Reservations, station operations, marketing, personnel, finance, route and schedule planning and general management were all under the control of the Saudis.

I appealed to TWA to send reinforcements in the form of airport managers to assist us in handling the growing size of the airline and the new international routes we were developing, and to cope with the Hadj

Downtown ticket counter Jeddah

pilgrimage that imposed enormous workloads on our meager staff.

Captain Bob Wells, my former assistant chief pilot from Riddle, and Bill Clarke, also from Riddle, were recruited to strengthen Flight Operations. At the same time we began to promote the most promising Saudi Nationals into management positions. We selected Captain Nahar to be Chief Pilot - a position he really did not want (he preferred to fly), but took nonetheless. Nahar was our only fully rated Saudi jet pilot, a product of extensive training by the RAF and an exceptional airman. He was promoted to Director General of the airline in the 1980s. Saudi Nationals also took over many foremen's positions in maintenance and stores. Our program of nationalization of the airline was, in my opinion, a major success - starting from ground zero at the time of my arrival and proceeding rapidly during my tenure.

But from the beginning the TWA pilot group was not eager to encourage in-flight training of the young Saudi pilots. The Training Department was educating them in English - the language of aviation - and sending them to academies such as Emery Riddle in the U.S. for basic training. After returning with their brand new commercial licenses, these young men were anxious to take the controls and polish their new airman skills. The TWA pilots wanted the young Saudis to sit like sacks in the right seat, keep their hands off the controls and be quiet. We had to improve the minds of the TWA pilots who made all of the takeoffs and landings and put the aircraft on autopilot for the duration of the trips.

When persuasion did not seem to produce immediate improvement, I directed Maintenance to remove all the auto pilots from the DC-3 and Convair aircraft, forcing the crews to hand fly them on the long, rough trips over the deserts of the Kingdom. This was not popular among the Americans, but it did the trick, and the TWA pilots were more than glad to turn over the drudgery of hand flying to the young Saudi copilots. We also required that the Saudis make all landings and takeoffs and record them in the logbooks. Their skills immediately began to improve and, after a year, we were able to begin the process of checking out the most promising as DC-3 and Convair Captains. Before my tour was over many of our young Saudi pilots had advanced to the DC-9 and Boeing jets. But for a year-and-a-half the British Advisors were a burr under TWA's saddle.

TWA Relations

Almost from the beginning my relations with TWA's home office in New York, and particularly with the Operations and Maintenance Headquarters in Kansas City, became testy. While Kansas City had no direct responsibility or authority over my operations in Jeddah, both they and New York felt they had a higher responsibility to assure that our operation met "TWA Standards."

The first area of friction already existed in the Saudis' beliefs, furthered by the British Advisors, that TWA was assigning inferior managers and staff to Jeddah and that these persons were perpetuating their own interests and not training the Saudi Nationals. We undertook to educate all concerned that TWA and our staff were in Jeddah primarily in the Saudis' interest and not in ours. We were there to help, to train, to "do the necessary" and not to hold them back.

We urged Kansas City to send us their best people, not their culls. When he arrived, each new employee sat down in my office for an orientation briefing in which I explained that we were guests in the Kingdom. There would be many things that were different and some that were disagreeable, but these must be accepted. We were there to help the Saudis, not to tell them. Politeness and persuasion were preferable to arrogance in the face of problems. Those who got the message generally had long and satisfactory assignments in Jeddah. Those who did not were sent home sooner rather than later.

Due to attrition and the termination of unsatisfactory pilots we were generally short handed. A generally low level of normal operations combined with four peak periods – the two Teachers' movements, the Holy Month of Ramadan and the Hadj – characterized Saudia's operations. Almost all of Saudi Arabia's schools employed foreign teachers from surrounding Muslim countries – Palestine, Syria, Iraq, Lebanon and Egypt – since a generation of indigenous teachers had not yet been developed. The opening and closing of school saw the movement of tens of thousands of expatriate teachers in and out of the Kingdom, posing a major overload on the airline.

During Ramadan all Muslims are supposed to fast from sunup to sundown for a period of one month. Many took the opportunity to leave the Kingdom during this period, again increasing traffic. And finally, during the Holy Month of Hadj, a million pilgrims from all over the Muslim world descended on Mecca and Medina, the holy cities. They came by truck and bus over the deserts and by ships, but mostly by air. Saudia carried as many pilgrims as it could and chartered services from foreign airlines for the balance.

Therefore, there was maximum pressure on the airline to fly as many flights as it could and carry as many pilgrims as possible. On the inbound Hadj flights aircraft ferried empty to the cities of the Muslim world where pilgrims were picked up and brought to Jeddah for onward passage to Mecca and Medina by bus. The pilgrims gathered in the holy cities for a week for prayer and then the return movement started, with flights departing full and returning empty for another load. Both the inbound and outbound Hadj lasted about two weeks.

During these periods I directed that all pilots should fly the maximum hours required to move the teachers, Hadjis and others. This involved flying the aircraft around the clock, consistent with necessary line maintenance. Overhauls and engine changes were scheduled for periods before and after the peak periods. I directed that the pilots fly up to ten hours daily (twelve hours for jets and DC-6s with a flight engineer) six days a week, or up to 240 hours per month. This was a problem with TWA Headquarters in Kansas City whose

Saudia Management

union rules permitted pilots to fly only 80 hours a month. TWA's Kansas City flight operations department was appalled when they found out what we were doing.

From my perspective the airline had to fly as much as it could to meet its responsibility to the Kingdom. When pilots were not flying they had nothing to do. They usually stayed home on the compound and fought with their wives or got drunk, or both. By keeping them busy flying ten to twelve hours a day they stayed out of trouble. The weather was always good, they got adequate rest every day or night, and there was no real safety concern. And finally, with our generous overtime pay scheme the pilots made a lot of money. For all of these good reasons I persisted with our heavy flying schedule and argued vociferously with Kansas City.

Kansas City sent out a survey team to see what else I was up to, and to impress on the Saudi Management the fact that my operating policies were "not in accordance with TWA standards." The team was under the leadership of Captain Exom, a typical tall, magnificent pilot affiliated with TWA's ALPA union. Captain Exom quickly reached an unfavorable impression of our operation and compliance disposition.

Our differences of opinion were aired in a conference with the Director General that was followed by a dinner and cocktail party at the D.G.'s home. Captain Exom, having perhaps partaken too copiously of Sheikh Suliman's Scotch whiskey, spoke disparagingly of the Saudi Nationals and the airline. The next morning at 6 A.M., he was awakened in his hotel, and his passport returned with his Saudi visa cancelled forever. He was escorted to the morning jet to Beirut and then on to Kansas City and home.

My relations with TWA's Kansas City staff and home office were never quite the same again. I remained determined to run the airline in the interests of safety, King Faisal and TWA – and in that order.

Making of a King

During 1964 the political pressure within the Kingdom of Saudi Arabia was increasing. On the one side were the followers and supporters of King Saud, the ruling monarch and second son of the legendary Desert King Ibn Saud, who built Saudi Arabia out of the wreckage of the Turkish Empire after World War I. On the other were the followers of several of his younger brothers and other relatives, more modern and liberal in their outlook. Each had their supporters among the Army, the Royal Family, the business community and the religious leaders.

Saudi Arabia is an absolute monarchy, ruled according to the Shirah, or

Islamic Law. Power is held by local leaders, princes and descendants of Ibn Saud (of whom there were many), local Emirs and Sheikhs, the Mutawa or religious police, and the Mullahs and ultimately devolved on the King himself, if matters ever got that high up the loose chain of command. While autocratic and absolute, without the benefit of Western type constitutional laws, lawyers and courts, the system worked and problems were solved. Minor criminals were given hearings, people with complaints or pleas for help or mercy could appear before the highest authority - ultimately the King himself - and be heard.

But by 1964 the old system on the national level had begun to break down. King Saud was incompetent and weak. His followers, hangers on, sons, and the loose band of adherents were corrupt beyond measure. Saudi Arabia was still a poor country. While ARAMCO was drilling and exporting oil from Dahran on the Arabian Gulf, the price was low (about $2.20 a barrel), the percentage paid to the Royal Treasury small, and the great oil fields had not yet been found. As this was about the only government revenue there was a chronic shortage of cash. King Saud used to make an annual pilgrimage to each of the desert sheikdoms making up the Kingdom, often traveling in "R-1," the DC-3 Saudi Arabian Airlines flew for the Royal Family and which was given to Ibn Saud at the end of World War II by President Roosevelt. The King dispensed bags of gold to the local chiefs. This comprised the "glue" which helped hold the loosely knit Kingdom together.

At the airline we found it difficult to get our bills paid. TWA was months in arrears receiving its management fees. Spare parts and overseas repairs were not paid until credit was shut off. Fuel credits were a problem outside the Kingdom, and other western businesses had the same problems. Efforts by the Finance Ministry under the direction of Prince Faisal, also a son of the "old King," Ibn Saud, were frustrated by the wasteful ways of King Saud and his extended family. Faisal was Western-educated (as were an increasing number of the younger princes and leaders in the Kingdom), and was trying to run the business affairs of the Kingdom properly.

Other leaders were frustrated as well. The military wanted more modern weapons and training. Businessmen needed foreign currency to expand commercial enterprises and imports. About the only unhampered import enterprise was the Cadillac Agency, run by the Zahid brothers, who brought two to three hundred new Cadillacs a year into the Kingdom for distribution to members of the Royal Family.

By the end of 1964, tensions between the followers of King Saud favoring the status quo, and of the more progressive faction loosely organized around Prince Faisal and his half-brother Prince Sultan, had reached the explosive point. The White Army, a Bedouin-based tribal army located in

Jeddah, supported the King while the Brown Army, containing the more modern units and located in and around the Capital, Riyadh, supported the Faisal faction. The streets were filled with rumors of impending civil war.

These events affected us at the airline. Our chairman, Jeddah businessman Achmed Jamjoon, supported the Royal Family and the King. Sheikh Suliman Romaih, the Director General and a taciturn desert Arab with roots among the people and the military, supported Faisal and the progressives. As the major transportation source in the Kingdom (there were only a few short railroads and no paved roads to speak of in the entire Kingdom), we knew that Saudi Arabian Airlines would have a part to play in whatever hostilities occurred. The fact that most of the pilots were Americans did not alter the fact that we were there in Arabia.

I maintained contact with the American Embassy during these times through Herb Ferguson, the Commercial Attaché, and Pete Hart, the Ambassador. Both were long time professionals in the Diplomatic Corps who kept me informed as I did them.

One mid-morning the phone rang on my desk at our airport offices. It was the Chairman, Jamjoon, speaking in his usual rapid-fire staccato style. "Mr. Beyer, please come to my office immediately!" "Yes, Your Excellency."

I woke up my driver, sleeping in the hallway, got into my Chevy station wagon and gave orders to be driven to the downtown Jeddah offices in the Bakashab Building, a shoddy six-story skyscraper housing the Arab administrative offices of the airline. Climbing to the third floor while sidestepping a few Moslems dutifully praying in the corridors, I entered Sheikh Jamjoon's waiting room, jammed as usual with local citizens and visitors attired in a mixture of Saudi galabiyas and/or western suits. I was immediately ushered into Jamjoon's luxurious office, with its multiple air conditioners, Persian rugs, opulent tapestries and gold trimmed furniture. Sheikh Jamjoon sat at a desk made more massive by his diminutive size, small ferret-like face and Arab headdress. He waved me to a big chair and ordered the half-dozen others in the room to leave – a sign of the extreme importance of our conversation.

"Mr. Beyer, you have heard of the trouble in Riyadh?"

I had.

"Mr. Beyer, we must save our King! Tonight we must move the White Army to Riyadh to save the King. I want all of the pilots to be ready. I want all of the airplanes to be prepared!"

"Your Excellency, I understand."

"Shokran."

"Masalamah."

"Salam Alakum."

I drove back to the airport and waited. In a few minutes the phone rang again. "Mort, this is Suliman." It was Sheikh Suliman Romaih, Director General of the airline. "Mort, you have talked to the Chairman?" I had. "I want you to come to my house. Come by yourself. Drive by the back ways to the side gate. It will be opened for you ..."

"Sheikh Suliman, I will be there in twenty minutes."

I got the Chevy keys from my driver and proceeded by the dusty, dirty unpaved side streets of Jeddah to Sheikh Suliman's walled compound on the northern outskirts by the sea. As I approached the great, black iron side gate, it slowly swung open and I drove in as it clanged shut behind me. A servant in dirty white galabiya showed me to the back entrance, where I climbed three flights of stairs to the living room.

It was a large room and very dark, with tapestries, rugs and over-large sofas and chairs. A bar covered part of one wall. The air conditioners whirred furiously, bringing the temperature down to about 70° – a contrast to the 100° outside. Suliman rose to meet me.

"Mort, would you like a drink?"

"Damn right!"

Suliman went to the bar, got two drinking glasses and filled them with Scotch, neat. He returned to the sofa and we sat down and sipped our drinks. Liquor was, of course, forbidden in Arabia. However, many of the richer, Westernized Arabs had their own sources and supplies. It tasted very good, and for several minutes we just sipped the Scotch and said nothing.

"Mort, the Chairman told you of the trouble in Riyadh? He told you to get all the airplanes ready and have all the pilots on the alert?"

"He did."

"Mort, all of the aircraft are broken, and all of the pilots are drunk..."

"Sheikh Suliman, I understand."

We finished our drinks in silence, I thanked him and drove back to the airport. Calling my assistant, Duane Busch, and Doral Hubbard, my maintenance manager, into the office, I directed them to organize a big party on the compound that night with plenty of Sadekie and steaks. I then directed Hubbard to decommission each aircraft as it came back to Jeddah that night by removing a propeller from one, a wheel from another, radios from a third, so that none could fly without these missing parts being re-installed, a job that would take several hours.

After a steak on the compound, and making sure that the party was well under way, I returned to my office. About 10 P.M. I heard the sound of many feet outside the windows and looked out to see the White Army shuffling by. Dressed in the native galabiyas dragging on the ground, with the Arab headdresses flowing, they were carrying camel sacks and were armed with 1879 Krag rifles. They were headed to the terminal to board their expected flights to Riyadh.

The phone rang. It was the Chairman. "Mr Beyer, Mr. Beyer! The Army is on the way to the airport."

"Yes, I know."

"Are all the aircraft ready? Are all the pilots on duty?"

"Your Excellency, I am sorry, but all the aircraft are broken and all the pilots are drunk."

"Aaaahhhheeeeeee..."

An hour later the regular Army units in Riyadh forced their way into the Palace and removed the King and his family. They were taken to the airport, where a Lufthansa B-707 awaited them. It had been on a scheduled flight from Bombay to Cairo, but one of the Saudi Hawker Hunters, flown by British mercenaries, had gone up and persuaded the German pilot to land at Riyadh to pick up some passengers desiring transportation out of the country. The Royal entourage was loaded on board and left the Kingdom, never to return.

Several days later the elders of the Kingdom elected Prince Faisal as the new King, and thus began an amazing and enlightened reign that was to have consequences for me as well as for TWA, the airline, and the Kingdom.

Shortly after Faisal became King there were organizational changes at the airline. Chairman Jamjoon was dismissed and replaced by Prince Sultan, newly appointed Minister of Defense and Aviation. Jamjoon's cadre of British advisors was also sacked.

Not long after installation of a new Board of Directors dominated by western-thinking businessmen, I was asked to have TWA present a proposal for a total TWA management contract for Saudi Arabian Airlines, replacing the narrow Technical Service contract which we had previously held.

Some six months later TWA's U.S. headquarters sent a survey team to review the airline. This group did not see eye to eye with my policies of operating the airline according to local customs and for the benefit of the Saudis, and attempted to impose TWA rules and regulations designed for a union-dominated U.S. airline on the Saudi Arabians. The group went back to New York and recommended to TWA's senior management that I be replaced. I was recalled to New York.

I entered Chairman Charles Tillinghast's office on schedule. He leapt from his chair, outrage spread across his face.

"Jesus Christ, Beyer, why didn't you tell us about this?"

"About what?"

"Goddammit, what you DID over there."

"What do you mean?"

Slowly, between gasps of rage, it came out. The previous day two gentlemen wearing trench coats and snap brim hats had arrived unannounced at Tillinghast's office and asked to be permitted to see him briefly. When queried about what, they showed their identifications and were ushered immediately into his office.

"Mr. Tillinghast, we understand you are recalling Mr. Beyer from Saudi Arabia."

"Yes, we certainly are. Tomorrow!"

"Well, Mr. Tillinghast, we wished to advise you that your action would not be in the best interests of the United States of America ..."

I stayed in Saudi Arabia for another two and a half years.

Under the reorganization of the airline following the accession of King Faisal I won a total management contract for TWA to run every department. Sheikh Suliman assumed full responsibility as Director General and Prince Sultan, the Minister of Defense and Aviation, became Chairman of the Board. I was named Deputy General Director and General Manager and new TWA executives were brought in to head all commercial, financial and administrative duties.

Under our new and expanded responsibilities we hastened the development of Saudia's route system to India, Pakistan, Italy, France and London. Minor routes included Iran, Iraq, Syria, Ethiopia, Sudan and more. This expansion has continued over the years since and today Saudia is the seventeenth largest airline in the world, serving thirty-seven nations with a fleet of a hundred jet aircraft.

We also entered IATA, the International Air Transport Association, and its related financial clearinghouse. Saudi Arabian membership in ICAO, the International Civil Aviation Association, was also sought. All Saudi Arabian operations and maintenance were brought into accordance with the requirements of the United States Federal Aviation Administration, including flight operations and maintenance. The FAA approved our manuals and procedures, and checked out our Saudi National pilots. This brought Saudia's entire operation up to the highest international standards, no longer subject to the whims of princes and politicians.

Over the years as Saudia operations grew, and as the programs that we had instituted took hold, TWA's influence receded and, finally, the last vestiges of the Management Contract were terminated in the early 1980s. We had indeed done our job.

*1965 Tillinghast
arrives in Jeddah*

TWA Chairman Tillinghast's Trip to Arabia

TWA had held a technical management contract with Saudi Arabia for sixteen years but a senior executive of the airline had never visited the Kingdom. So early in my assignment I began working to persuade TWA's Chairman, Charles Tillinghast, to come to Jeddah to visit the airline and pay his respects to the Saudi management and the King. The American Ambassador, Pete Hart, also provided support. In the spring of 1966 it was arranged that Tillinghast would come.

We had already won a total management contract following King Faisal's elevation to the throne and the dismissal of the previous chairman Achmed Jamjoon and his British Advisors, and were expanding our routes into Europe. TWA's new managers for marketing, finance and administration, along with their staffs were already in place. Saudi Arabian Airlines was becoming an increasingly important part of TWA's overseas operations.

Charlie Tillinghast was a courtly Wall Street financier who had been recruited to run TWA following the ouster of Howard Hughes. He had brought improved profits to the company and a down-to-earth management style in sharp contrast to mercurial Mr. Hughes.

I selected Don Logan, newly seconded to us by TWA to run Administration at Saudia, to organize the Tillinghast visit. He arranged a schedule that included the Saudia Board, a meeting with the US Ambassador, discussions with our TWA employees and, of course, an audience with King Faisal.

On his arrival Tillinghast was carefully coached on the affairs of the airline and the local social customs. In Arabia it is extremely bad form to point the soles of ones feet at another person. The feet are considered unclean and presenting the soles of your Floresheims to an Arab is a mortal sin. Tillinghast was carefully coached to keep his feet flat on the floor when having his audience with the King.

As Tillinghast's visit approached I developed a case of laryngitis, and by arrival date could do little more than croak and whisper – a horribly frustrating situation under the circumstances. Don Logan had to take over – which he did well for the entire trip – while I stood by mutely.

As the audience with the King approached, Don once again briefed Mr. Tillinghast on the proper form in addressing the King: "Your Majesty." Speak when you are spoken to, and keep your feet on the floor.

But once in the throne room and under the King's interested questions, Tillinghast grew increasingly effusive and enthusiastic – waving his arms for

The Signing Ceremony

emphasis and, finally, crossing his legs and shining the sole of his shoe directly in the King's face. We cringed in embarrassment, tugging vainly at Tillinghast's sleeve, only to have the King wave us off with a smile while he let Tillinghast finish his colloquy.

The visit was highly successful, and a few months later Tillinghast called Don Logan back from Jeddah to become Assistant to the Chairman in New York.

My voice returned slowly.

Saudi Days

Living in Saudi Arabia was a unique experience for the family and me. The two girls, Barbara and Nancy, were too old for the school (up to grade 8) that I ran for children of the TWA group and other Western children. The

*1966 Jimbo at an
Embassy party*

Dinner in a Saudi home

principal was hired by TWA and the teachers were selected from the wives of other employees. So Barbara and Nancy were sent off to a succession of boarding schools in Switzerland, Holland, Beirut and the U.S. They flew in and out and halfway around the world by themselves, developing a great sense of independence. The two boys, Jim and Will, attended our TWA school.

The kids loved life in Jeddah – the trips to the desert and flights to exotic places. We had a small cabin on The Creek, an estuary off the Red Sea some twenty miles above Jeddah. It was reached by driving over open desert. The snorkeling off the reef was great, as was the fishing for tuna, barracuda and wahoo – all fish similar to those found in Florida. All four children picked up conversational Arabic quickly and could bargain with shopkeepers and travel on the Four Gersch (about 5¢), brightly painted and gaudily decorated mini buses that meandered through the city.

Virtually all of the TWA staff drove relatively new Cadillacs. This was not the result of good pay but rather the result of a custom adopted by the Royal Family As I have mentioned before, the progeny of the extended Royal Family‘ received a new Cadillac every year.. These vehicles were driven hard, usually over the open desert since there were no paved roads outside the cities – except between Jeddah and Mecca, Medina and Taif, the summer capital high in the mountains. Even to Riyadh, the capital, one either flew or took the twenty lane superhighway, a track across the open desert between Jeddah and Riyadh, some four hundred miles. So at the end of one year the Royal Cadillacs were usually somewhat worse for wear when the princes got their annual new vehicles and gave the old ones to favored servants. Many of these servants did not drive and were happy to sell the autos to the TWA staff for 5,000 Riyals – about $1,100.

It was a common sight to see Arab men walking down the streets holding hands – an established custom and not a homosexual relationship. But it did give new visitors to the Kingdom a bit of pause at first. Also, the Arab men's customary greeting was kissing each other, and in the days before Arafat became a household TV sight, this too created consternation among our guests from the home

1965 Tillinghast arrives in Jeddah

office. Finally, the Arab sign of greeting, instead of a "howdy" or a wave, was what seemed to be an obscene gesture with the middle finger extended and the hand moved vertically in an "up yours" motion. It all took some getting used to.

Early on when I first arrived in Jeddah, Westerners were hesitant to drive their own cars as, in the event of an accident resulting in death, the Arabic penalty was execution on the spot of the driver at fault – an eye for an eye was the law of the land. But early on the King believed that they were losing too many good drivers, so he modified the penalty to an indemnity system. The driver at fault paid 16,000 Riyals (about $3,500) if he killed another Saudi, and 12,000 Riyals if he killed a Muslim from another country. These penalties were doubled in the holy months of Ramadan and Hadj, with much lower penalties for killing camels, sheep or goats. The penalty for killing a Christian was 10 Riyals.

The Saudi culture believed in direct action. Many citizens loved loud horns in their cars, an effect achieved by hooking up a six-volt horn to the

12-volt electrical system common in most cars. The result was a cacophony of auto horns that deafened pedestrians and home dwellers alike. This noise offended the King, who had two palaces on the Mecca and Medina roads, in front of which were roundabouts. One morning as we were driving to the Creek for the day, we noted a dozen soldiers stationed on the roundabout, each armed with enormous bolt cutters. Any car that sounded its horn as it rounded the curve was halted, the hood thrown open and the horns amputated and thrown on a growing pile in the middle of the circle. By the time we returned that evening the pile of horns was several feet high. Jeddah was a much quieter town after that

The Yemeni War

Yemen was a small Arab kingdom located at the southwest corner of the Arabian peninsula, surrounding the British port of Aden.

From 1964 to 1967, a war raged in North Yemen between the Royalists and liberal factions supported by Egypt. Saudi Arabia backed the Royalists, much the same as the U.S. intervention on behalf of Saigon in Viet Nam. Saudi Arabian Airlines played a key role in the Saudi campaign to sustain the Royalist cause - all entirely unknown to TWA in its ivory towers in New York City.

Saudia's activities were almost entirely logistical. We flew munitions and equipment to Yemen through the airports close to Yemen primarily in the southwestern corner of the Arabian peninsula at Nejran and Khamis Mashet, using our DC-6A and DC-3 cargo aircraft. We brought in guns and ammunition for the Royalists and carried out casualties.

The Egyptians were infinitely better armed and equipped than the Yemenis, with tanks, armored cars, and scores of MiG fighter bombers from Moscow. But as so often happens in war, tactics and morale outweighed equipment ten to one. The Egyptian generals sent their columns up the dry wadis and riverbeds seeking Yemeni insurgents. The Yemenis, equipped with 1879 Krag rifles and hand-made explosives, waited behind boulders and scarce trees. As the tanks lumbered by, they would spray them with rifle fire, jump on top, whip off their turbans, and stuff them down the exhaust pipes. Soon the tanks would stall and the acrid fumes from the engines would drive the Egyptians out where the Yemenis lopped off their heads with their tribal swords, or lobbed plastic explosives down into the open turret.

The Egyptians soon lost all appetite for this kind of warfare and turned to their superior air power (the Yemenis had none). Prince Badr, one of the Royalist leaders, had a palace a few miles from Nejeran on the southern border that he refused to leave, claiming he was protected by Allah. For more than a year the Egyptians bombed the Palace almost daily, tearing up the desert for nearly a mile in every direction. However, the Prince was right. They never hit the buildings and the Palace and the Prince inside were unscathed.

Toward the end of the hostilities the Egyptians turned to more violent means, using poison gas to attack the Yemenis. At one point they managed to kill a herd of sheep. The Yemenis demanded that the United Nations investigate this atrocity. The U.N. requested that the sheep be delivered to Jeddah for clinical examination. Saudia was requested to send a DC-3 to Nejeran to pick up the dead sheep and bring them back for examination. We assigned a Saudi crew to go get them and they departed the next morning. Arriving in Nejeran, they were revolted by the stench of the rotting sheep that were now several days old, and refused to transport them. Because of their refusal I had to assign two American pilots to complete the task. I gave them gas masks. They flew to Nejeran that afternoon and returned in a few hours with the putrefying carcasses of the animals. After tests were completed the U.N. examiners concluded that the Egyptians had indeed committed a grave breech of international law by using poison gas.

Throughout my entire stay in Arabia the Yemeni War was a minor but constant element of our existence. While we were Americans with no official responsibility, we were nevertheless there and responsible for "doing the necessary" in support of the Kingdom. And so we flew a veritable Saudi Military Airlift Command, without official sanction from either the U.S. Government or TWA, in support of the Yemeni Royalists. In a few years the Egyptians had had a belly full, like the Americans in Viet Nam, and they left. The Yemenis sorted things out for themselves for the time being and Saudia's role diminished to one of technical and marketing support for Yemen Airlines, their national carrier.

Arabian Justice

Saudi Arabian justice was swift and severe, and surprisingly effective. Shortly after our arrival one of the Princes of the Royal Family had attended a party at one of the Embassies. He had become drunk and raped the wife of the Consul. The next day the King sent a messenger offering the aggrieved lady a choice: his son's head on a plate, or an invitation to leave the Kingdom and enjoy a lifetime pension of $50,000 a year. She left.

Common thievery was still punishable by amputating the right hand (the left hand was used for bodily cleansing and thus was considered unclean). This was performed surgically, with antiseptics and bandages. Rape, murder and crimes against the State (including unionism) were punishable by beheading. In cases of rape or murder, a member of the aggrieved family was permitted to perform the beheading. This often proved difficult and required repeated hacks with the sword. All executions were performed in the Souk in Saturday, with the criminal kneeling with his head toward Mecca. The public was invited.

Stoning was the fate of prostitutes. Only one such incident happened during my stay in Jeddah. A hole was dug about four feet deep and the woman placed in it while the hole was filled up to her waist. The multitude of watchers was then invited to stone her. There were street vendors selling bags of nice sized rocks for one Riyal a bag. On this instance the King pardoned the unfortunate woman at the last moment.

Occasionally we had robberies in the TWA community, usually performed by third national houseboys seeking to supplement their incomes. In a typical instance a house was ransacked and radios, furniture, silverware and jewelry were stolen. The Jeddah police were notified. They investigated and, a few days later, turned up with the loot and the houseboy. When asked, "how did you do it?" the Chief of Police answered simply, "He confessed."

My son Will and another boy were exploring an abandoned house located on the mud flats in front of Jeddah on the Red Sea. Once inside they were attacked by an Arab, and the other boy – a roly-poly youth – was violated by the Arab. They ran home to report and soon the police appeared to get the facts. Will asked:

"Dad, what should I tell the police?"

"Tell them the truth," I told him.

"Well, Dad, his dad has told him to identify whoever they bring in, but he and I are not so sure they have the right man."

"Well, you tell them exactly what you think."

"OK, Dad."

The next morning Will, his friend, his dad and I all appeared at the Jeddah Jail and were taken to the office of General Shaheebe, the Chief of Police. The Jeddah Jail was indeed an unpleasant place where one would not wish to be confined. A wretched looking young man clad in a dirty galabiya was dragged in and pinned against the wall by two guards. The General began his interrogation:

"Is that the man who buggered you?"

"Yes, General, that sure looks like him. He did it."

"William, is that the man who buggered your friend?"

"Well, General, we talked about it, and the man says he is innocent. What happens if I am sure that he did it?"

"We will torture him until he confesses."

"And what happens if we are not sure?"

"Then we will torture him not so much."

We left, and a few days later saw the wretch standing on a street corner looking somewhat worse for wear. Evidently they had tortured him not quite so much and let him go. Had he been found guilty he would have been beheaded and the boy's dad would have gotten the job.

The Arabs were a very law abiding group by nature and had a very religious upbringing. We never had the slightest reluctance to walk alone at night or visit the darkest streets of the Souk.

The Secret Service was very effective. One night Barbara was at a party at the Embassy in the company of a young American businessman who had been visiting various companies in Jeddah during the day. He was making sarcastic remarks about the Saudi system, so Barbara introduced him to a young Prince who was in charge of the Jeddah District Secret Service. She explained to the Prince that her escort was making disparaging comments about the efficiency of the police. The Prince said: "Mr. Johnson, would you like to know what you did today? Yes? Well at 7:15A.M. you had breakfast at the Haramain Hotel, left at eight to go to the offices of the Zahid brothers where you stayed for an hour and a half before going to the British Embassy. Then you went to the United Arab Bank for lunch." Mr. Johnson was humbled. The Saudis knew all that they wanted or needed to about the activities of foreigners in the Kingdom.

Showdown

As TWA's staff grew under our new contract, I was anxious to strengthen our Flight Operations Department and to accelerate the training of the young Saudi National pilots. Earl Drew, whom I had known from the Congo operations with Air Ventures and Airlift, was now in Beirut as Operations Manager of Lebanese International Airlines. I thought it would be appropriate to recruit him to help me in Jeddah. He joined us a few weeks later and quickly set about speeding up training and implementing the programs necessary to bring Saudia into full compliance with FAA, ICAO and IATA programs.

Earl was ambitious and a consummate politician, eager to improve his status and position within the airline. I wanted the pilots to progress rapidly but safely, from positions as DC-3 and Convair copilots to captains, but was cautious not to overreach since most of these young men had only minimum flight time and no command experience. Drew was more aggressive and had identified more and more with the most militant of the young pilots and their desire for promotion.

I was away from Jeddah for ten days in Europe and the States. Upon my return Bill Clark, one of my trusted associates, met me at the plane. He advised me that Earl Drew had taken over and was sitting at my desk. Since it was already evening I elected to go straight home. I planned to show up at the office early in the morning – which I did – before Drew arrived.

When Earl sauntered in he was surprised to see me at "his" desk, and proceeded to tell me that he had taken over and that he had the support of the pilots, both American and Saudi. He was implementing a more aggressive program of advancement for the pilots. He claimed also to have the agreement of the Board of Directors and the Director General of the Civil Aviation Division, Sheikh Kamil Sindi.

I told Drew that we would see about that, and handed him a letter of resignation that I had prepared that morning for his signature, and demanded that he sign it. Evidently believing that he had the necessary backing from the

pilots and, through them, the Saudi management, he defiantly signed the letter and threw it back at me.

I took the letter and called Sheikh Suliman Romaih, the Director General, and asked him for an appointment later that afternoon. When I arrived at his office

Heil shepherds

there was a large number of Saudi pilots packed inside. One could hear them roaring from way down the hall. When I got to his office he invited me in and asked the pilots to leave. We talked and I explained the background of the situation as I saw it – my concern over too early advancement of the young pilots and the self-appointed promotion of Earl Drew. Sheikh Suliman quietly took Earl's letter of resignation and scrawled "APPROVED" over the face of it. He then called the Administrative Department and ordered them to arrange for Drew's departure on the Boeing jet the next morning.

I returned to the office and had my assistant Duane Busch set up a general meeting of the Saudi and TWA personnel for that afternoon, where I explained our actions. I then advised TWA in New York that they could expect a visit from Earl Drew in a few days.

Irrigation project at a Saudi Farm

Desert Trek

When the UNYOM (United Nations Yemen Observation Mission) left Jeddah, they sold me their Jeep and gave me their remaining supply of Scotch and gin - both welcome donations. We also hired their Sudanese man-servant/cook and his son. The Jeep was handy for weekend trips to the Creek north of Jeddah and for forays into the desert around Jeddah.

One July day my two sons, Jim and Will, and a young friend of theirs, Glenn, planned an all-day trip to the mountains east of Jeddah. We stocked the Jeep with food, water, a rifle and other miscellaneous supplies and equipment. I checked the gas gauge, which pronounced the tank "FULL." We set off at 8 A.M., soon leaving the roads for the camel tracks over the desert - between the dunes, over the hills and down the ravines. By 10 A.M., we were well into an utterly barren, desolate, treeless wasteland.

Then the Jeep stopped. A check of the gas tank showed the gauge had lied - it was empty! We were at least twenty miles from the nearest road, which we knew lay somewhere to the south of us - the Jeddah-Mecca highway.

We faced a choice; pitch a tent and wait for someone from the airline to come looking for us - possible twenty-four hours hence - or walk out. I talked it over with the boys and we elected to walk. We took five gallons of water in a large can and set out south.

We could maintain a rudimentary southbound course by watching the sun, just like the navigators of old. But we were often forced to detour around huge dunes – nothing is more tiring than walking through sand – and avoiding sudden hilly ridges and deep wadis (gulches). Every half-hour we stopped to rest for five minutes and take a few ounces of water each. Then we pressed on.

As the sun rose toward mid-afternoon, the temperature increased to well above 110°. Only an occasional hot puff of a breeze provided relief. But the boys kept going. We didn't have the energy to talk but did enough to keep each other's spirits up. Once we passed an Arab walking in the opposite direction and asked him for directions:

"Marhaba, Kiefhalak?" (Hello, how are you?)

"Fain Al Tarik Al Kabir?" (Where is the big road?)

He points in the direction we are going.

"Kam Saah?" (How many hours?)

"Katir." (Many)

"Kam?" (How Many?)

"Mumkin Khamssa." (Perhaps five)

With this not too encouraging word we pushed on. The sun slowly moved downward toward the Red Sea, and about six o'clock in the evening we crested a hill to see the Mecca Road a mile or so ahead of us, streaming with cars. It was a welcome sight. We gulped our last water and set out at a brisk pace. Twenty minutes later we were hitchhiking toward Jeddah. A tanker truck driven by an Arab stopped and we piled into a crowded cab. I explained our destination: the Aramco Compound on the Mecca Road. The driver understood and chattered away in Arabic that we only partially understood. The boys were better at street Arabic than I by this time. The 25 miles back to Jeddah went fast enough.

When we walked into the house we were greeted with worried glances and questions. The airline had been alerted but had not sent out any rescue parties. We were glad not to have caused too much of a stir, but we were also glad we were missed.

The boys and I all headed for the shower, plenty of ice water and bed. I think I lost 10 pounds that day. I'm sure the boys held up better.

The next day the maintenance staff drove out to the stranded Jeep and brought it back in. We had buried the gun, wrapped in a blanket, and parked the Jeep over it. The footprints of the dozens of local Arabs who had visited our Jeep during the twenty-four hours it sat there – filled with our supplies- surrounded our Jeep. But true to Bedouin honesty, nothing had been touched and everything was recovered.

The Farisan Islands

The Farisan Islands lie off the West Coast of Saudi Arabia, in the Red Sea, just north of Gizan. For hundreds of years they were used as the Arab's "Devil's Island," a dumping ground for unwanted criminals whose crimes were too serious to overlook but not serious enough to merit execution. Several thousand people lived on the half-dozen islands of the group, totally dependent on their own resources for food and the other necessities of life.

Daniel Ludwig was the 70-year-old owner of a billion-dollar shipping and resource development company. He had poured tens of millions of dollars into unsuccessful rubber development in the Amazon, and specialized in the mining and importation of salt and other minerals to the U.S. One day his emissary showed up in Jeddah and asked to charter one of our DC-3s for a trip to the Farisans. Since his financial credentials were acceptable, we provided a plane under the command of Captain Bob Wells and Bob McDougal for the flight. It was on a weekend, so the boys and I went along, as well as Shorty Davis, a geologist.

We flew south along the coast, watching the ever-changing scenery. About 250 miles below Jeddah, off Marsa Hali, there was an Italian submarine sunk in about 300 feet of water. From our cruise altitude we could see clearly her outlines on the white sand bottom, and only speculate on how she met her fate in World War II.

Arriving over the Farisans – which had no airport – we slowly cruised up and down the island group, surveying the terrain and looking at the beaches. Finally Captain Wells lined up with a long white beach, put wheels and flaps down full, and glided to a perfect landing on the hard sand. No sooner did we roll to a stop than a Jeep full of Saudi police appeared. Ludwig's shipping official engaged them in conversation, explaining that our mission was to look for signs of oil seepage and salt outcroppings that his company was interested in developing. This mystified them greatly, but the production of a long parchment scroll, covered with green writing and the gold seals of the House of Saud convinced them that we were serious. So Ludwig's man, the boys and I piled into the Jeep for a tour of the largest island, leaving Captain Wells and McDougal to guard the plane.

An hour's tour of the Farisans was a remarkable experience. Roads were mere two-rut Jeep trails. Houses were built of stone, with palm-thatched roofs. Small agricultural plots supplied the natives with food, along with scores of goats. We were surprised by the industry, neatness and orderliness of this community despite its isolation from the mainland and the world.

An hour of driving produced little evidence of either oil or salt, and so we returned to the DC-3, climbed aboard, thanked our hosts and left. We taxied out to the end of the beach and, using the packed sand as a runway, were soon airborne and away.

Over the years we flew other expeditions for Mr. Ludwig, but never any as interesting as the trip to the Farisans

Flight to Addis Abbaba

TWA also had a management contract with Ethiopian Airlines on the other side of the Red Sea. In the 1960s the Ethiopians were far more technically advanced than Saudis. We signed a contract with them to overhaul some of our engines in preference to sending them to Europe for servicing. The Saudis resented any invidious comparisons and there was always some friction between the two carriers.

We carried our engines back and forth from Jeddah to Addis on our DC-6 cargo/passenger aircraft, and occasionally some of our Saudi managers and I went along to talk contract with our counterparts in Addis.

On one flight in 1966 we arrived in Addis Abbaba shortly after Emperor Haile Selassie had put down a coup attempt by an element of the Army led by the Emperor's eldest son. The crackdown had been quite severe with several hundred mutineers hanged or fed to the pride of lions that the Emperor kept on his palace grounds for reasons of security From the hotel across the street one could hear them roaring in the night.

As we drove down the autopista from the airport to the city, we noticed what appeared to be scarecrows - often with vultures perched on their shoulders - dangling from each of the tall light posts that lined the roadway. Upon inquiry about this strange phenomenon we were advised that they were the bodies of the hanged mutineers. The Emperor's son was spared and sent to Europe to improve his mind.

Voyage of the MAVIS II

I was relieved of duty as General Manager of Saudia by TWA in April 1967. The change had become increasingly obvious as TWA sought to exert its control over Saudia, and I continued to press for the development of the desert Kingdom's airline for its own citizens. Finally TWA's Chief Financial Officer in Saudi, Larry Staley, advised me that Lou Geiser was being sent out to take my place. Geiser was a maintenance supervisor from Kansas City without appreciable credentials in the field of managing foreign airline enterprises. I talked with my friend Suliman Romeh the Director General. He advised me to accept the situation, which I did.

For almost a year I had planned to buy a cabin cruiser and bring it to Jeddah. I looked at boats in the U.S., but finally ordered a new Ancas Queen built in Norway and powered by two inboard/outboard GM/Volvo V-6 engines. In November 1966 the boat was loaded on a ship bound for Aden on the Southern tip of the Arabian Peninsula. In Rotterdam a careless crane operator dropped 20 tons of steel girders on it, crushing the hull. The boat went back to Oslo for repairs.

In the meantime, the political situation in Aden deteriorated. Local Nationalist forces fought with the British for control of the port city. I planned to have the boat delivered in Djibouti instead, a French enclave on the Horn of Africa across the Red Sea. But the Norwegians had no boats headed for Djibouti, so the cabin cruiser was scheduled for delivery to Aden anyhow.

The boat, christened MAVIS II, was due to arrive in Aden by deck freight in mid-April 1967. I organized a crew consisting of my youngest son William, wife Jane, Frank Williams (a TWA mechanic working in Jeddah) and Don Logan (now assistant to TWA Chairman Charles Tillinghast) who flew over to help crew the voyage).

We left Jeddah the afternoon I was terminated by TWA, flying Middle East Airlines to Aden. We landed at the Aden airport to find it closely guarded by British soldiers. Rolls of concertina wire circled the buildings. Machine gun nests in sandbagged revetments were manned at all corners of the facilities. We got a taxi and were whisked to the Aden Roc Hotel near the port entrance. We registered and went up to our room overlooking the harbor and a small park. A bottle of Scotch was broken out and we were all sitting around on the veranda when there was a sudden "BOOM" a hundred yards down the road at a bus stop. Sirens screamed and British soldiers drove up in Rovers and ambulances. The next morning we learned ten people had been killed in the bomb explosion just below us.

The British occupied the buildings across from the Aden Roc, which they had covered with chicken wire. This prevented bombs from being thrown through the windows. British children driven to and from school were moved in armored buses covered with wire again. These buses were led and followed by Land Rovers equipped with machine guns and driven by British soldiers, twenty thousand of whom occupied Aden.

The next morning we were advised by the shipping agent that our boat had arrived and that we had to come down to his office in "the Crater" of Aden – a native quarter that was the center of the civil uprising and considered too dangerous for Europeans to go into. We went anyway, and there we found this lovely Brit (acting as our Agent) who had made his life in Aden, in his little Customs office.

Over the next few days we got our papers cleared, supervised the unloading of the boat onto the dock and hired a crane to lower it into the harbor.

Fuel was brought quayside, and with tanks filled we performed initial sea trials that went well. The boat was fast, clean and seaworthy. Two 55-gallon drums were found and secured on both sides of the cockpit to hold the extra fuel we would need to reach Assab on the Ethiopian coast, our first planned stop.

We met the Saudi Arabian Airlines agent, a young Adenese, with a Volksvagen van clearly marked with the Airline name. As the days passed, he drove us back and forth to the hotel, the docks, the port authorities and the ship's chandlers where we bought supplies for our voyage.

Supplies were endless; rope (lines), cooking implements, crockery, cutlery, staples, cases of wine and booze, spices, the list went on and on. I acquired a compass and two-way radio from the airline and these were hooked up. A small Zodiac was purchased and tied down on the foredeck, along with life vests. Fishing rods, hooks and lures were placed. A final sea trial was next.

It was a bright, sunny morning as we cast off and cruised out the mouth of the Aden harbor into the Indian Ocean. The water was calm so we tried various speeds and maneuvers. All went well and we turned toward the harbor well satisfied with our preparations. At three-quarters throttle, about 2,400 RPM, MAVIS II was comfortably on the step at about 20 knots. Suddenly there was a heavy thump and one engine stopped. Smoke billowed from the engine room, but there was no fire. We limped back into the harbor to survey the damage.

The entire top of the engine was split open, revealing broken camshafts and valves. The basic block, pistons, cylinder and crankshaft appeared okay. Volvo had an agent in Aden who was summoned to the quayside, along with two native mechanics – none of whom had ever seen engines such as those installed in our boat. Williams, an aircraft mechanic, began to disassemble the top of the engine, removing broken parts. Using the engine parts manual we were able to prepare a list of what we required for repairs and immediately had the agent cable Volvo in Stockholm to airfreight us the needed parts.

Surprisingly, they did so, and two days later the material arrived at Aden airport on Middle East Airlines. The two Arab mechanics and Williams began rebuilding an engine they had never seen – without the benefit of a repair manual. Through trial and error the job was finally accomplished, and the engine started without a problem on the first try. We let it idle throughout the night to test and run it in. In the morning we set to sea.

Reaching the open ocean we changed course to the west along the

Yemen coast, headed for the Bab el Mendabh, the entrance to the Red Sea. Comfortably on the step at 20 knots we hoped to reach Perrin Light, a massive lighthouse in the middle of the Bab el Mendabh in four hours, then Assab, Ethiopia six hours later. It was not to be. An hour out the second engine blew up just as the first one had.

We faced a choice: continue on the one remaining engine that we had just rebuilt, or go back to Aden where open revolution had exploded the previous night according to our radio, tuned to local Aden stations. Don Logan had left us just before we sailed, unable to stay for the voyage due to the delay caused by the loss of our first engine. He made it to the airport on the floor of the Saudi VW bus and departed on MEA's last flight before the airport was shut down.

We decided to go back and limped into the harbor and back to our anchorage behind the rusty old Ethiopian coastal freighter loading at the dock. The Donatella, as she was called, had been built in Liverpool in 1915 and now plied the Arabian Gulf and Red Sea supplying the riffraff ports of the region. She belonged to an Italian Captain who had survived the Ethiopian wars and now lived in Massawa, Eritrea – once an Italian colony but now incorporated into Ethiopia (Eritrea has subsequently won its independence from Ethiopia).

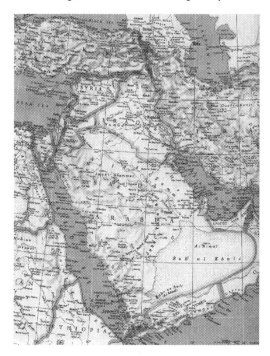

Aden was aflame. Clouds of smoke from burning houses and facilities hung over the city. The crump of artillery and the stutter of machine guns could be heard all too plainly as the British garrison battled the revolutionaries. We wondered if we had made a wise choice.

Loading of the Donatella stopped as the Adenese port workers abandoned their posts. While British gunboats patrolled the harbor we were concerned that we might suffer a local attack. So we got out our two American flags for prominent display (in those days Americans were still relatively well liked in the region). Captain Gepetto, sensing our distress, offered to let us tie up alongside the Donatella rather than at our exposed position beside the dock. We gladly accepted.

As sundown came, Captain Gepetto appeared at the rail above us to invite us aboard, brandishing a bottle and shouting, "Cognac! Spaghetti! Vino!" We all eagerly clambered up the iron ladder on the ship's side to partake of the Italian's hospitality. For the next ten days we did this often, usually supplying the cognac from our stores and enjoying the delicious spaghetti and wine from the Donatella's larder.

There was nothing to do but wait out the war on the shore. The battle intensified as one local group of revolutionaries slew the three sons of the leader of the other faction and started a three-way war with the British. Sniping, bombing and artillery were used against the British strong points and patrols, and hourly bulletins were issued over the radio. Our Saudi agent braved all of this to visit us daily, bringing water, food, needed supplies, and more cognac. We waited.

The Donatella was going to sail for Assab and Massawa as soon as she could be loaded. This would hopefully occur when (and if) the troubles died down. I met with the Captain to negotiate a tow to Massawa since there was little merit in trying it on our own, and little chance to repair the second engine. For $250 he agreed to tow us from Aden to Massawa where, hopefully, we could get repairs or a further tow to Jeddah.

After five days the battles on the shore subsided and a modicum of peace was restored. The dockworkers came back and finished loading the Donatella. The next morning we both cast off and set to sea, with MAVIS II trailing the Donatella out of the harbor on one engine in order to avoid questions about maritime law and local regulations. Once outside the harbor we threw the tow line aboard the Donatella and set out at a stately five knots for the Bab el Mendabh, Assab and Massawa.

It was a beautiful day and there was a light breeze from the southeast, so we broke out our fishing rods to catch a midday meal. Fish were plentiful – wahoo, tuna, dolphin. The Donatella's cook was also fishing, with his lure dragging alongside our boat. So we snagged his line and loaded it up with two fish at a time, leaving him to bemusedly haul them aboard to feed his crew.

Seviche is a Peruvian dish consisting of raw fish marinated in fresh limejuice. The fish are cut in small squares and allowed to soak for an hour or two in the limejuice and then eaten. It is possible to survive for weeks on seviche alone, and during our two weeks traveling up the Red Sea we had plenty.

As evening came the Donatella turned north to head into the straits of the Bab el Mendabh. The wind had been rising in late afternoon and now increased to a Force Eight gale with huge breaking whitecaps rising behind us and carrying the MAVIS II forward under the stern of the Donatella. The two ropes fell slack and our little cruiser turned sideways in the troughs between the waves. Then the next wave swept the Donatella forward and the towline snapped taut, jerking MAVIS II back on course. Would the ¾" nylon rope break, or pull the fittings out of our hull? The long nylon towrope was actually quite elastic, so it was able to absorb what would have otherwise been a severe shock to the structure. I started our single remaining engine to offset the effects of the huge waves.

It is a phenomenon of the seas known as the Venturi effect that when a strait of water passes between two land masses, especially of any height, winds tend to increase sharply. This is what happened to us in Bab el Mendabh. We had no idea how bad it could get, but it did. The strait is marked with a huge lighthouse on Perrin Island, with a beam that can be seen for twenty miles or more, sweeping great arcs through the darkness. Inside Perrin Island is a small sheltered lagoon and it was tempting indeed to just cut loose and make a run for Perrin as the seas grew worse and poured over the rear deck of MAVIS II.

But we stuck it out and as we passed the gates of el Mendabh the winds moderated. The sea this night was also filled with great tankers and occasional container freighters heading in and out of the Red Sea on the route between Suez and the Arabian Gulf.

Morning found us in the Red Sea headed for Assab, Eritrea. We reached Assab the following day. Untied from the Donatella, we entered the Assab harbor under our own power and not as a "prize of the sea" as we would have been under tow. We cleared Customs and Immigration much to the bemusement of the authorities who evidently had never seen a small American yacht so far from home.

Awaiting the Donatella's putting to sea again, we walked the streets of Assab, finding an icehouse where a local Abyssinian sold 50-pound blocks of the dirtiest ice I had ever seen. We bought one block and lugged it back aboard to preserve our fish and cool our drinks. Also, we were introduced to Dongolo Water, a local natural sparkling water that came from a cave in the mountains above Assab. Most water used in drinks has the effect of diluting the flavor and taste of beverages, but Dongolo Water had an entirely opposite effect. It enhanced the flavor of scotch, bourbon or wine. Even mixed ten-to-one it gave you the impression that you were drinking straight alcohol. We hired a local bearer to carry several cases back to the boat.

Our immediate objective was to find another tow to Jeddah, another five hundred miles up and on the other side of the Red Sea. Since our surviving engine was doing nicely we would even have settled for a tow to Port Sudan on the west shore of the Red Sea opposite Jeddah. From there we could take a run across the Red Sea under our own power. But no ships could be found that were going our way or that would take us. Nor were any freighters going to Jeddah that could carry our boat as deck freight because it was the Hadj. An enormous ocean liner loaded with some two thousand Hadjis made port while we were in Massawa, but that was not much help either.

Sleeping accommodations on the MAVIS II were cramped, but adequate. Will and Frank shared a "V" shaped bunk in the cabin forward, and Jane and I a double bunk in the main cabin that also contained the lavatory. Cooking was conducted topside in a galley fueled with bottled gas, but meals were served on a table in the main cabin. Our two auxiliary 55-gallon drums of gasoline sat forward in the cockpit - one on each side. Fortunately, they did not leak, as Jane was a prodigious smoker. A leak or puncture would have had unfortunate consequences! We decided to tie the MAVIS II up, lock it securely and hire a local Abyssynian guard, then head back to Jeddah to close up our villa on the Aramco Compound and transfer back to the United States. Passes were arranged on Ethiopian Airlines from Asmara to Beirut, and from there to Jeddah on Saudia. We rented a car to drive from Massawa on the seacoast up 7,000 feet to Asmara on the high plateau.

In the early 1900s the Italians had built a narrow gauge railway up the escarpment, followed by a road. In World War II the railroad had been destroyed but the road - narrow, partially paved, steep and tortuous - had survived. The trip up this road was beautiful and somewhat adventuresome since it was inhabited by bandits and revolutionaries who preyed on unwary travelers. Our only mishap occurred when we were stoned by a tribe of real baboons pelting our car with rocks as we passed.

The next morning the Donatella cast off and we resumed our tow north along the coast of Eritrea, an arid and utterly uninviting shoreline without a sign of life - no villages, no small boats, no camels, no nothing. After three days and nights at sea we reached Massawa where we parted company with the Donatella after one last night of "Cognac! Spaghetti! Vino!" with the Captain and Canatello, an enormous man of imposing girth, who regaled us with tales of the war and his survival to become a successful Ethiopian Red Sea ship operator through the Ethiopian territory. We boarded our flight and arrived in Jeddah that night.

Return to America

Upon our return to Jeddah we packed our possessions, closed up our villa, said goodbye to our Saudi and TWA friends, and flew back to the United States and our farm in Virginia. Our tenants were still there but the place had deteriorated during our absence. The Black Angus herd that we had sold them was gone, the fences collapsed, the machinery broken down, and our dog had forgotten us. We gave the renters notice and, in the meantime moved into a friend's large basement apartment.

We still had to get MAVIS II back from Masawa and I had to find a new job. The MAVIS II had been so miraculously spared, we renamed her "INSHALLA". TWA offered me a management position – Director of Stores for the Maintenance Department – in Kansas City as they had promised. While this was an important position overseeing some $50 million worth of inventory, it was not at the same grade level as my position in Jeddah, would not pay me as much, and had greatly reduced pass privileges for my family and me. I thought I deserved better, and turned the job down. I did not fancy a role as a smaller fish in a bigger pond. I would look elsewhere.

Meanwhile, back to Massawa. On my return I took my eldest daughter, Barbara, who had stayed behind in Jeddah during the original cruise from Aden. We arrived at Asmara again by air, rented a car and once more descended the road to Massawa, avoiding both bandits and baboons. INSHALLA was there, spick and span, with everything in place thanks to our guard. I had arranged to have her deck freighted on a Norwegian freighter that was scheduled to stop in Massawa in the near future. The freighter would ultimately land in Baltimore, Maryland, some thirty days later. I had saved the timbers that were used to cradle the boat when she was originally delivered in Aden, disassembling the cradle and carrying the timbers on deck during our earlier voyage. So, we reassembled the cradle and made INSHALLA ready for her long journey to the States. Since we had several days to kill until our freighter appeared, I donned a face mask and proceeded to clean the bottom and outdrives of the myriad barnacles that had accumulated on her in the warm waters of Massawa Harbor during the time we were gone. This proved to be a mistake. Cleaning barnacles is a messy job and I suffered numerous cuts and scratches. In retrospect, the waters of Massawa Harbor were 50% water and 50% sewage. I got a serious case of hepatitis that, fortunately, did not manifest itself until after Barbara and I had returned to the States. (When it did, no doctor could diagnose it and I became sicker and sicker. Finally, one night a bright young intern stopped by my hospital room to ask how I was. "Lousy," I said. He asked a series of questions and quickly got to the cause. "Hepatitis," he declared. Proper treatment was prescribed and I recovered.)

The freighter arrived, and at the last minute Barbara and I decided to board her – passengers were permitted – and sail with her up the Red Sea through the Suez Canal to Palermo, Sicily where she was scheduled to be dry docked and overhauled for two weeks. We paid our small fare and were escorted to a generous cabin behind the bridge. The food was ample and good, the days of reading on the sundeck delightful, and our fellow passengers most interesting. One was a rich, seventy year old heiress of a Detroit auto fortune who had been on the ship for months in the Indian Ocean, the Arabian Gulf, and was now going home. Even more interesting was a British priest and his wife who had spent five years in Ethiopia converting (or trying to) the Amharic Jews to Christianity.

We steamed through the Suez Canal while watching camel caravans and small palm-studded villages along the sides. The Egyptian canal pilots strutted and preened themselves until we dropped them off in Alexandria. Ships moved through the Canal in convoys, passing each other in the Great Bitter Lake in the center of the Canal. Going in one direction or the other, this usually involved an overnight delay, but our convoy was the one scheduled through that day. The next morning we were in the Mediterranean heading for Sicily while listening to the news on the radio about the start of the Six Days War that closed the Canal for some three years.

Leaving the ship at Palermo, we rented a car for the leisurely twelve hour drive – according to the Italian rental agent – to Rome where we were due to board TWA for the flight home. Armed with a loaf of Italian bread, a kilo of cheese and two liters of Dago Red, we set out. It took twenty-two hours driving straight through and we made the plane with half an hour to spare. Barbara created a small sensation in the airports in Rome and New York by carrying a four-foot sawfish bill – complete with its hundred long teeth – which we had bought in Massawa as a souvenir.

Epilogue – Saudi Arabian Airlines

I left Saudi Arabian Airlines after four years during which the airline effectively was transformed from the 13th century on the Arabic calendar (1964 was the Arabic year 1385 on the Islamic calendar) into the 20th Century. We had brought Saudia into compliance with the FAA and ICAO safety standards, entered IATA (the International Air Transport Association), extended Saudia's operations from the Middle East to Asia, Africa and Europe and, most importantly, begun the transition to a truly Saudi Arabian national airline through training and promoting the Saudis themselves.

TWA had been awarded a total management contract and had regained the confidence of the Saudi Government. New DC-9 and B-707-320C aircraft were being delivered, and more were being ordered. The airline began a program of growth and expansion as well as the withdrawal of TWA and other expatriate personnel. By 1998 Saudi was the seventeenth largest airline in the world, completely managed by Saudi national staff and executives.

In September 1998 Saudi Arabian Airlines invited me back to Jeddah as a consultant to help them dispose of their fleets of B-737s and Lockheed TriStars bought 25 years before and now being replaced by more modern jets. ✈

CHAPTER VIII

Modern Air

The Rosen Boys

In 1963, after leaving Riddle, I operated as an independent consultant to Aerovias Sud Americana, Ray Tonks at Aerodex, and others in the Miami area. I was contacted by the Gulf American Land Company, which operated a five-plane DC-3 fleet between Miami and Ft. Myers, the location of their real estate development operation. Prospective land investors were flown from Miami to Ft. Myers for a day's visit to Gulf American's Cape Coral land development, where resort communities were being carved out of the mangrove swamp. Deep canals were dug and the fill used to raise the land level to minimum building elevation. Sample houses were built, roads cut, and a "show place" clubhouse constructed as a focus for the new communities. Hopeful investors were urged to buy land still under water, to pay small monthly installments, and to take possession of a finished lot when their payments were completed. Gulf American Airlines was a key part of this strategy, bringing the buyers to the properties. And buy they did, often 80 to 90% of those brought to the properties. Properties were often "double decked," sold to two or more investors at the same time. The developers expected that many would not complete their payments and would default, permitting them to deliver the site to the second purchaser.

The Rosen brothers, Jack and Leonard, got their start as push cart salesmen on the streets of Baltimore and parlayed their earnings into a land development company in Florida. Using high interest loans from Jay Pritzger, they financed their boiler shops in the Northeast and Midwest, sending tens of thousands of potential land investors to Florida to see the properties. The operation was a typical "cat and rat farm." The investments of the purchasers financed the development of the properties and the sales of even more properties to new investors.

Gulf American Airlines was having problems: unreliability, high costs and unionization. The Rosens contacted me to take over at the then munificent salary of $25,000 a year. I almost took it, but TWA intervened with an even more interesting offer in Saudi Arabia.

When I had returned from Saudi Arabia in 1967 Gulf American was still there. The Rosens had now acquired Modern Air Transport, a certificated charter airline with five DC-7Cs and five Martin 404s which had been acquired by Gulf American. The airline was in chaos. President Al Rozawick was an old Miami hand hamstrung by interference from the Gulf American ownership in the person of Sol Sandler, Executive Vice President and brother-in-law of Jack Rosen.

I was invited to Miami for interviews with Jack and Leonard Rosen who still wanted a new CEO for their airline. Modern Air was a challenge and an opportunity and I accepted it, launching a very interesting four-year career.

Jack Rosen was a small, precise, neat and pious practicing Jew. Leonard was big, crude and sloppily dressed. He kept girls on a houseboat and his wife in a Venetian Island mansion. He would often appear at a Board meeting, belching and farting, in dirty tennis shorts and his yarmulke. They were indeed a pair, and brought me right into their "family" at Gulf American, insisting that I attend Bar Mitzvahs and circumcisions. It was a contrast – going from the airline of the King of the Muslim world to one owned by Jews.

Reorganizing Modern Air

During November and December of 1968 two major restructuring changes took place at Modern Air Transport. The company had three groups of airmen. This was a result of the prior merging of Modern Air, the DC-7 charter airline, the old Gulf American Airlines (whose pilots were flying the DC-3s and Martin 404s across the Everglades to Ft. Myers), and a new ex-military pilot group hired to fly the new Convair 990 jets which were being acquired. The management had promised each group "super seniority." The Modern and Gulf American pilots were members of ALPA, but the jet pilots were non-union. The Teamsters (IBT), who also represented the flight attendants, represented a fourth group – the old Modern professional flight engineers.

The seniority problem was resolved through binding arbitration. I hired an arbitrator who built a single seniority list, a task he completed with considerable skill based on group and date of hire. This, however, left many of our most qualified ex-military pilots at the bottom of the seniority list that determined flight status. They flew as copilots on the DC-3s across the Everglades while the old senior Gulf American DC-3 pilots and Modern Air DC-7 pilots vied for captain positions on the jets. We were given a couple of months' grace period to straighten this out due to delays in jet deliveries.

Of secondary concern were the two B-727-100 jets I had leased to replace the DC-7s and capable of flying directly into Ft. Myers on flights bringing prospective land purchasers to Gulf American's Cape Coral development. The ALPA pilots refused to fly the B-727s with a Teamsters Flight Engineer, declaring it to be "unsafe to have two unions in the cockpit," and further it was "against ALPA policy" even though they had been flying with the IBT flight engineers on the Modern Air DC-7s for years.

Bob Berghel, with whom I had worked at Riddle and whom I immediately retained to help sort our labor mess, agreed that we had a firm contract with the Teamsters and that we should honor it. The pilots were adamant, so we canceled the B-727 lease and returned the two aircraft. Pilots scheduled to fly the B-727s were furloughed. The problem of what to do about our newly merged seniority list proved more difficult. We now had a mixed fleet of two Convair 990 jets, with three more on order. Then there were the five DC-7C long range piston planes inherited from the merger with Modern, plus five Martin 404s and five World War II DC-3s from the old Gulf American Airlines fleet. Under ALPA contract rules the senior pilots got to fly the biggest and fastest planes and received the highest pay. The junior airmen were supposed to fly the least desirable aircraft.

To make things worse, business was getting bad. When Modern Air was moved to Miami from Trenton, New Jersey and merged into Gulf American, it lost most of its old commercial charter revenue base. Already ten years into the jet age, the old slow DC-7Cs had lost their passenger appeal and were increasingly expensive to operate. The Martin 404s' and DC-3s' usefulness was all but wiped out when we decided to put the CV-990s into Ft. Myers. The five thousand foot runway was barely adequate for this high performance four-engine jet, but it met the minimum FAA specifications, so Modern Air began direct land-buyer flights from the cities of the Midwest and Northeast to Ft. Myers. All but fifteen of our two hundred man pilot force were laid off in mid-December. With the delivery of our three additional CV-990s we were determined to rebuild as an all-jet airline.

This simplified the job of training pilots following the arbitrator's establishment of a single seniority list. We proposed a simple "up or out" program in which every pilot was to be given an opportunity to qualify on the CV-990 in the order of seniority. If a pilot passed, he flew, if he failed he was terminated. Pilots were required to pass each step and given two tries to do so.

The steps were:
>- Ground school, with written and oral exam.
>- Flight training, with company check ride.
>- FAA final check flight.
>- En route check ride and release to the flight line.

Mindful of the rapid shrinkage of the pilot ranks in the last several months following the return of the B-727s, and the grounding of the piston fleet and our determination to "do it right," the pilot union agreed to this procedure. January 1st the "up or out" training program began.

We needed twenty more pilots to man our five Convairs. We went through more than sixty pilots getting there. Two dozen flunked ground school and the written and oral exams. The technology of the jets was just too much for many old World War II or Korean War pilots who had not attained or maintained their skills. We had no flight simulator so all training was real time. Another twenty failed flight training. Each night's training flights, which we conducted on the Freeport, Bahamas' under-used runway across the Gulf Stream, produced a new series of horror stories. The basic curriculum was twelve hours at the controls. An initial check would indicate if sufficient progress was being made, after which a few more hours of training were offered to the more promising candidates. But many washouts occurred early.

A few of the more horrendous stories are worth recounting. Once, a practice landing maneuver a trainee got the plane on the ground, threw his hands in the air and then watched spellbound and transfixed as his plane hurtled at almost full throttle toward the end of the field. The check pilot pulled up at the last minute.

An old captain, eyes glued to the instruments, made a perfect approach to the open ocean a quarter of a mile to the left of the runway, only to be saved by the instructor.

Another pilot, asked to hold course and altitude, made the aircraft wallow and stagger plus or minus a thousand feet from designated altitude and 30° right or left of the course. A trainee, instructed to emulate a fire emergency and "shut down four," (the #4 engine) managed to turn off three engines before the instructor intervened.

The next one rotated the aircraft on takeoff, and kept on rotating, until the nose passed thirty degrees nose up and the shudders of final stall shook the plane from nose to tail – until the instructor took over. Getting the gear down or the flaps positioned for landing was always an iffy proposition, as well as getting them up and stowed on a "touch and go." The trainees attempted many a "wheels up" landing before being instructed to do a last minute go around.

And so the training proceeded slowly into the spring, as we finally checked out enough qualified pilots to fly our growing jet fleet; almost all were from our least senior ex-military group. Two aircraft were dispatched to Germany to start our new contract operation from West Berlin to the sunspots of the Mediterranean. But forty-six pilots had failed and been discharged, by far the largest number ever to be disqualified for incompetence at a single airline in the annals of ALPA. To make matters even more embarrassing to the pilot union, the failures included every member of ALPAs Master Executive Council (MEC) and negotiating committee.

Over a dozen pilots had the good grace to recognize they had been given a fair chance and left. The other thirty filed a "grievance" under the union arbitration machinery with the company. The company/union "System Board" quickly decided to agree to disagree, and the National Mediation Board was requested to appoint a neutral arbitrator.

The man selected was Judge Brown, a State judge from Sherman, Texas and a pilot in his own right. Fair and firm, he did not tolerate the histrionics that so often dominate such cases. Bob Berghel was, of course, our Counsel, and I was the company member of the Board.

For two months the judicial hearing process droned on, individual case by individual case. The Company presented each pilot's training file. Captain Hal Neff, our Chief Pilot, and Ross Zimmerman, assistant chief pilot and chief instructor, went through each training flight maneuver by maneuver. The full ALPA MEC (Master Executive Council) was present, since every officer of the Union had been disqualified in the jet training program and was now a grievant. This led to endless huddles at the ALPA table as they all sought to coach their somewhat beleaguered ALPA lawyer.

Every opportunity was sought to impugn the skill and veracity of Modern's witnesses.

Captain Neff: "I asked Capt. James to proceed thirty seconds on a heading of 270° and then turn to 180°."

Mr. Berghel: "And what did he do?"

Captain Neff: "He passed thirty seconds and then kept going for another thirty seconds until I directed him to turn."

ALPA Lawyer: "Did you look at your watch?"

Captain Neff: No"

ALPA Lawyer: "How did you know it was thirty seconds?

Captain Neff: "Because I can tell time .."

ALPA Lawyer: "Can you tell thirty seconds now without looking?"

Captain Neff: "Try me."

ALPA Lawyer, looking ostentatiously at his massive Rolex: "OK, now."

Dead silence filled the room as everybody gazed at their watches and Neff stared at the ceiling. Tick, tick, tick ...

Captain Neff: "Now!"

It was exactly thirty seconds. The review of Capt. James' training records continued.

In his final decision the Judge upheld the Company on twenty-eight of the thirty cases. Two pilots were reinstated for renewed training. One, a former high officer in Castro's Cuban Air Force, agreed to take a modest payment in lieu of more training. The second was checked out with some difficulty as a copilot on the CV-990. A year later the aircraft he was flying hit the radar shack during a night landing in a thunderstorm in Acapulco, Mexico. Both pilots involved were believed to have had their "heads out the window" instead of one watching the instruments on the landing. Only the crew were onboard and all survived. The aircraft was destroyed. It was Modern's only accident.

Following this ignominious defeat the ALPA elected a new MEC and Modern enjoyed peaceful labor relations.

Berghel and Bill

Bill Genovese was the fiery leader of the Airline Division of the Teamsters' Union, the IBT. During my years at Modern Air we had many face offs with Bill, who represented our Flight Engineers and Stewardesses. Bob Berghel always handled the negotiations until, like a summit meeting, it was only necessary for me to appear for the final critical give and take and settlement. But God help the airline executive who let himself get involved in a slugfest with Bill Genovese whose brutal, profane style was designed to intimidate and humiliate the management, make them lose their tempers, their control, and their good sense.

My first experience with Bill Genovese was shortly after I joined Modern Air. He was meeting down the hall with our personnel manager negotiating some grievance, when I walked in and introduced myself. To my amazement I was greeted with a torrent of profanity. "You goddamned, motherfucking, cock sucking son of a bitch. When are you going to straighten out this fucking place and treat my people right?"

"Bill, when you care to talk civilly, I will be glad to meet with you," I responded and turned and walked out, leaving Bill yelling. "You can't walk out on ME, big bossman ..." The door closed.

Over the years Bill Genovese and I grew to understand and respect each other. Although a tough and flamboyant union leader, he was as aware as I of keeping our company going, his members employed, and the dues flowing. Would that I could say as much for the leaders of the ALPA (the pilot union), IAM, and the BRC who represented mechanics and ground crews.

Bob Berghel represented management at many other smaller airlines as well. Negotiations opened at Saturn Airways, a charter airline, with the stewardesses represented by the IBT. Bill Genovese always liked to handle the stewardess negotiations personally. So on opening day he and his two leading Union Local officers, both senior girls long inured to the tough life of a non sked hostess, lined one side of the table. Berghel and two Company representatives faced them.

Preliminary pleasantries over, Bob launched into THE SPEECH, pointing out recent company losses, industry setbacks, government charter contracts restrictions, and increased competition. As he became more and more articulate in outlining the Company's inability to pay, he fired up his invariable cigar and bathed Bill and his girls in cloud after purple cloud of fumes. The Teamster's girls gasped and choked slightly, hardly relishing either the speech or the gas attack with which it was being delivered.

After a half-hour of monologue, Bill Genovese abruptly interrupted. Leaning forward he snarled, "Bob, when are you going to stop the bullshit and tell me what you are going to do for my cunts?"

A shocked silence ensued. Moments passed ...The two IBT girls got up red faced and fled the room leaving Bill alone.

Unfazed, Bob Berghel continued his monologue where he had left off.

The Convair 990

After acquiring Modern Air Transport, a small supplemental charter airline limited to U.S. domestic, Canadian and Mexican authority, the Rosens

1969 Modern Air Convair 990

agreed to purchase five Convair 990 four-engine jets that were being disposed of by American Airlines. The Convair 990 was built by General Dynamics and was an improved version of the original CV 880. The aircraft was smaller than the Boeing B-707s and the Douglas DC-8, and carried only 125 passengers. It was designed for speed and American Airlines bought it to try to win the transcontinental speed contest against United and TWA. No other U.S. airline purchased them, but SAS and Swissair both acquired small fleets of Convair 990s. The CV 990 could operate at Mach .98, just under the speed of sound, but fuel consumption was an enormous twenty-five hundred gallons per hour at this speed – far greater than the B-707s and DC-8s with 30% more seats.

When I came aboard at Modern Air we already had two aircraft delivered and three more being readied. The CV 990 was relatively cheap to buy because it was expensive to fly. We could either abrogate our contract with American, losing millions in cancellation fees and advance deposits, or go ahead and try to make the best of it. I chose the latter alternative. We later acquired five more CV-990s but sold one to Spantx (a Spanish charter airline) and lost one in an accident at Acapulco, Mexico.

My first action was to increase the seating capacity. The luxurious American Airlines seats were scrapped and replaced by a "slim line" seat that could be mounted on 31" spacing without reducing legroom. This permitted us to increase seating capacity from a 125 to a 149, the exit-limited capacity of the aircraft. This brought a 20% reduction in cost per seat-mile (one seat flown one mile, the index of aircraft efficiency) since it took no more crew, fuel or maintenance to carry a hundred and forty-nine passengers than it did to carry a hundred and twenty-five.

We then turned our attention to the question of speed vs. fuel consumption and aircraft range. At the high-speed cruise being used by other airlines, the CV 990 burned 2,500 gallons per hour. By reducing speed to Mach .78 we reduced fuel burn by 30% per hour and, due to lower speed, we had less "drag" and much improved range. At full Mach .98 the aircraft burned so much fuel it could barely make the transcontinental flight. At Mach .78 we had a transatlantic aircraft.

Our final move to improve efficiency occurred later when we purchased American Airlines' entire spares inventory and engine tooling. We also acquired American Airmotive, a large independent maintenance facility on the Miami airport. We could now do our own engine and airframe overhauls, improving reliability and reducing costs.

The seat-mile costs of the Convair were still higher than our competitors, but we had a smaller aircraft that suited some charter programs better than the larger DC-8s and B-707s, and we had a homogenous fleet. Had it not been for the negative influences of our parent company, GAC, in later years our fleet would have grown to perhaps twenty aircraft and our efficiency and market mass would have improved to the point where Modern made a net profit.

Modern Air Expands Berlin Tour Flights

Aviation Week announcement

The Berlin Operation

Shortly after joining Modern I received a call from John McDonald, who had worked for me at Riddle Airlines a few years previously. John was General Manager of Benny Goodman's Saturn Airways operation in Berlin, Germany. Under the Potsdam Agreement ending World War II, Berlin became an enclave governed jointly by the Four Powers, U.S.A., France, the U.K. and the U.S.S.R. In 1948 the Soviet Union had erected The Wall dividing the East and West parts of the city, and imposed a total blockade of all ground support to the West, shutting off coal, oil, food and transport. President Truman broke the Blockade with the Airlift, but Berlin remained a divided city with all land access to Berlin shut off by the Russians, the only way to get in and out of Berlin was by air. The Russians also controlled the air space and established three corridors ten miles wide and ten thousand foot maximum altitude that had to be used by airliners and allied military jets. The Russian MiGs patrolled the corridors and threatened to shoot down any aircraft that got out of the corridor. While this never happened, it was because the corridors were strictly respected.

No German aircraft could fly to Berlin, and only the airlines of France, the U.K. and the U.S.A. could serve West Berlin. Thus Pan Am, British Airways and Air France provided scheduled service from Berlin to a half-dozen cities in West Germany and to Paris and London. As Europe emerged from the aftereffects of the war, an increasingly active charter business developed, offering low cost tours to the Mediterranean and beyond. A British charter company and Riddle (of which I was then Senior Vice President) set up charter operations from Berlin to Palma de Majorca. Shortly after I left, Riddle shut down Berlin, and after a succession of operators, Saturn Airways and Capitol, another U.S. charter airline picked up the U.S. side of the Berlin Charter operation. John McDonald was appointed General Manager. Saturn ran the operation until 1967 when Benny Goodman sold Saturn to Howard Korth, and Korth decided to abandon Berlin. McDonald called me in Miami to explain the opportunity.

Our two charterers were the Flugring and the Flugunion. Flugunion was a consolidator for the biggest tour operators in West Germany – Neckerman (the department store), TUI (the German railways) and others. Flugring was strictly a Berlin operation, serving some 70 small mom-and-pop travel agencies in the cities. The principals were Dr. Hasselbach and Herr Kuhn. Dr. Hasselbach had been a Colonel in the German Army in World War II. As the Russians closed in on Berlin, Hasselbach had been ordered by Hitler to set off the mines in and around the Templhoff Airport that was largely intact despite the Allied bombing and Russian shelling. The airport housed an immense production factory under its terminal where the Germans were turning out Heinkel fighter bombers right up to the end of the War.

Hasselbach blew up the pumps that were keeping the factory dry, and let the waters of the Spree River inundate it. Then he locked down the doors. He then deactivated the mines under the runways and main terminal, determined "to save Templehoff for the German people" – defying the Fuhrer's orders.

The Templhoff airport is chiefly remembered from the Berlin Airlift. Who can forget the stream of Allied transports flying low between the apartment buildings to land on its 5,000-foot strip. The terminal was unique, a huge horseshoe where the roof completely covered the dozen transports parked under it. Despite being the target of the American's vaunted "pinpoint bombing," it had seldom been hit and was totally intact at the war's end.

While suitable for Saturn's DC-7Cs and Pan Am's B-727-100s, Templehoff's short and obstructed runways were too short for Modern's Convair 990s. We were fortunate that Tegel Airport was just being opened to charter traffic in the French Zone of Berlin. With a longer runway and clear approaches, it could handle the largest jets.

John McDonald was hired as Modern's Vice President-Berlin, and won the Flugring and Flugunion contracts and organized our ground and in-flight service staff at Tegel. Pilots had to be American citizens from the States, but all other staff were local Berliners, including Udo Fritsch and Horst Wuttig, who had worked for me in Saudi Arabia and who headed our new Berlin maintenance department.

Over the next four years our Berlin operation grew, reaching five Convair jets in 1971. The first winter we kept one aircraft in Berlin even though we had no business in the beginning. We were able to persuade our contractors to start a new speculative charter program to the Canary Islands, the first-ever winter charter program by any airline from Berlin. We also structured a series of weekly flights to Istanbul and Ankara, carrying Turkish

Kommt ein Vogel geflogen...

Cartoon from Der Tag

"Gastarbeiters" (guest workers) home. As Modern's operation expanded, we added more and more destinations in the Mediterranean and beyond, and engaged in a three-year battle to obtain rights to operate scheduled as well as charter flights from Berlin to West Germany.

Modern's Berlin operation was the only profitable sector of our operations, keeping the company going and subsidizing our U.S. commercial charter operations – chiefly to Las Vegas and Mexico – in the Americas. We also engaged in extensive domestic military charters, called CAMs ("Civil Air Movements" under contract to the DOD, generally carrying reservists on assignment around the U.S.A.). Ultimately Modern overcame all competitive charter airlines from the U.S.A., U.K. and France in Berlin and had 85% of the charter market. As the Berlin Der Tag's cartoonist pictured "Kommt ein anderen Vogel geflogen, " (Here comes another bird flying).

I flew to Berlin to meet with McDonald and the two German tour operators who organized the charters. The Convair 990s with 149 seats were too large for a single tour operator to fill, so we had to negotiate and bring them together to utilize the aircraft. The alternative for them would be the use of separate aircraft of smaller capacity but higher cost per seat. This gave us a negotiating advantage, but we also faced the problem that without both of the tour operators we would not have enough flying to justify the basing of

Modern Air Photo – Newspaper article

two CV 990s in Berlin.

The travel season began on May 1st and lasted five months. During this period we ran one or more weekly charters to some dozen points in the Mediterranean: Palma, Ibiza, Malaga, Bastia, Tunisia, Dubrovnik, Split, Athens, Crete, Cyprus and others. A flight would carry 149 passengers in, then return with the passengers who had been brought down a week or two before.

These were scheduled charters, permitted in Europe but banned in the United States by the Civil Aeronautics Board. The CAB was trying to protect the larger scheduled airlines from the charter airlines. However, when in Berlin, we were outside the jurisdiction of the CAB. We operated by the more liberal European rules.

After several days of negotiations, we concluded contracts with both tour operators totaling over $5.5 million covering operation of 500 trips during the summer season. We considered this a major coup given the guaranteed revenue, high utilization and the foothold it would give us in the international markets. In the U.S., Modern was restricted to domestic charters only, a restriction the CAB did not see fit to lift during my years with Modern.

Night Flight to Budapest

On the 19th of August 1968, Modern flew a charter from Toronto to Budapest with one of our Convair 990s. We were scheduled to pick up a load of passengers there for return to Canada. We knew there might not be an aircraft air start unit available in Budapest to restart the engines, and carefully instructed the pilot not to shut down all four engines until he was absolutely sure he had an operable ground unit available. With one engine still running it was possible to start the others with the cross air bleed from the compressor of the operating engine. The captain carefully interrogated the MALEV agent who met the plane and was assured that an air start unit was available. He shut down all four.

He was wrong – terribly wrong. There was no start unit within 500 miles of Budapest. Pan Am had removed the last unit three days before. Nobody else used them.

The crew tried everything they could think of. Two air conditioning trucks were backed up to an engine and the hoses inserted in the intake. Not enough air. A MiG fighter was borrowed from the Hungarian Air Force, started up (it used a battery cart), and backed up so its exhaust blasted toward the engine on the CV 990. It was three feet too low to the ground and just blew under the wing.

The captain called Berlin where we had an air start unit. A plane was inbound from Palma de Majorca and, as soon as it landed, we proceeded to load the air start unit in the belly. It would not fit through the cargo compartment door. We removed the unit's wheels, the tow bar, the cowling and the air hose. It barely squeezed in, mounted on its skids. At 9 P.M. that night we took off down the south corridor over Fulda and Frankfurt, heading for Vienna and Budapest. I went along on the flight. Tension in the area had been increasing between Russian and the satellite countries, which were restive. We were keenly aware of this in Berlin, a hundred miles deep inside East Germany and jointly occupied by the Red Army and the Allies. Czechoslovakia was particularly restive and its Communist president, Antonin Novatny, had been ousted during the previous spring. He was replaced briefly by a succession of generals. In April 1968 Alexander Dubcek became president, promising democratic reforms. In July Russia and its satellites had demanded the Czechs end their reforms.

It was a calm and peaceful night as we flew east along the Czech border. We could see the lights of Brna and Bratislavia to our left. Suddenly the radio became alive with traffic. The lights in the Czech towns blinked out. Russia and four satellite allies, including Hungary where we were going, were invading Czechoslovakia and we were flying right into it.

Hal Neff, our Vice President of Flight Operations, was flying. We conferred a few minutes, listened to the traffic, and called Berlin. It did not appear that the invasion was going to be contested and there was no sign of ground fire or enemy air activity. Modern's plane was still immobilized on the ground in Budapest. We did not have the slightest idea if the Russians would try to seize West Berlin as well, but thought there was a fair chance that they would, in which event we could do nothing about it. We decided to press on and try to complete our mission.

The bedlam on the radio continued. Hungarian air traffic control verified that our clearance to land was still valid, as did the tower as we approached Budapest. The runway lights came on and we swept in for a landing, taxiing up to where our sister jet was parked. This time we did not shut down the #1 engine but kept it running in case we had trouble with the air start unit.

We removed the unit from the belly after locating a Russian-built forklift and figuring out how to make it run (a $20 U.S. bill helped). While the outbound passengers were rounded up and counted – they had been cooped up in the terminal for eighteen hours by this time – we reassembled and attached the air start unit and fired up the grounded jet without difficulty. By 2 A.M. everything was ready, the air start unit was reloaded, everybody was onboard, and we had our outbound clearance to Berlin and Canada, respectively, from air traffic control. Both planes taxied out and took off.

At 3:30 A.M. we entered the Berlin Corridor at Fulda, descending to ten thousand feet as required. A pair of Russian MiGs made a close pass to check us out and perhaps harass us. We didn't know. The long summer day was about to begin and, if the Russians were going to come, now was the time they would show their hand. So in apprehensive silence we flew on until we could see the bright lights of West Berlin glowing on the horizon. A slow turn over perpetually darkened East Berlin and we were lined up with Flughafen Tegel's Runway 27 for landing. It had been a long night. The Russians were not there to greet us. I drove to the Ambassador Hotel for a short sleep.

General Acceptance Corp. Buys Modern Air

In 1969 the Rosens sold Gulf American Airlines to GAC, the General Acceptance Corporation. GAC had made its fortune in the business of auto loans and was now branching out into real estate development. Modern Air was part of the transaction. Airlines and aviation was not a business that GAC understood, but they quickly appointed Jim Brown – their Treasurer – as President of Modern Air in place of Jack Rosen (who unfortunately died a short time later). Rosen's brother Leonard lived on, as did the colorful stories of his peccadilloes.

Jim Brown was a straight-arrow business executive and a quick study. He developed a genuine interest in Modern Air. Once a week I would meet him at a local IHOP for breakfast and a briefing. Using the resources of GAC we were able to buy American Airmotive, a large engine and airframe overhaul agency that operated on the Miami airport and provided maintenance services to airlines and the U.S. Air Force. We also bought three more Convair 990s from VARIG – the airline of Brazil – and American Airlines' vast inventory of aircraft and engine spares and tooling. We were thus freed from dependence on costly outside contractors and could provide all of our own engine and airframe maintenance, making our operation much more efficient and self-sufficient.

Brown was always critical of the fact that Modern never made a profit, but was satisfied to support us enthusiastically as long as we were narrowing the gap. We had an excellent working relationship as long as he was our responsible contact with GAC. But when he was appointed to a new position in GAC's hierarchy, they sought to replace Brown with their head of Personnel as President of Modern. I was willing to work with Jim as President, but believed that I was entitled to the position when he moved up. He agreed as well, Mr. Personnel was dropped and I became President of Modern in my own right. However, from that time forward my relations with GAC declined, especially as they got in trouble financially and with the law.

GAC did not know how to run a land development business with its high-pressure boiler room sales, double decking practices and entrepreneurial tactics. Sales fell off, costs increased, and GAC decided to enter the building of high-rise condominiums on the waterway north of Miami. With enormous amounts invested in suitable land, they became involved in zoning problems and attempted to buy their way out, by way of payoffs. This added further to their financial woes and added legal problems as well. GAC slowly slipped toward the brink and eventually declared bankruptcy. But long before this they were applying more and more pressure to Modern Air, which continued to lose money as a result.

GAC went through a series of internal reorganizations as it struggled with its problems, and with each change in management there was a change in tactics. Use of Modern Air flights to bring buyers to GAC properties was curtailed suddenly, and we were left with idle capacity with no lead-time to secure alternative business. Consultants were hired to advise us without conferring with us. GAC offered six months' salary to any executive who didn't agree with new policies and wanted to leave.

Over the Poles

Sometime in the early 1950s, when I was with Capital Airlines, a little man came into my office and introduced himself as Commander Dustin, USN Retired. He had a unique proposal. Commander Dustin, as a lowly seaman 3rd class, had been Admiral Byrd's dog sled driver when he explored Antarctica and reached the South Pole in 1928 and 1933. Byrd was now dead and the Commander wanted to honor him by a commercial flight around the world, over both the North (which Byrd had also conquered) and the South Poles. He wanted to charter a plane from Capital for the venture and sell seats to adventurous rich people.

The idea had appeal. It was technically feasible with our long range DC-4s, making fueling stops at Little America and in Northern Greenland. The only question was money. The trip would take 30 days, cover 30,000 miles or more, and take 150 hours. Our cost was around $50,000 and we had to have the money up front. Commander Dustin took this information and went off to raise money. I did not hear from him again for eight years.

Sometime in 1962 I was sitting at my desk in Miami at Riddle Airlines. We were in one of our periodic poor spells with little flying. In walked Commander Dustin, still small, but full of enthusiasm for his idea, which had not changed. This time I had a far superior airplane, the Douglas DC-7C, capable of 4,500 miles nonstop with a full passenger load. But Commander Dustin still did not have any money. We again reviewed the opportunity and I sent him away with a proposal to charter him a DC-7C for $100,000 for the adventure, payable in advance. Commander Dustin did not reappear for eight more years.

In 1970 I was again in Miami, running Modern Air with our fleet of eight Convair 990 jets. Fall was coming and business was dropping off for the slow winter season. Once again, out of the blue, as it were, came Commander Dustin. This time he had MONEY. He had teamed up with an entrepreneurial professor at Harvard Business School who enjoyed extra curricular privileges and they had organized a company to fly the Byrd Memorial Flight around the world, over both Poles.

It would be the first passenger flight to circumnavigate the globe by this route. With the horsepower of the Harvard Business School behind them they were able to promote the flight professionally. I signed a contract with the Dustin group to operate the Convair 990 on a special Round the World Charter for $250,000. The flight would take one month and would visit every continent. The aircraft was specially configured with eighty seats (down from a normal one hundred forty-nine) for added passenger comfort.

Captain Hal Neff, our Chief Pilot, was to command. We scheduled departure from Boston (Harvard's backyard) on December 15th. Our first stop was the U.S. Air Force Base at Thule on the northern tip of Greenland. From there we would fly to the North Pole and then head south (which was in all directions) to Anchorage, Alaska for our second scheduled stop. The flight ultimately passed through or over thirty countries, all of which had to grant special fly over and landing authority. The U.S. FAA and CAB also got into the act, as did the State Department, eventually.

Commander Dustin and the professor did a magnificent promotional job. They sold 70 places on the flight to a wide and wild variety of businessmen, playboys, retirees and others, at $10,000 each. This meant they raised a cool $700,000 of which they kept half. There were no women in the group.

We had a great takeoff party in a Boston hotel the night of December 14th and Dustin gave me their cashier's check for $250,000 as per our agreement. The party was vigorous and lasted well into the wee hours, until even the most robust participants staggered off the bed to prepare for the takeoff at noon the 15th.

As departure time approached, the somewhat bleary-eyed passengers assembled at the loading area and slowly filed on board. It was cold and sleeting outside.

I put the $250,000 cashier's check in an envelope and gave it to our Superintendent of Ground Operations with strict instructions to proceed directly to Miami and deliver the check to Finance. Unfortunately, he was still drunk. Instead of following directions he accidentally left the check in a phone booth and then disappeared for two days. Luckily for us, an honest man found the check and mailed it to our Miami office. A few days later our Superintendent was asked to seek other employment.

We buttoned up the flight, taxied out, and took off. The Convair 990 was fully loaded with fuel. We carried a below normal load of 70 passengers but several tons of spare parts, wheels, tires, brakes, accessories and other tools and equipment we might need far from home. The Convair did not enjoy a wide operator base and, therefore, there was virtually no technical support for the aircraft outside of Modern's system. We carried our own support on board, including a trained mechanic to supervise whatever might have to be done.

The Boston runways were covered with slush. As we took off a wake of icy water sprayed out from under the wheels up into the wheel wells covering the landing gear. When we reached flying speed there was a loud "BANG" and the plane shuddered. Red warning lights flashed on one main gear but then all three gears retracted normally and we climbed out slowly to the north toward Thule, 2,500 miles away on the northern tip of Greenland.

Three hours out, I was sitting on the jump seat talking with the crew when we received a radio contact from Boston. "Modern 907, Boston Control here, we have found one of your wheels on the runway!"

We discussed this bit of bad news. We did not believe we had thrown a wheel on takeoff but fortunately we had two spares in the belly if we needed them. We called Boston back and asked them for a re-check. "Modern 907, Boston here, we have checked. No, you did not lose a wheel. You just stripped off the retreads on one of your tires. Over and out." This occurs infrequently on aircraft as it does on trucks.

We all remembered the loud bang on takeoff and a momentary red light indication as the wheels came up. This squared with the loss of the retread rubber. We debated whether to return to Boston or continue. A return would have brought all kinds of problems with our passengers. Since we had everything on board to care for either a wheel replacement or a tire change we decided to press on. By this time we were over Labrador and the long winter night was closing in.

It was snowing heavily as we approached Thule. We had approximately two hours of reserve fuel left as we lined up for approach. Flaps down, we slowed to approach speed. Gear down. The right main showed red lights, indicating that the gear was not locked down. The left gear indicator was green. The nose gear did not come down at all. The prospect of landing with the nose gear up, right gear red and left gear down was not reassuring. Hal Neff called the tower and told them of our problems. Ambulances and fire trucks rushed from their shelters to the runway and positioned themselves for our approach.

We recalled the slush on the runway at Boston and figured that the nose gear might have frozen in the "up-latched" position due to the slush freezing as we climbed into colder air. Our flight engineer lifted the floor hatch in the cockpit and climbed down into the nose wheel well. This was hardly an enviable situation since the doors were open and the icy blast of the arctic slipstream was roaring by at 200 miles per hour. The flight engineer took a hammer and a large screwdriver and began to chip away at the ice-encrusted up-latch while Neff cycled the gear. With a final crack the iced up hinges gave way, the nose gear swung down and locked into place.

Neff and I discussed our alternatives. Go in with three gears down and take our chances with the red lights on the right gear, or go in belly up with all three gears retracted. A gear-up was a no-no since it would wash out the entire trip as well as the aircraft. We opted for a full gear down approach given the probability that the gear was down and the red light an erroneous warning, and descended for our final approach into Thule. And indeed it was a final approach. We had no fuel to go anywhere else by this time and there was no place else to go anyway.

As we lined up on the runway, the fire trucks and ambulances were waiting for us, with light beams rotating through the snow. All gears were down, flaps full, minimum speed. We swept in over the approach lights and settled solidly on the runway. Captain Neff held the right wheel up as long as he could before easing it onto the ice-covered runway. All gears were firm and we rolled to a stop turning to the giant hangars whose doors opened to welcome us.

The passengers disembarked and were bussed by friendly Air Force staff to the BOQ where Fran Daniels and her Baltimore Broads were entertaining for the evening with music, sing alongs and spicy fun. Our passengers, slightly shaken by our stressful approach to Thule, were in the mood to join in and celebrate. And so, far into the night, the revelry in the BOQ continued.

Down at the hangar we jacked up the Convair 990. The failed retread from one tire had stripped wiring out of the brake lines and retract switches on that gear. The gear warning lights had also been damaged so that we had to replace the wheel, the plumbing and the warning circuits. The job took about four hours with lots of enthusiastic help from the Airmen on station who otherwise had so little to amuse them. Meanwhile, the party at the BOQ roared on.

At approximately 2 A.M. we had the gear repaired, jacked and tested. It was time to get our passengers. Busses were dispatched and soon began to roll up, discharging totally inebriated travelers who staggered and crawled up the stairs into the jet. At 3 A.M. we had everybody accounted for, had thanked our gracious hosts, paid our bills and taxied out for the next leg of our flight to the North Pole and then south to Anchorage, Alaska.

For two hours we flew north, calculated our position over the Pole with Doppler and announced the Pole crossing to our passengers. We then turned southwestward toward Anchorage, two thousand miles away over the Arctic icecap and the mountains and tundra of Alaska. Outside it was the inky blackness of the Arctic night, with the overcast extended so high that we were still in it and could not see the stars or the famed Aurora Borealis. The landing at Anchorage was uneventful except for a whiteout on final approach that caused the runway to disappear until we were almost on it.

One of our passengers was a younger businessman from Seattle who said he enjoyed an income of a quarter of a million dollars a year, had one employee, and manufactured "shit house door knobs for Boeing." There were evidently a lot of these knobs on a 747 because he made a good living. He was a ladies' man and told me during a recess in the entertainment at Thule that he had taken one of Fran Daniel's Baltimore cuties to the BOQ, rented a room for an hour from an obliging desk sergeant, and had a good time. He was seated next to me on the Thule-Anchorage leg so I had to listen to him. He had a folio of pictures (all nude) of many of his previous conquests and explained to me that, with his Mercedes convertible, he preyed on the international

Convair 990 landing on the ice at McMurdo, Antarctica

stewardesses overnighting in Seattle between flights. The action must have been pretty good because he had lined up a girl in advance to meet him at almost every airport at which we were scheduled to stop. I learned later on from my crew that this was, in fact, the case. So I guess my seat-mate was also establishing a record for round-the-world sexual prowess on our flight.

I left the flight in Anchorage and flew back to Miami while the trip continued the next day to Tokyo. On this leg one of the elderly passengers died of a heart attack. We had to make arrangement to have his remains shipped back to the U.S. before the trip could continue.

From Japan the CV-990 visited Manila (Philippines), Darwin (Australia), Christ Church (New Zealand), and finally hopped off on the 2,500 mile leg to McMurdo Sound on the Antarctic Continent.

In Antarctica it was summer, with continuous daylight. The U.S. Navy, which ran the station at McMurdo close to Admiral Byrd's old camp, smoothed a 7,000-foot runway on the eight-foot thick ice of the Sound and we came in just as if it were a normal runway. All the passengers were dressed in Arctic parkas and off they went, with Commander Dustin in the lead, to visit Admiral Byrd's old quarters which were still standing, perfectly preserved in the cold, dry climate.

The Commander had arranged for us to refuel from Navy stocks. The flight was reboarded and set out to cross the Antarctic Continent, a feat never before attempted by a civil airliner. The route first lay nine hundred and fifty miles to the South Pole itself where a few small huts could be seen, and then flew north some two thousand six hundred miles over the polar icecap, over Graham Land peninsula, and over Cape Horn to its next destination of Punta Arenas, Argentina.

It was a magnificent flight over a totally barren and unknown territory.

One did not like to think about the possibilities of surviving an emergency landing, but then fortunately, none was necessary. From the tip of South America the route took the Convair to Manaos, Brazil on the Amazon and then across the Atlantic to Dakar, Senegal in West Africa. Stops were made for a day in each place for sightseeing and visiting local dignitaries.

In Dakar we changed aircraft. The original one developed engine trouble so I ordered one of the two based in Berlin for the winter ferried down to Dakar as a replacement. The plane with the bad engine was ferried on three engines back to Berlin for repairs, and was again switched back a few days later in Copenhagen.

A five-day stop in Rome had been planned since the Commander was a good Catholic as were many of the passengers. A Papal audience was scheduled. However, some passengers were restive and one was a close friend of U.S.S.R. Ambassador to the U.S. Anatoly Dobrynin. He phoned the Ambassador from Rome, requesting permission for our aircraft to fly to Moscow and mentioned that Russian visas would have to be issued for our passengers. He led the Ambassador to believe that all were high-ranking American businessmen. Surprisingly, the answer was an immediate "yes."

In Miami we scrambled to get clearance from our totally non-plussed FAA, who literally did not know what to make of it. The State Department also consented reluctantly, not quite believing what they were doing.

In Rome the sixty passengers who wanted to go to Moscow trooped down to the Russian Embassy for visas. Our flight was dispatched to Copenhagen, where it picked up an Aeroflot navigator to help manage the fight over the U.S.S.R. and into Moscow.

It was mid-January when Modern landed at Moscow's airport in the inevitable Russian winter snowstorm. The group was met by three Commissars from Industry, Finance and Agriculture, and a convoy of Zivs to transport them to the Metropole Hotel, where all foreigners stayed. During the next two days the party was briefed by the Russians about Aeroflot, their heavy industry and agriculture. They were wined and dined, with many vodka toasts to celebrate this first flight by an American commercial airline to Russia. And strangely, no American Embassy personnel ever showed up. It was as if our group did not even exist.

The Polar group finally closed out the Russian interlude and flew back to Copenhagen where they met up with the rest of the original group who had been flown in on a commercial aircraft from Rome. From Copenhagen we flew on to Boston, landing 30 days after departure.

So ended Commander Dustin's dream flight. It was the first flight by a commercial passenger aircraft around the world over both poles. We touched

The Passengers on the ice at McMurdo, Antarctica

all seven continents and were the first American commercial airline to fly to Moscow, in a world still deep in the Cold War.

Round the World Polar II

Modern operated a second around-the-world flight in 1970, this time captained by Ross Zimmerman and chartered by a group whose members each had visited at least a hundred foreign countries – quite an achievement in those days. As expected, all participants were old and rich – the average age was over seventy. The aircraft made up in Los Angeles, crossed the North Pole from Anchorage to Europe, made its way through Africa, across Southern Asia, and then across the South Pacific with a stop at Easter Island.

Captain Zimmerman noted from his initial flyby and from the tower when questioned, that there were a lot of rocks and debris on the Easter Island runway. This is extremely hazardous for jet engines that are likely to ingest such materials, particularly on landing and takeoff when engines are reversed or at high thrust. Zimmerman made the slowest possible approach and landed without using reverse thrust. The passengers went off for a brief bus tour of the island.

The local authorities expressed indifference to the debris on the runway and refused to provide manpower to clean it up. Zimmerman was, therefore, left to his own devices and he came up with about one hundred paper sacks. When each passenger returned, he was briefed on the problem the rocks presented on takeoff, when ingestion into one or more engines could cause engine failure and possibly a crash. All the crew and passengers were given bags and formed a ragged line across the runway to pick up rocks and debris. At the end of an hour, the long march down the runway had been completed and the runway was clean. The aged and exhausted passengers were loaded back aboard and the flight proceeded to Santiago, Chile.

Since Captain Dustin of the Byrd expedition was no longer available, we were unable to make arrangements with the U.S. Navy to refuel at Antarctica's McMurdo Sound ice airport. Therefore we planned to fly from Argentina's Puerto Arenas Airport to the South Pole and return. Unfavorable weather at the alternate airport made a full penetration to the South Pole impossible, but our passengers got a breathtaking four thousand mile roundtrip over the icecap anyhow.

White Hats – Black Hats

Every morning we held a staff meeting to review past and current operations. I used these meetings for general staff motivation, praising good work and commenting on areas where improvement was required. A bit of symbolism was always effective. When V.P. Sales Ralph Sacks successfully negotiated a multi-million dollar Mexican charter program with a major tour operator, I obtained and awarded him a huge black sombrero resplendent with gold trim. Ralph proudly hung it on his wall.

As we went through our long and arduous upgrading flight training program on the new Convair 990s, weeding out weak pilots (including the entire ALPA Master Executive Council) and terminating them, it became obvious that Hal Neff, our Chief Pilot, was much smoother in his handling of the pilots than his Deputy, Ross Zimmerman. Both were veteran Air Force pilots who had joined Modern when the Convairs were purchased, and both were well-qualified check airmen. But Neff was more popular than Zimmerman.

One morning in our staff meeting I thought it would be appropriate to recognize Hal's and Ross's efforts. So I purchased two hats and stuffed them in a box under my desk. At the appropriate time I outlined my intention to award hats to Hal and Ross. I proceeded to praise Neff's efforts in training the pilots, finally handing him a white Western hat complete with Modern emblem. I then turned to Ross, praising him, but pointing out that he was much less appreciated by the pilots. I told him I would have to recognize this in awarding him his hat. One could tell from his face that Ross knew what was coming . . . I then reached under the table and drew out . . . another white hat.

Topless to Paris

On Father's Day, 1969, Modern Air flew the world's first and only topless stewardess flight. It was a special charter for a Berlin nightclub and operated from Berlin to Paris over that weekend, carrying over a hundred men and three women on one of our Convair 990s. The flight was billed as a "Weg vom Mutti Fliegen" (Get Away from Mother Flight). John McDonald, our irrepressible Berlin Vice President, organized the trip, and it received wide notice in the Berlin press. As a result, five hundred interested spectators showed up at Tegel Airport at departure time and the police had to dispatch several vanloads of reinforcements for crowd control to keep spectators off the ramp. The next morning the Berlin tabloids featured front-page stories and pictures. One was headlined "Fatti Tag - Der Polizie Hat Viel zu Tun" (Father's Day - the Police Had Much To Do). The wire services picked up the story and flashed it overseas. I received a call from the Miami Herald that resulted in a front-page story "German 'Busenvoegel' Flight? It Definitely Gets X Rating." I gave the Herald a complete story, including little incidents like the three women who sniffed, "No good can come of a flight like this," as they boarded.

My mentors at the General Acceptance Corporation – owners of Modern Air – had a fit when they saw the story. It did not fit the GAC image of propriety and political correctness. I was called on the carpet not only about the flight, but also because of my remarks in the press.

I had not known of the flight in advance, McDonald having wisely concluded it was better not to ask. This contributed even more to GAC's outrage. We had to promise never to repeat the performance.

The story found its way into papers all over the world and, for a long time, whenever I traveled and was identified by the flight attendants as head of Modern Air they would attack me. "Oh, you're the one with the topless flight!" I readily admitted this was true and there immediately followed either a tirade about respect and things like that, or expressions of greater interest. Modern's hostess applications (we did not hire young men in those days) increased five fold following the publicity.

The topless girls were not actually our stewardesses, but rather German showgirls provided by the Daily Girl Club. The regular complement of German stewardesses - known the world over as "Die Tiger Madchen von Modern Air" due to their distinctive yellow and

Father's Day flight

black striped uniforms - was aboard and well dressed in their regular uniforms.

The Civil Aeronautics Board
By the early 1970s the Civil Aeronautics Board (CAB) had created four classes of certificated airlines: the Trunk (now Major) airlines such as United, American and Northwest; the Local Service airlines such as Piedmont, North Central, Southern

(now all extinct and merged into the Majors); the All-Cargo airlines such as Airlift, Seaboard and Flying Tigers (now all bankrupt except Flying Tigers – merged into FedEx); and finally the Supplemental or Charter airlines, sneeringly referred to as non skeds (for non-scheduled). Modern Air was a non sked – one of eight – also now all gone except for World. As of 1970 the non skeds included big carriers with full international authority (Capitol,Trans America, Saturn and World), and those with limited domestic and Mexican authority (Johnson, Perdue, Universal and Modern Air).

The large Trunk airlines were restricted to specific routes, but were permitted to operate charter and cargo services on an unrestricted basis in competition with their lesser brethren, the Local Service, All Cargo and Supplemental carriers. Further, charters were very narrowly defined and were not open to the general public or individual holiday-seekers as in Europe. In order to travel on a charter flight that offered savings of up to 75% from scheduled services, one had to be a member of an "Affinity Group" and travel together going and coming. An affinity group was something like an American Legion Post, a B'nai B'rith organization (no Goys allowed), or a University Alumni group. Passenger lists had to be submitted to the CAB in advance for screening. All charter fees were held in escrow until the flights were completed.

Modern's most annoying (and debilitating) CAB restriction was the one that limited our operations to the domestic U.S. and trans-border Mexican and Canadian flights. Modern, and several other small non skeds, were prohibited from flying to Europe, Asia, South America or the Carribean – all charter destinations of greater potential. Modern was also permitted to carry domestic military charters (CAMs) but was banned from operating intercontinental military chargers for the Military Airlift Command (MAC) since they would not accept our Convair 990s that could not be converted to cargo.

It was in this constrained regulatory atmosphere that Modern fought for existence. We were able to develop our Berlin operation outside the CAB's stultifying jurisdiction and also got "exemptions" from the CAB for two trans-polar around-the-world flights. But these were the exceptions.

We sought liberalization of U.S. charter rules and were able to persuade the CAB to permit "split" charters where two affinity groups shared a single flight, and we later won the ability to operate exclusive tour charters operated by a single tour operator/agent. But as a group the American charter carriers were never able to match the success of the European charter airlines. Following airline deregulation in 1978 all of the U.S. charter airlines were liquidated or bankrupted except World, which merged to save itself, and struggled on, principally as a military contract airline.

Schedule Service from Berlin

Modern Air established itself as the largest charter airline in Berlin, but our operations were strictly confined to charters only. Pan Am and, to a much lesser extent, British Airways and Air France were providing scheduled services to all of the major cities of West Germany. The Government of Berlin also gave them excessive subsidies and these airlines charged egregious fares. Lufthansa and other German and international airlines were prevented from flying to Berlin by the Russians under the restrictions they imposed on Berlin airspace as permitted by the Pottsdam Agreement.

All flights to and from Berlin had to pass through East German airspace to reach West Germany, and by Russian decree were limited to three corridors – each ten miles wide and ten thousand feet high. Operations outside or above the ten thousand feet corridors were subject to Russian interference. It was a common experience to have a MiG escort when in the corridor. However, despite the risk, there never was a civilian or military incident during the thirty years the corridors were in existence. On one occasion I was riding in the cockpit of a Pan Am DC-8, flown by a New York-based pilot who scornfully dismissed the corridor restrictions as "bullshit." He proceeded to climb straight out of Flughafen Tegel, reaching twenty thousand feet as we passed over Fulda at the end of the central corridor. Fortunately, the Russian gunners were asleep and the subsonic MiGs could not scramble fast enough to intercept us. At Modern we did not consider flying the corridor "bullshit."

In 1969 Modern began to agitate for rights to fly scheduled services between Berlin and West Germany, promising the City of Berlin that we would do so without subsidy and 50% off Pan Am's egregious fares. The IGS, Pan Am's Internal German Service, was the most (and later only) profitable service according to their own financial reports to the CAB. Our application was

Modern Convair 990

outside the jurisdiction of the CAB and the Germans quietly supported it, but were in no hurry to anger their American overlords in Brussels and Washington. Pan Am rolled its mighty lobby machine into action saying Modern's proposed competition was unsafe and would financially harm them to the degree that they would have to abandon Berlin. Modern's deserving application for scheduled service rights to Berlin vanished into the black ooze of international and power politics.

Modern eventually did win rights to provide scheduled jet service from Berlin to Sarbrucken in West Germany, and we purchased a twelve passenger German Hansa jet to provide the service. It was the first small Regional Jet service in the world and we operated three flights daily. Unfortunately, the economics of the Hansa Jet were better suited to executive transport than scheduled service, and our experiment slowly died of starvation. We also tried to establish a Hansa Jet service Berlin Tegel to Stockholm, matching SAS's service to East Berlin's Schonefeld Airport, but for some reason could not win the approval of the Swedish authorities. Meanwhile, Pan Am started a B-727 service to Zurich and Vienna, both destinations that Modern had sought.

Cats to Berlin

My daughter Barbara had always been interested in aviation, and when she graduated from high school in the States I had an opening in the Print Shop at Saudi Arabian Airlines. In this position she managed the shop and a half-dozen Arabs – an unheard of situation in the Kingdom. When I moved to Modern, Barbara became a flight attendant until GAC took over and their Personnel Department ruled it a case of "nepotism." Therefore I let her go to Berlin, out of reach of the GAC, where she found a position in the Finance Section. Barbara lived off the economy in Berlin in a small apartment on the Ku-Damm.

Barbara loved cats, so when our cat in Miami had kittens we were only too glad to take them to Barbara in Berlin. I took them in a "cat box" on my next trip to Berlin and the following dialogue took place at the airport in Miami:

"Mr. Beyer what is in that box?"

"Cats."

"You cannot carry them in the cabin."

"Why not?"

"They are in a Pan Am cat box. You can only carry them in the cabin in an Eastern cat box."

"How can I get an Eastern cat box?"

"You have to go to the baggage service desk in the B Terminal and get one."

"But if I do that I'll miss the plane!"

"Well, you can ship them as baggage, but have to sign a waiver because they are in a Pan Am cat box . . ."

"Well, okay," and I signed a long disclaimer form, consigning the cats to the baggage pit.

On arrival in Washington the cats did not appear with the rest of my baggage. I went to the gate and out onto the ramp where our plane was still being unloaded. The cat box was mashed flat under a piece of heavy freight. I rolled the freight to one side, retrieved the cat box, patted it into shape and opened it. The four kittens were mashed flat on the bottom . . .

Scratching them on their backs revived them. We got a taxi and proceeded to the Statler Hilton Hotel in downtown Washington, where the cats escaped into the lobby through a broken window in the cat box. A ten-minute chase by a couple of bellboys retrieved them, the window was repaired with tape, and we headed off to our room. The next evening we boarded a Pan Am flight for London, cats in hand in their box.

"What have you got in that box?" asked a young couple on their honeymoon.

"Cats for my daughter in Berlin."

"Why can't she get cats in Berlin?"

"They ate them all in the war."

"Oh! Can we see them?"

"Sure."

"Can we take them back in coach with us for the night?"

"Sure, gladly."

They took the cats for the night and returned them as we approached London the next morning.

When we arrived at the gate, the British authorities boarded the aircraft and announced that all passengers could disembark except "the man with the cats." I sat there as the passengers streamed off. Finally, two Airport Police approached me.

"Are you the man with the cats?"

"I am."

"Why are you importing cats into the United Kingdom without a quarantine permit? All pets brought into the U.K. are required to have a permit and are placed in quarantine for six months. This is a health measure."

"I am not importing the cats into the U.K.. I am in transit on Lufthansa to Hamburg."

"Where are your Lufthansa tickets?"

"I don't have them yet, I have to pick them up at the Lufthansa ticket counter where they are in the 'will call' box."

The police retreated to call headquarters for further instructions while I waited apprehensively as the minutes ticked away to my departure on the connecting flight. A delegation was waiting for me in Hamburg.

"All right, please come with us." I descended the aircraft stairs onto the tarmac where a police van awaited me. I got in with two officers. Two more officers took the cats in a separate van. We motored across the airport to Lufthansa's gate at Terminal 2.

I checked in at the Lufthansa desk, was given my ticket to Hamburg and paid 50 marks extra for the cats. I then went to the departure gate.

"What have you got in that box?"

"Cats. Here are their tickets."

"Wait a minute, I must see ..." The agent disappeared, and after several minutes returned.

"You cannot carry the cats on this flight."

"Why?"

"It is Lufthansa policy."

"Yes, but I have tickets for them ..."

"It does not matter, it is Lufthansa policy that we do not carry cats and dogs on the same flight."

"How many dogs do you have on this flight?"

"One dog."

"How many baggage bins do you have on this flight?"

After some thought, "two."

"Would it be possible to put the dog in one baggage bin and the cats in the other?"

"Ah ... I will see." Another backroom conference, whereupon it was announced that indeed I could take the cats.

We arrived in Hamburg without further incident, where I was taking delivery of our Hansa Jet. The Hansa Jet was manufactured by Hamberger Flugzeugbau in Hamburg, and we were ferrying her to Berlin. Captain Bob Wells was the pilot in command. After appropriate ceremonies at the delivery, we departed for Berlin.

Television, radio and the press were on hand for our arrival at Tegel. It was a bit of an occasion since our flight was the first in a German aircraft into Berlin since World War II. The cats were featured as "Die Erste Passagieren Zu Berlin" on the newscasts.

Modern Air had a high profile in the Berlin press and also in the fashion

*Modern Air
Hansa Jet and Mort*

industry in Berlin, often serving as a backdrop for new fashion designs. The Hansa was frequently featured.

Modern also up-scaled our stewardess uniforms, adopting long capes and stunning dresses. Modern's girls were great attributes to our charter services. Early on we introduced duty free sales on board the aircraft, and gave the girls a generous portion of the proceeds that were actually enough to pay the full salaries and expenses of our flight attendants.

Even on the shortest flights it was customary in Europe to give passengers snacks and sandwiches, along with a beer (one mark). Early on John McDonald organized our own kitchen on the Tegel Airport where we saved three marks per passenger by preparing and packaging our own catering for the roundtrips to the Mediterranean. Return meals were stuffed in the bellies of the aircraft and moved topside on turnaround in order to avoid the expense and uncertainty of catering in Tunisia and Turkey or other foreign destination.

During our first year in Berlin one of our Convair 990s got a bad reputation for unreliability with our charterers. This was undeserved in our view, but they demanded that we replace the aircraft in our next season's contract and send a new plane in its stead. We dutifully took the aircraft, NC907, back to Miami that winter, changed the registration number to NC912, and sent it back the next summer with a new (and undiscovered) identity.

Visit to the Congo

In the late 1960s Capitol International Airways was operating a single DC-8-20 aircraft from Brussels to Kinshasa, capital of Zaire (formerly the Congo) on charter to Air Congo, the national airline.

Duncan Tolmie called me while I was on one of my visits to Berlin and offered to get Mobutu, Dictator of Zaire, to transfer the Air Congo contract to Modern Air. (Duncan was formerly Assistant to the Chairman of Capitol and he had been fired when his mentor, the Governor of Tennessee, had been defeated for reelection.) Our Convair 990 could do everything the Capitol DC-8-20 "water wagon" could at lower cost. The DC-8-20 was the first of the DC-8 series and was equipped with the much less efficient P&W JT-4 engines that required water injection on takeoff to provide sufficient cooling at full power – hence the name "Water Wagon."

I had known Duncan when he was Capitol's representative in Washington and he had helped me in an unsuccessful run for Congress in the 1950s. He had gotten the Congo contract for Capitol and, now that he had been fired by Jesse Stallings, he wanted to get even by having the Congo contract transferred to Modern.

John McDonald and I agreed to meet Duncan in Brussels where he would arrange transport to Kinshasa and a meeting with Mobutu. Duncan was living by his wits in Paris and was noted for his consumption of alcoholic beverages, winning his nickname of "Drunken Duncan." Tales of Duncan's escapades were legion. He stayed for some months in the Hilton Hotel in Frankfurt, Germany, where he could not pay his bill. The hotel seized his baggage and would not let him leave. Duncan went out and had several thousand shares of Air Haiti (a non-existent Haitian flag airline that he claimed to control) printed. He then sold the bogus stock to Steadman Hinkley, President of Overseas National Airlines, for $10,000 which he used to escape from the Hilton.

Duncan was noted for inviting numbers of friends and associates visiting Europe to elaborate lunches at posh watering holes with pricey tabs. As luncheons ended and pay-up time came Duncan was noted for his propensity to disappear into the lavatory, leaving his guests staring at the check in embarrassed silence. Finally someone would pick it up and pay, whereupon Duncan would reappear, promising to buy the next one for sure.

On one occasion Duncan hosted a lunch for 20 at the Georges Cinq in Paris. When the check arrived this time he paid, asking the waiter if a check would be acceptable, then writing one out for 3,500 Francs.

"Ah, oui, oui, Monsieur, tres bien," as Duncan added a liberal tip.

The waiter disappeared only to return a few moments later with a troubled look on his face.

"Monsieur Tolmie, I am very sorry but we cannot accept your check since your last two were no good."

"Oh, I am so sorry to hear that. Le me give you a check for 10,000 francs which will cover all three."

"Ah, oui, oui, Monsieur Tolmie, tres bien."

Duncan sponged unmercifully on his friends, but was a charming chap and was usually forgiven by his associates.

At the appointed time Duncan did not appear at the Brussels Air Congo office. McDonald called him in Paris where Duncan was holed up with a cherie. He promised to be in Brussels the next day, so we waited. Shortly before noon, Duncan turned up soused to the gills, staggering down the street. We managed to arrange three first class tickets to Kinshasa and went back to the hotel to await our flight, and to sober up Duncan. We left Brussels at 10 P.M. and by morning arrived in the Congo, taking a beat-up taxi through the dirty, shack-lined streets to the Sabena Staff House where we had arranged rooms. During the afternoon Duncan arranged an audience with Mobutu for two days hence. We prepared a contractual agreement for presentation, then had it translated into French and typed by a nice lady in the American Embassy.

That evening Duncan took us to a cozy bar run by a Belgian lady where all three of us ordered our favorite dry martinis, with Duncan giving precise instructions to the lady in his impeccable French. A few minutes later the lady appeared, bringing three huge glasses filled with gin and sweet vermouth. John and I decided that was not what we had ordered while Duncan insisted it certainly was, and proceeded to drink all three himself. John and I went behind the bar and gently persuaded the lady to let us make our own gin martinis with dry vermouth.

From the Belgian bar we proceeded to the American Officers' Club, where we got some nice rare Kansas City steaks and a few more martinis. On our way back to the Staff House we were accosted by a very black "lady of the evening" offering us her extraordinary services. She was dressed in an immaculate Paris high fashion gown and reeked of high-octane perfume. For myself, I decided an immediate return to the Staff House was the wisest course of action.

The next morning John and I were in the breakfast room eating a tolerable portion of scrambled eggs and bacon. Duncan failed to appear. After half an hour we apprehensively called Duncan's room:

"Duncan, where the hell are you?"

"Help me, I can't get out of my room!"

"Why not?"

"I can't, she's lying on the floor outside my door!"

We went up to Duncan's room and there, sure enough, was the Congolese whore curled up on the floor outside Duncan's room.

We were ushered into the Congolese presidential throne room, dark with Parisian tapestry and gleaming with golden ornaments. Mobutu sat on a slightly raised dais at the end of an enormous conference table lined with gold-painted Louis XVI Parisian chairs. Several Congolese officials and Board Members from Air Congo were present. Duncan, John and I were ushered in, shook hands and sat down.

Duncan made the introductions since he knew Mobutu and had been Capitol's representative, explaining that Modern brought a more up to date, faster and more comfortable jet aircraft. I took over, expanding on Duncan's presentation and particularly stressing the added comfort and legroom of the Modern Air Convairs. I leaned back expansively in my gold encrusted Louis XVI chair only to have it slowly collapse under me, depositing me ignominiously on the floor.

For some reason Modern's offer to improve Air Congo's air service to Europe was not accepted by Mobutu.

Years before, after I had left Riddle in 1963, I had been President of Air Ventures, an operation owned by The Company that provided air services to Katanga, supporting Moshe Tshombe who opposed Patrice Lumumba, Mobutu's predecessor as ruler of the Congo. I doubt that this had anything to do with our failure to win a contract for Modern Air.

Journey to Biafra

In 1970 Nigeria was rent with revolution as the eastern region rose against the dominant West based in Lagos. The United States sided with the established government, but there was a thriving private airlift conducted from Europe that supported the rebels in Biafra. Entrepreneurs such as Hank Wharton were paid thousands of dollars per trip to fly old Connies and DC-7s into Port Harcourt, the rebel base, carrying arms and medical supplies. The war raged for some two years until the Lagos faction finally began to prevail with American help.

Believing there might be an opportunity for Modern Air flying airlift support for the national government (Lagos) forces, I made arrangements to fly to Lagos on Pan Am to visit my friends at Pan African Airways, still owned by The Company at the time. Don Sitman, an old acquaintance, who was now President of Pan African, met me upon my arrival and made me comfortable at the Pan African staff house at the airport. A trip into the city was an adventure in itself, especially at night when one was stopped at frequent military roadblocks. Having a 16-year-old-soldier stick an AK-47 in my face and demand to see my papers, even though he probably couldn't read them, was a bit disconcerting.

The Government forces had just recaptured Port Harcourt, and Pan African was flying into the just captured airport that was still under fire by the

Biafran rebels in the jungle. We flew in one morning in a DC-4 carrying ammunition, passing over the still smoldering wreckage of Pan African's other DC-4 that had been shot down by the rebels two days previously, just a mile short of the runway. We made a steep "canyon approach" to stay as far above the rebel machine gunfire as possible. Landing on the shell-pocked runway, we missed as many holes as possible and pulled up to the terminal building where our cargo was unloaded at panic speed while the rebels limbered up with a new barrage that, fortunately, missed our aircraft but tore up the runway even more.

Our return load consisted of some one hundred wounded government soldiers who all seemed to be injured in the foot and, being unable to walk, were loaded onto the aircraft on pallets by a forklift. This too proceeded at warp speed. We sat them all on the floor, started the engines, taxied out at full speed, and took off – again avoiding the shell holes.

Circling sharply after takeoff we tried to avoid more rebel ground fire and slowly climbed out toward Lagos. En route our DC-4 ran into a fierce line squall and a sinister black roll cloud at two thousand feet. The thunderstorm was filled with heavy rain that beat on the metal hull like machine gun fire, and by blinding bolts of lightning. The aircraft pitched and rolled, and with every downdraft agonized howls from the wounded filled the cabin. I was riding in the cockpit and looked back into the cabin through a window in the cockpit door. Each time the aircraft dropped in a downdraft the soldiers were lifted into the air to crash back onto the floor with the next updraft. All one could see in the intermittent flashes of lightning were hundreds of white eyeballs and screaming mouths filled with white teeth.

We returned to Lagos without further incident. It did not appear that there were further airlift opportunities for Modern in Nigeria, so I got on the next Pan Am flight west and returned to Miami.

An Unexpected Diversion

Walter Jenkins, who had been Assistant to President Johnson before an unfortunate incident in a public washroom, was subsequently a representative of the Mexican President Aleman. Modern Air had obtained a contract for several hundred program charter flights from New York to Mexico City and Acapulco. However, landing rights proved difficult to obtain in Mexico until we retained the services of Mr. Jenkins. We paid him $750 per flight with the understanding that this would be distributed to the authorities concerned in Mexico and that landing rights would be granted. They were.

From time to time we would pay a courtesy call on President Aleman to express our appreciation for his assistance in removing restrictions on our operations in Mexico. I took a nonstop flight on Pan Am from Miami to Mexico City. After a day of meetings I was returning on the next morning's Pan Am trip from Mexico City to Merida in the Yucatan and thence to Miami. I was late and barely made the flight.

Approach to Merida was routine until at about 5,000 feet the pilot announced over the loudspeaker, "Ladies and gentlemen, I am sorry to inform you that we have a young man on board who has expressed a desire to visit Cuba. We are therefore overflying Merida and proceeding directly to Rancho Boyeros Airport in Havana. The bar is now open and complimentary cocktails will be served." I saw a young man seated in the first row in First Class holding a 38 caliber automatic in the ear of one of the stewardesses who had a pained look on her face.

The aircraft flew on to Havana without further incident and taxied to the terminal. Thoughts of my role in the Bay of Pigs attack were uppermost in my mind as the police entered the aircraft, then disarmed and carried away the young man who had caused our difficulty. The ground crew came aboard and several of them instantly recognized me from my Pan Am days twenty-five years before.

"Oh, Mr. Beyer, it is so good to see you again!"

"Yes, Jose, it is good to see you too ..."

We were escorted off and into passport control where the Cuban authorities examined our papers minutely. I sat as quietly and unobtrusively as possible, dreading what my dossier from Cuban intelligence might hold. At last our passports were returned and we were invited to visit the old Pan Am Clipper Club which was now titled the "Arriba Cuba!" – or something like that. Outside the windows we could see scores of Russian jets on the ramp, some with the old insignia of Cubana, the Cuban National Airline, and some with the hammer and sickle of the U.S.S.R.

We were each offered a pack of the finest Cuban cigars and a handful of propaganda in Spanish extolling Castro and his Cuba. An attentive waiter asked what I would like to drink.

"A Cuba Libre."

"Si si, Senor."

A lady reporter from TV Havana showed up to interview the passengers and I waved her away. "No comprende Español."

After approximately three hours on the ground we were ushered back onto the Pan Am jet. We taxied out and took off for Miami where we were met by dozens of FBI, CIA, Customs and Immigration agents all wanting to interrogate each passenger.

"Who do you think did it" I asked one agent.

"I don't know, but someone said one passenger showed up at the last minute in Mexico ..."

I assured him that I knew nothing and had seen nothing. They let me go, but only after Customs had confiscated my Cuban cigars. They let me keep the Cuban propaganda.

I went back to my office and called Jim Brown to advise him that I was back and okay, but that I had lost his cigars – Jim was a lover of fine cigars and would have appreciated them.

"Goddamn you, Beyer, you always get to have all the fun!"

In the late '60s hijackings to Cuba were frequent. The young man who had taken our plane was the son of a U.S. Army officer stationed in Mexico. According to one of our stewardesses he had "uglied himself up" by shaving off his long hair and had stolen his father's gun. He was going to Cuba for a new life. We understood that Castro, who didn't want these crazy Americans, sentenced him to ten years on the Isle of Pines, the Cuban Devil's Island.

A Modern Farewell

I was in Dubrovnik on holiday when the final, crushing straw was dropped on Modern Air. Haywood Wills, Chairman of GAC Corporation, appointed his personal assistant as Chairman of Modern Air without consultation with me or anyone else. Because he was formerly a flack for Claude Kirk, flamboyant governor of the State of Florida, he was totally inexperienced and unqualified for any position with our airline

Our new Chairman immediately moved to set Modern right, firing "Big Ernie" Gerber, my vice president in charge of the American Airmotive shops because he did not have "the GAC Image." Big Ernie was a remarkably competent technician who did not suffer fools graciously – and said so. It was obvious that things would go from bad to worse, so I took advantage of Wills' offer to the officers and resigned, accepting my six months' severance pay. Haywood Wills declined to pay me some four months accrued vacation time so I sued GAC for it. Haywood showed up at the trial with a phalanx of GAC lawyers. After an all day trial it took the jury exactly three minutes to rule in my favor.

I accepted an offer made a month earlier by Jesse Stallings, owner and President of Capitol International Airways, one of the largest supplemental (charter) airlines, to head his airline as President and moved to Nashville, Tennessee.

Modern's losses mounted swiftly under the new management. Domestic operations were terminated and all aircraft moved to Berlin where there was not enough business to support the whole fleet. Then Modern lost the Berlin tour operator contracts due to poor reliability and due to being outbid by Joel Eisenberg's Air America. Finally the company collapsed entirely when GAC itself went bankrupt and could no longer provide support. ✈

CHAPTER IX

Capitol International Airways

Recruited by Capitol

In April 1971 Jesse Stallings – owner, Chairman and President of Capitol International Airline, a major Supplemental airline – called me and invited me for dinner at Miami's Aviation Club. Capitol had a fleet of eight DC-8 aircraft, most of which were cargo/convertible models capable of quick changes of configuration between passenger and freight operations. The company had worldwide authority and was one of the four supplemental "have" airlines. But, like the other members of the charter industry, Capitol was having financial difficulties and was losing money. Its operations were increasingly unreliable due to weak management.

Jesse Stallings himself was in poor health, as was his airline. He was very much a "hands on" manager, reluctant to relinquish control. But he was in trouble, and offered me the Presidency of Capitol and a generous salary. I was not having a good time at Modern as GAC and its lackeys were interfering increasingly in Modern's operations. I told Jesse that I wanted two weeks to think over his offer. He agreed and flew back to Nashville. I departed for a visit to Berlin and a brief vacation in Dubrovnik, a charming Yugoslavian resort on the Adriatic. While there, Jim Brown from GAC called me to suggest that I come home since GAC's Chairman Haywood Wills was taking over Modern.

Returning to Miami I found that Wills had, in fact, installed his assistant as my Chairman. He had dismissed Ernie Gerber and was making other moves that were incompatible with my policies. I resigned, seized my golden parachute and called Jesse Stallings to accept his offer of the Presidency of Capitol. Two days later I departed for Smyrna, Tennessee, leaving my family in Florida.

Capitol was based in Smyrna, Tennessee, where the airline occupied the facilities of a small USAF base that had been closed down. We had eight DC-8s of various types: two original DC-8-20s, four DC-8-54 convertibles, and two stretched DC-8-61 passenger aircraft. Our principal operations were transatlantic passenger charters, military contract operations in the Atlantic and Pacific, and some domestic charters. Jesse had just closed the major crew base in Philadelphia and ordered all crews to move to Smyrna where he could keep a better eye on them. Operations were controlled from Smyrna as was marketing. Maintenance was performed in a large hangar on the Smyrna airfield.

Chief officers were "Mac" Rowe, Executive Vice President; the Vice President of Maintenance; and Jack Lagerquist, Director of Operations. Hank Benagh managed the operations control function. Doris Basford was Stallings' long-time assistant and treasurer, keeping a steely hand on the checkbook. I was moved into a modest office next to Doris, with Jesse in the next office beyond hers. It was a cozy arrangement designed so that Doris could overhear almost all of my conversations by phone and in person. But since I had always operated in a goldfish bowl, and did not believe in closed door policies, I went along with it.

Capitol: The First Day

On arriving at my office the first day I set up a practice that I had followed at Riddle, Saudia and Modern; a brief, regular morning staff meeting to review the previous day's operations, see what was planned for that day, and discuss any general problems. We had a good bit to discuss. A few weeks before, the Military Airlift Command had threatened to "red line" Capitol, refusing to give us any more business until the reliability of our operation improved. MAC awarded contracts on a monthly, daily and yearly basis, and could rescind them at will. The previous day they had implemented the "red line" and we would get no more military contract business until we cleaned up our act. An early visit to MAC was in order and I went the following Monday.

Secondly, we had a problem with our commercial transatlantic charter operation. We had three charter groups of passengers in hotels in Frankfurt, Germany due to mechanical delays and poor planning. The aircraft were in New York and had to be ferried empty to pick up the passengers in Frankfurt. Due to Stallings' recent "move" order the crews were all in Smyrna. I ordered three crews rounded up at Smyrna and sent by commercial jet to New York

---

[2] *Not to be confused with Capital Airlines, for whom I worked for 12 years until the airline was merged with United.*

to ferry the aircraft to Frankfurt to pick up the passengers before we lost another $100,000 per day, NOW!

I headed for my office only to be accosted by Hank Benagh, the Operations Control officer.

"Mort, we have a passenger problem in Pittsburgh."

"Yes, Hank, what is it?"

"The passengers are rioting. We have called the police."

"What are they rioting about?"

"Well, we have the groups going to Las Vegas and we loaded the B'nai B'rith group in New York and they are sitting in the front of the plane and won't move."

"Yeah, so?"

"Well the group getting on in Pittsburgh is the NAACP and they won't sit in the back of the plane. What are we going to do?"

I pondered a moment and suggested to Benagh, "There are three seats on each side of the aisle aren't there?"

"Yeah."

"Well, why not seat the NAACP on one side of the aisle and the B'nai B'rith on the other?"

After reloading the flight proceeded to Las Vegas without further incident.

The visit to MAC at Scott Field produced no immediate result. The military staff expressed their concerns with Capitol's performance, late flights, cancellations, mechanical difficulties and dirty, unkempt aircraft. Provided that we operated our basic contract without incident for the next 60 days, MAC would restore our eligibility for "expansion" flights – extra trips over and above our basic contract.

A few weeks later we experienced an engine failure on one of our cargo flights in Japan. Our next flight was 30 hours later out of Travis AFB in California. We had 30 hours to get the aircraft back to Smyrna from Japan, change the engine, and reposition the aircraft at Travis. The aircraft was ferried on three engines back to Smyrna, the new engine readied for arrival and changed in less than three hours, an unheard of performance, and the aircraft repositioned to Travis within the allotted time. We had saved our military contract.

Marketing and Planning at Capitol

A specific agreement covered each charter flight contracted showing chartering party, price, time and place of origin, destination and return, and aircraft number assigned. All aircraft itineraries were maintained on a huge

Planning Board for the next six months showing each contracted flight and its relationship with all other flights. Flights were indicated by wooden blocks for each trip, color coded for each aircraft. When a flight was instituted a block was prepared showing vital information. The block was placed on the board to graphically illustrate departure and arrival time at each station. To change departure/arrival times the block was moved right or left, and in the event of a cancellation the block was removed. The Board was inviolate, and only Hank Benagh was supposed to touch it.

Capitol had a Dutch tour operator who gave us several millions of charter passengers each year. He was often dissatisfied with the operating times of the flights allocated to him, preferring Friday and Saturday night departures from Europe and Sunday night returns from the States. We could not satisfy his preferences, especially since he also got the lowest charter prices. Once he showed up in Smyrna for a sales conference and, taking advantage of his chance, stayed after the meeting adjourned, went to the Planning Office and rearranged the schedule blocks on the Board to times more to his liking. As a result flights for which we had signed contracts had been "rescheduled" to other times and other days. We faced utter chaos.

I called our Contract Coordinator to my office and we made a complete list of all of our signed contracts for the next six months, showing times and dates of operations and specific aircraft allocated. We then took this back to the Planning Board and began to systematically plot every commitment that we had made. The results were even more chaotic. On many days we had contracted more aircraft than we owned, with two or three flights on the same aircraft. At other times flights could only be covered by extensive empty ferry flights for which we received no revenue. At the end of a week we had rescheduled every aircraft and every contracted flight at times when we could perform them. The Marketing Department was instructed to go back to our clients, including our Dutch tour operator, and work out the new schedule with them.

A corollary of this exercise was the virtual elimination of "empty legs" or ferry flights. Most of Capitol's charters were "ad hoc," or in other words single flights or small groups that operated on specific days, such as flying Amsterdam to New York on the 26th of July and returning on the 15th of August. If we did not have an aircraft in Amsterdam on the 26th of July we had to ferry one there – perhaps from another point in Europe, but often clear across the Atlantic. Up to my arrival 20% of all of Capitol's transatlantic flights were such empty legs, positioning aircraft to operate a revenue flight from the other side of the ocean. These ferry flights constituted almost 20% of our cost with no revenue.

Our answer was threefold:

1- Try to reschedule already booked flights to match up with existing ferry legs.
2- Sell the remaining empty legs by offering discounts to charter groups or swapping with other airlines with similar problems.
3- Avoid committing for charter flights that created empty legs in the future.

Through this strategy we cut Capitol's 1971 empty legs from 20% to 8%, saving $2.8 million that first summer alone.

Capitol had a long time Senior Vice President of Marketing, an old crony of Jesse Stallings' named Frank Sparacino. I felt that Frank was not supporting my efforts to have a more organized and disciplined marketing program. Jesse said that he would reassign Frank to our Los Angeles regional office and give me approval to hire a replacement – Archie Leonard, a marketing vice president from Pan Am – as our new Senior Vice President of Marketing.

Archie duly reported for work, but Jesse changed his mind and kept Sparacino on. Therefore, and until after I left Capitol, we had two Senior Vice Presidents of Marketing sitting in adjacent offices. Archie advised each of our District Sales Managers that he was coming to visit them personally. Frank summoned all of the District Managers to Smyrna, so that when Archie arrived in Chicago, Detroit and Cleveland he was visiting empty offices.

Goodbye to Navigators

When I arrived at Capitol we were still carrying navigators on our trans-ocean flights. Doppler Radar had been installed in all of the aircraft some time earlier, making the function of the professional celestial navigator superfluous. So now I sought and obtained FAA approval to cease carrying navigators on Capitol flights, saving considerable amounts in salaries and expenses.

The pilots' ALPA contract was somehow silent on the subject of navigators, but they perceived an opportunity to get more money by demanding that the former navigators' wages be paid over to them since they were obviously doing more work and carrying additional responsibility. As a matter of fact the Doppler Radar made ocean navigation much easier and its operation tended to keep pilots busy and awake on long over-ocean stretches.

When we declined to give the pilots additional compensation for flying without a navigator, they threatened to strike if we implemented our plan. I advised the MEC, the Master Executive Council, that we would proceed with implementation at 9 A.M. the following morning on a flight to be captained by the Chairman of the pilots' union. The next morning he flew without further protest and the navigators were withdrawn. Several who had pilot certificates were retained as first officers.

It was my experience in airline management that strikes only occur when one side or the other mistakes the firmness of the other. If your unions know for certain that you mean exactly what you say, and will do what you promise, a strike is highly unlikely. In thirty years in airline management I never had a strike, and never gave anything away. As Harold Gibbons, VP of IBT, once said to me as we concluded a negotiation: "Goddammitt Beyer, I hope that some day you go to work for a rich airline." I never did.

Goodbye to Capitol

After a year at Capitol I had made a significant improvement in the quality, and particularly the financial performance, of Capitol. We had won back the confidence (and thence the patronage) of the Military Airlift Command. Our commercial program was working well and our wasted ferry mileage had been reduced by over 60%. I had moved the flight crew base back to Philadelphia where it was central to our commercial charter base in the Northeast, saving millions of dollars in crew deadheading and layover expenses. Plans were being made for the acquisition of new widebody jets, the Douglas DC-10-30s, for our passenger and military contracts.

However, Jesse Stallings' health was also improving along with his wealth, and he was taking a much greater interest in the operation of his airline. And, thus, he and I were more and more in conflict.

Jesse had always run the airline "on the cheap," with an inadequate and poorly paid but subservient staff. I felt that this was false economy – that we could be more profitable by doing a quality job and not making stupid mistakes. We also fell out over policy questions. I wanted to make inroads into the Berlin market that Capitol had once shared with Saturn, but Jesse adamantly opposed and sabotaged a contract after I had won it for Capitol.

My initial agreement with Jesse was a one-year deal, and when the year was up he decided he wanted his airline back, as it were. He gave me a not-too-generous thirty day severance payment and I left to seek other employment.

I had bought a lovely new home on a four-acre point of land overlooking Old Hickory Lake, a TVA dammed portion of the Tennessee River, and brought my cabin cruiser, INSHALLA, up to dock her at the house. The lake was great for weekend cruises.

The supplemental airlines as a whole were having a poor year, and Universal Airlines – one of the biggest – went bankrupt. I was offered a chance to buy it and pull it out.

My backers and current owners of Universal owned all the common stock and gave me control of it without cost to me. If I were to succeed I would be granted a controlling share. If not, I would simply have to return the shares.

Sequel

Capitol was one of the largest of the supplemental airlines, with complete domestic and international authority. By all odds it had the best chance to survive the transition to airline deregulation, but did not. The company did reasonably well during the '70s after I left, particularly benefiting from significant MAC contracts to Vietnam. Owner Jesse Stallings died and the company was sold to his daughter. However, the sale collapsed and Capitol was finally taken over by George Bachelor, a legendary aircraft lessor and broker from Miami. This change was unsuccessful as well. Bachelor leased Capitol several DC-10-10 widebody aircraft that were deployed in scheduled services from New York and Los Angeles to Miami, but this operation failed due to increased competition and the increasingly poor reliability and cost control at Capitol. Capitol finally collapsed into bankruptcy in 1984 and was liquidated, with much of its equipment transferred to George Bachelor's other airline, Arrow Air. This airline went bankrupt itself following the bombing of a military charter flight it was operating at Gander, Newfoundland.

I had only peripheral contact with Capitol in later years in my capacity as a consultant with AVMARK Inc., but never was afforded the opportunity to straighten it out one more time. ✈

CHAPTER X

And Subsequently

Universal Airlines – the Phoenix That Would Not Rise

Universal Airlines was one of the larger Supplemental, or charter, airlines, with a fleet of four DC-8-61 and 13 Lockheed Electra aircraft. The DC-8s were engaged largely in domestic passenger charters and the Electras on a domestic military contract called Logair. The company sought refuge in Chapter 11 bankruptcy in 1972.

I was contacted by Ted Harris, a young airline entrepreneur, with the idea of obtaining control of Universal, finding new financing, and resurrecting it from bankruptcy. I spent the next year on what turned out to be a mission impossible.

I was given stock in the company on a consignment basis. If I pulled it out, I paid for the stock, if I failed I owned nothing. I obtained about $20,000 in outside financing and for the rest paid out of our own pockets. We had five tasks:

1- Develop a believable new business plan.
2- Keep the bankruptcy judge and creditors from liquidating the company.
3- Keep the certificate alive at the FAA and CAB.
4- Win new certificated route authority from the CAB in the ongoing Supplemental Renewal Case.
5- Find significant new financing for Universal.

Basically, we succeeded on all but the last requirement. Financing proved a bridge too far due to industry losses and finally the second Arab-

Israeli war that quadrupled oil prices. I traveled from coast to coast visiting possible investors, making presentations to cities and civic groups and offering to locate our airline at their closed Air Force facilities. Everywhere we went people were long on hopes and dreams, but short of cash.

One of our hopeful investor targets was Jimmy Hoffa, legendary leader of the Teamsters Union, the IBT. The Teamsters had organized Universal prior to its bankruptcy and were also active in other airlines, such as Pan Am, Capitol and Modern, where I had negotiated with them. Our contact was Louie, one of Hoffa's henchmen who headed a limo service owned by Hoffa. It served the Detroit Airport. Louie offered to take me to Hoffa who had the capability of providing financing for Universal, directly or indirectly. Louie picked me up at the Detroit Airport in a chauffeured stretch limousine and we drove to Hoffa's house.

Jimmy lived in a modest house in the suburbs on the edge of a lake, surrounded by a four-foot chain link fence and guarded by a large but well behaved Doberman – he obeyed Hoffa's command to "heel" as we let ourselves in. We sat in a sunny drawing room overlooking the lake. I outlined my plans for the resurrection of Universal and the benefits to the Union of helping Universal back on its feet. Jimmy listened interestedly and finally, as I finished, asked, " Mort, what happens if I invest $5 million and things don't go as you expect?"

"Jimmy, you lose it."

Louie interjected, "No, this is a sure thing, Jimmy, you won't lose it. This thing is gonna work."

Jimmy brushed Louie aside. "Shut up Louie," he said. "If it goes down the shitter I lose my money." After some further discussion, Jimmy turned to me:

"Mort, I want to think this thing over. I am going fishing in Florida for a few days, and I'll call you . . ."

I thanked him and left. Several days later, true to his word, Jimmy called me.

"Mort, I have been thinking about your proposal. I think the economy is going down the shitter, and the airlines with it. I don't want to be mixed up in it."

I thanked him for his consideration and frank assessment. Despite our best efforts we could not raise the funds we needed to fulfill our business plan and meet our commitments to the creditors, the Court and the CAB. I returned the Universal stock and we called it quits.

Johnson Flying Service

Shortly after abandoning our efforts to resuscitate Universal Airlines, I was contacted by Delford Smith, Chairman and owner of Evergreen Helicopters, a large company that was engaged in various types of specialized operations from work in the oil patch in Alaska to logging in the Pacific Northwest and fire fighting all over the country. A few months earlier he had agreed to purchase Johnson Flying Service, a small CAB certificated charter airline based in Missoula, Montana and owned by Robert Johnson, an aviation pioneer now seventy years old and seeking to retire. Johnson had sold the airline twice before, once to the Pennsylvania Railroad, but the CAB had refused to approve the acquisition due to fear that the railroad ownership would upset the balance in the U.S. airline industry. Johnson was running out of money and was anxious to sell out.

The airline was equipped with numerous helicopters and light planes, two Lockheed Electras, several DC-3's and Ford Tri-Motors, plus five World War II TBM's, modified as water bombers. Smith had been looking for a president to replace Johnson.

Del Smith invited me to his hotel in Washington to discuss his ambitions for Johnson. A dynamic and charismatic man, who had built Evergreen Helicopters into a worldwide operation from a one plane, two-seater Allouette operation in Alaska, Del was an eloquent advocate of his plans for Johnson. He dreamed of using it as a platform for an expanded aviation operation. He wanted me to manage the needed CAB approval of the acquisition, and meanwhile start the building process of the airline merger with his helicopter company. It was rumored, correctly, that Smith had ties with the CIA and conducted sensitive missions for them in the backwaters of the world. In view of my previous ties with The Company, this provided an additional incentive to come aboard.

I visited McMinnville and then flew to Missoula to meet Bob Johnson and his staff. I was impressed by Del Smith's aggressive ambition and with Bob Johnson's gentlemanly mien, so I agreed to accept the position as President. I went to work as soon as I could get in place in Montana.

Johnson International Airlines

When we were engaged in actual fire fighting activities, we prayed for dry summers and hot "fire seasons." A veritable Air Force of small private contractors served the US Forestry Service all over the Pacific Northwest and other regions, using World War II DC-4s and retired Connies, DC-6s and DC-7s as "water bombers." Conversions consisted of installing water-retardant tanks in the bellies. Even to this day these aircraft are still in service, although now supplemented by more modern ex-military Lockheed Hercules and Consolidated P-2-Vs combined jet and prop planes.

But Johnson Airlines was limited to fire fighting, which was too thin to support a year-round airline, and my first task was to expand Johnson's operation. The Electras were only used an hour or so each day. Johnson was eligible to operate domestic military passenger flights (CAMs) but had not sought the safety clearance required from MAC at Scott Field, nor filed the necessary insurance and contract information needed by MATS (Military Airlift Transport Services) who contracted on a competitive basis for flights. We immediately applied and were soon heavily engaged in CAM operations. Since one was paid only for the "live" legs and not for ferry flights, the trick was to try to link up live flights in an optimum sequence to satisfy the military scheduling requirements at minimum cost to them – and to Johnson. Football and other sports and commercial charters were mixed and matched with military contract operations, and Johnson's utilization increased sharply.

We also determined to cut down on the less viable parts of our Forest Service operations, so the TBMs were sold to a Canadian operator for $500,000. He used them for spraying pine forests infested by the Spruce Bag Worm, a pest that denuded millions of acres of native pine each year. The Ford Tri-Motors were also sold, and DC-3 utilization increased by extending our range of operations outside the Northwest Region.

In keeping with our new expanded operations and hope for the future, we changed the name of our little airline to Johnson International Airlines even though we did not as yet have any international authority. Del Smith wanted to adopt the name of Evergreen International, but I was able to persuade him that this would be unwise since the CAB had not yet approved the acquisition.

Already working for Johnson was Sam Hunt, a dispatcher with whom I had worked at Capitol. I soon offered a position to Bill Clarke who was with me at Riddle, Saudia, Modern, and Capitol.

Our office headquarters were in a double-wide trailer at the Missoula County Airport. Bob Johnson, then in his late seventies, showed up every morning and sat at the end of my conference table to open the mail, reading every letter and counting every check. He sat in on our daily morning briefing before proceeding to the engine shop where he preferred to spend the day rebuilding engines. We had the in-house capability of building every type of piston engine we operated, up to and including the 18-cylinder R2 800s used on the TBMs.

Daily operations included the dawn patrol of helicopters and light planes to check northern Montana for fires started during the night by lightning storms or careless tourists. Electras were dispatched to all corners of the U.S. serving our increasing charters, and the DC-3s took on their cargoes of smoke jumpers – usually college kids earning an extra buck during the summer. Smoke jumpers parachuted into remote areas from our DC-3s and Ford Tri-Motors – now almost fifty years old. The U.S. Forestry Service paid a small fixed "availability" fee and a high "activity" fee.

The Company (CIA) owned a small ex-Air Force base at Marana, Arizona. The facility had a five thousand foot runway, two hangars and a staff house complex, along with several thousand acres of desert. The Company also had a small fleet attached to it; a real Boeing B-17 modified to a water bomber, an Electra and several Twin Otters and Bell Helicopters. In the winter of 1973 The Company approached me to see if Johnson and Evergreen wanted to buy the facility at Marana and the associated aircraft. This was definitely of interest since our facility at Missoula was too small and too out-of-the-way for future development. Our hangar could not handle even our Electras. After obtaining Del Smith's approval I traveled to Marana where we made a deal to buy everything for $2.9 million. The money was advanced by Evergreen.

In due course, the CAB set down a proceeding to consider Evergreen's acquisition of Johnson that was duly opposed by all of the trunk airlines that feared the consequences of the acquisition to their vast intercontinental systems. This kind of knee-jerk opposition to any form of new entry or expansion of low-cost services was in large part the cause of airline deregulation several years later – with consequences that few perceived. Despite the opposition, the CAB finally approved the Evergreen acquisition, but not in time to save Bob Johnson from another financial haircut.

Del Smith had promised to pay Johnson several million dollars and had advanced a small amount to run the company in the interval between the agreement and the CAB's approval. If the CAB delayed approval, the agreement became null and void.

When the CAB delayed approval, Del Smith demanded the acquisition agreement be revised to reduce Johnson's payment to half of the agreed amount. I believed that this was an unconscionable attempt to take advantage of Bob through no fault of his own, and argued with Del Smith about it. His reply was to send his Financial Director and Operations Manager from Evergreen over to Missoula to issue a directive to the Johnson Board of Directors to fire me. They promptly did. I believed that Del owed more than this to Bob.

Almost immediately following the CAB's final approval, Johnson's Missoula operation was closed down and transferred to McMinnville, Oregon – the Evergreen headquarters. The name of Johnson was expunged and changed to Evergreen International. A few of the Johnson staff, principally flight crews, were retained. In later years Marana became a major storage area for hundreds of grounded surplus transport aircraft during the recessions of 1980 and 1990, and is again today in the downturn following 9/11. Evergreen became a major owner, lessor and operator of chiefly cargo jet aircraft, but built up hundreds of millions in debt in the process.

The B-17 that we acquired from The Company with Marana was modified back to its original military configuration and became the centerpiece of Del Smith's unique personal aeronautical museum that now includes Howard Hughes' gigantic World War II Spruce Goose, now in McMinnville.

Berghel – Montana

We introduced Bob Berghel to the "Foot Tall Martini" at the Lost Mine Saloon in Missoula, Montana. It was October, 1973, and Bob had come to help Johnson International Airlines negotiate a new contract with its eight-man group of IAM mechanics. Probably one of the most docile labor groups in the West, the Johnson local was bolstered by a representative from headquarters in Minneapolis.

The day had been spent driving up over the Mission Range on a one-lane gravel road, enjoying the scenery and wildlife. We even saw a black bear. Evening took Bob, Bill Clarke, Sam Hunt and me to the Lost Mine for two-pound sirloins and Foot Tall Martinis. The Foot Tall Martini was served in a deceptively slim bell flower glass with a globe on the bottom, and it really was a foot tall. How many ounces it held I don't know. But the ambiance of the place with its huge roaring fire, moose and grizzly heads hanging from the rafters and relics of the pioneer Lost Mine all around, made for easy drinking. More than one round was consumed, washing down the enormous steaks. Toward midnight we delivered Bob to his room at the Red Lion Motel after scheduling breakfast for seven the next morning in order to prepare for the day's negotiations.

At seven Bill, Sam and I were seated in the Cafe waiting for Bob. Two cups of coffee and twenty minutes later he still had not showed. Thirty minutes, still no Bob. A phone call to his room was unanswered. We became apprehensive, called the manager and trooped to Bob's room. We knocked loudly ... Silence ... More knocking ... More silence ... With increasing alarm we began to wonder. Is he dead or something? What had we done to Bob last night? We asked the manager to unlock the door and entered. A low groan rose from the bed. A shake of the shoulder produced some signs of life. Bob rolled over and slowly opened a blood-shot eye. We laughed, a huge burden of concern having been lifted from our shoulders. Bob slowly sat up, grunted a "good morning," and headed for the bathroom as we admonished him for his slug-a-bed nature. Downstairs we had breakfast. Bob joined us for coffee only. "No thanks, no eggs and deer sausage... Ugh!"

Negotiations went well. Louis Wolfer, our Chief Mechanic, and the IAM man from Minneapolis sat on one side of the table. Bob Johnson, Bob Berghel and I sat on the other side. After brief statements on both sides we settled down for a point by point discussion of the union demands and the Company position. Bob pulled out his inevitable huge Cuban-type cigar, lit up, and proceeded to launch his ultimate negotiating weapon — enveloping the other side in cloud after cloud of fragrant, heavy blue cigar smoke.

To some, the smoke of Bob's legendary cigars had always seemed sweet and aromatic. To others it must have appeared pungent and acrid. At any rate, it was a powerful negotiating weapon. Negotiations were finished by noon, the new contract initialed, and Mr. IAM was back on his Northwest plane to Minneapolis by 12:30 P.M.

That evening we took another tour up Lolo Pass where Lewis and Clark had crossed more than 150 years ago on their way to the Pacific. At dinner that evening at the Hungry Horse Saloon Bob showed no interest in Foot Tall Martinis, reverting to his more traditional favorite drink, the Stinger.

The Founding of AVMARK

AVMARK, an acronym derived from Aviation Marketing, was conceived and founded by four of my associates in 1962, while I was working with Riddle Airlines in Miami and commuting back to my farm in Virginia on weekends. National Airlines flew the Miami-Washington route and extended free passes to me as an airline executive on an industry courtesy basis.

Fellow founders included Ralph Kaul, a local developer, and Joe Murphy, editor of the trade publication American Aviation. We each contributed initial capital of some $1,000. AVMARK was conceived as a monthly newsletter reporting on purchases and sales of new and used transport aircraft. In 1962 this was an infant industry. A new four-engine Boeing B-707-320 might cost $3 million, and used aircraft such as DC-3s and DC-4s could be purchased for $25,000 to $50,000.

By publishing our newsletter listing actual transactions and showing aircraft on offer, we hoped to get "in the middle of" aircraft deals as brokers. A broker might make $25,000 to $50,000 on the sale of a million dollar aircraft and, thus, the incentive to become a deal maker was strong. We sold our AVMARK newsletter for $25.00 for twelve monthly issues, and in due course built up a paid circulation of over a hundred subscribers among airlines, manufacturers, brokers and others. We did not, however, get in the middle of any deals.

I wrote the newsletter anonymously since, in those days, the CAB frowned on anybody in the airline industry having any interests in "other phases of aeronautics" as they phrased it. But when I took the job in Saudi Arabia I could no longer "ghost write" the newsletter from Jeddah. It was turned over to Joe Murphy, who continued the publication – but just barely. Upon my return from Jeddah I found that our circulation had been reduced to just fifteen subscribers – all unpaid.

When I moved to Miami with Modern Air Transport, I again commenced publishing the AVMARK Newsletter, with my wife Jane as Secretary/Treasurer. We took in Jordan Greene as Vice President and front man for AVMARK. Jordan was a self-made mechanic who was putting himself through law school. When he graduated he became the only full-time employee of AVMARK in our office on 36th Street in Miami.

Our revival of AVMARK was successful. The industry was growing rapidly with the development of the DC-9, B-727 and B-737. Widebody Boeing B-747s, Lockheed L-1011s and Douglas DC-10s were entering production. AVMARK filled a niche in the airline food chain and had no competitors. We got our first airline appraisal, a Curtis C-46 cargo aircraft, for which we furnished an opinion letter for $10. We ultimately got up to two hundred and fifty times more for our appraisals.

Captain Mort, 1999

By 1975, when I left Johnson, the circulation of the AVMARK Newsletter was in the four hundred range, all paid at $100 per year. It provided a livelihood for Greene in Miami and good extra cash for us in Montana. We were also beginning to generate more aircraft appraisal work as transactions, leases and financings became more prevalent nationwide. We even began to develop foreign subscribers. The newsletter was growing from simply reporting transactions and offering listings to editorializing on industry affairs and analyzing aircraft and airline economics.

I was now living in Montana – two thousand miles from the East Coast – and removed from the West Coast as well. A survey of the airline industry – then just recovering from the second Arab oil crisis – did not show much promise on the job market. The market for used airline presidents was extremely thin. I hung out my shingle as an airline consultant, using AVMARK as my vehicle, and taking the titles of Chairman and President.

AVMARK grew slowly at first. Our first active client, the Pan Am Flight Engineers Union needed expert witnessing services in a major grievance proceeding against the company. This arbitration started us down one of the many roads that AVMARK traveled in the years to come.

Jordan Greene and I had a messy corporate divorce in 1982, with the court allowing both of us the continuing use of the AVMARK name. I eventually bought him out and went on to develop AVMARK, which I sold to Barbara in 1989 – accepting a three-year contract.

When my three-year contract expired in 1992, I founded Morten Beyer and Associates (MBA) to continue my association in the industry, building a new stable of clients and starting a new monthly commentary, the MBA Aviation Oracle. In 1997 we merged with Agnew & Associates to form Morten Beyer & Agnew – still "MBA." Bob Agnew became President while I held the Chairmanship.

As I write this conclusion sailing between the South Atlantic Islands of St. Helena and Tristan de Cunha, I look back on an interesting and rewarding career in aviation following my guiding philosophy – "when you needs me, call for me, and when I gets there, tell me what you want." And after sixty-one years in the airline business I look forward to continued participation in the ever-changing kaleidoscope of the world's most dynamic industry: Aviation. ✈

Mort and a 747 in
Dothan, Alabama
1990